Laura Cornelius Kellogg

The Iroquois and Their Neighbors
Christopher Vecsey, *Series Editor*

Frontispiece, first edition,
Our Democracy and the American Indian
(Burton Publishing, 1920).

LAURA CORNELIUS KELLOGG

Our Democracy and the American Indian
and Other Works

Edited by
Kristina Ackley and Cristina Stanciu
Foreword by Loretta V. Metoxen

Syracuse University Press

All royalties from the publication of this book will go to the Cultural Heritage Department, Oneida Nation in Wisconsin.

Parts of the introduction originally appeared as "Laura Cornelius Kellogg, Lolomi, and Modern Oneida Placemaking" by Kristina Ackley and "An Indian Woman of Many Hats: Laura Cornelius Kellogg's Embattled Search for an Indigenous Voice" by Cristina Stanciu in a special issue on the Society of American Indians, *American Indian Quarterly* 37, no. 3: 117–38; *SAIL: Studies in American Indian Literatures* 25, no. 2 (Summer 2013): 87–115. Reprinted with permission of University of Nebraska Press, publisher of both journals.

The introduction contains unpublished material from the Ernie Stevens, Sr. Collection, located at the Division of Land Management, Oneida Nation in Wisconsin.

"Overalls and the Tenderfoot," originally published in *The Barnard Bear* 2, no. 2 (March 1907). Reprinted with permission of Barnard Archives and Special Collections.

For a listing of books published and distributed by Syracuse University Press, visit www.SyracuseUniversityPress.syr.edu.

ISBN: 978-0-8156-3390-7 (cloth)   978-0-8156-5314-1 (e-book)

Library of Congress Cataloging-in-Publication Data
Available from publisher upon request.

Manufactured in the United States of America

For our parents, children, and the Oneida Nation

Kristina Ackley, PhD, is a tenured member of the faculty in Native American studies at The Evergreen State College. A citizen of the Oneida Nation in Wisconsin, she received her PhD in American Studies from the State University of New York at Buffalo, and her MA in American Indian law and policy from the University of Arizona, and was a postdoctoral fellow in American Indian Studies at the University of Illinois at Urbana-Champaign. Kristina has published her work in *American Indian Quarterly, Studies in American Indian Literature, American Indian Culture and Research Journal,* and edited collections. She generally teaches in programs that prepare students for work in the fields of education, government, law, social services, and public history. Kristina is at work on a book manuscript on Oneida placemaking.

Cristina Stanciu is an assistant professor of English at Virginia Commonwealth University, where she teaches courses in American Indian studies, US multi-ethnic literatures, and critical theory. Her work has appeared and is forthcoming in *American Indian Quarterly, Studies in American Indian Literatures, MELUS: Multi-Ethnic Literature of the United States, College English, Wicazo Sa Review, Intertexts, Film & History, Chronicle of Higher Education,* and edited collections. Cristina's research on her current book project—*The Makings and Unmakings of Americans: Indians and Immigrants in American Literature and Culture, 1879–1924*—has been supported by fellowships at the Beinecke Rare Book and Manuscript Library, Yale University, and the Newberry Library, Chicago.

Contents

List of Illustrations   *ix*

Foreword, LORETTA V. METOXEN   *xi*

Preface, KRISTINA ACKLEY AND CRISTINA STANCIU   *xiii*

Acknowledgments   *xix*

Chronology   *xxiii*

Introduction
  Laura Cornelius Kellogg: Haudenosaunee Thinker,
  Native Activist, American Writer
     CRISTINA STANCIU AND KRISTINA ACKLEY   *1*

Our Democracy and the American Indian

  Publisher's Introduction, 1920 Edition   *65*

  Chapter Synopses, 1920 Edition   *67*

  Our Democracy and the American Indian:
  A Presentation of the Indian Situation as It Is Today
  (full text, with annotations)   *69*

Other Writings

  Short Stories and Poems
     The Legend of the Bean (1902)   *111*
     The Sacrifice of the White Dog (1902)   *113*
     A Tribute to the Future of My Race (1903)   *114*
     Overalls and Tenderfoot (1907)   *119*

  Essays
     Building the Indian Home (1901)   *133*
     She Likes Indian Public Opinion (1902)   *138*

Industrial Organization for the Indian (1911)   *140*

Some Facts and Figures on Indian Education (1912)   *154*

Public Speeches and Congressional Testimonies

Presentation at the Dedication of Lorado Taft's
   Indian Statue Black Hawk (1911)   *167*

Testimony during Hearings on H.R. 1917:
   Statement of Laura C. Kellogg (1913)   *173*

Statement, US Senate Committee on Indian Affairs:
   Statement of Mrs. Laura Cornelius Kellogg (1916)   *197*

Testimony before Senate Subcommittee on
   S. Res. 79: Survey of Conditions of the Indians
   in the United States (1929)   *202*

Appendix
   List of Selected Articles from Local, National, and
   International Newspapers   *251*

Notes   *253*

References   *281*

Index   *291*

Illustrations

1. Laura Miriam Cornelius, 1902   *7*

2. Grafton Hall, Fond du Lac, Wisconsin   *7*

3. Laura Cornelius in Southern California, 1902   *12*

4. Laura Cornelius in Southern California, 1903   *13*

5. *Miss Laura M. Cornelius*   *14*

6. *Laura Cornelius: A Redskin Princess*   *15*

7. *Miss Laura M. Cornelius, Indian Student at the University*   *17*

8. Laura Cornelius as a student at Barnard, 1907   *22*

9. Laura Cornelius at the first meeting of the SAI, 1911   *27*

10. *Some of the Indian Members of the First Conference*   *28*

11. *Laura Kellogg, Daughter of Long Line of Indian Chiefs, Laughs at the Old Idea of Downtrodden Squaw*   *31*

12. Title page, first edition, *Our Democracy and the American Indian*   *32*

13. Oneida Boarding School, ca. 1910   *40*

14. Oneida Boarding School, ca. 1910   *41*

15. Oneida children learning to darn socks at the Oneida Boarding School, ca. 1910   *42*

16. Oneida Boarding School, *Going Home Day*, ca. 1910   *44*

17. Former Oneida Boarding School grounds after the sale to Catholic Diocese, ca. 1956   *46*

18. Receipt given to supporters of the fundraising efforts of the Six Nations Confederacy, 1924   *50*

19. Photo of Kellogg and Oneida chiefs, 1925   *51*

20. Photo of Oneida women, 1925   *53*

21. *Federal Court Upholds Jones Chief of Six Nations*, 1929   *58*

Foreword

Laura Miriam Cornelius was born in 1880 in a log home on a trail in the center of the Oneida Indian Reservation. The trail was to become Old Seymour Road and Laura was to become known as Laura Minnie Kellogg. It was a time of extreme conflict between the Oneida Nation and the United States of America on the issue of "allotment," a process of allotting parcels of tribal property previously held in common to individuals of the tribe. Therefrom sprung confusion and conflict among various "parties" of Tribal members, who held strong opinions as to their future survival. Laura grew up surrounded by family members, friends, and leaders in the Oneida Community who were in constant debate as to what course of action would be in their best interest.

Now, at long last, 135 years from her birth, we have this opportunity to view her thoughts and motives. There is much in her work to review and contemplate, for her words and inspirations may be as appropriate now, or even more so, than they were at the time she wrote or said them.

Cristina Stanciu and Kristina Ackley have reviewed her works and recognized her genius, with the consideration that Laura is a Native American woman of the nineteenth and early twentieth centuries, when women—especially Native women—were not recognized throughout the general population for national and worldwide leadership qualities.

Laura Minnie Kellogg did everything in her power to assist her own tribe, the Oneidas, to overcome all the diseases, effects of wars, removal from their homelands, and loss of homes and large land masses. She urged her fellow tribesmen and women to learn the system available to them to address their grievances and wrongs. She did this eloquently.

It is time, now, thanks to the research and editorial work of professors Stanciu and Ackley, to learn what Laura Kellogg is continuing to teach us, Native people as well as non-Natives: that the improved welfare of certain original populations of this land prevails and elevates the status of us all.

This work is timely in that tribal members need to reflect on their histories to come to grips with their present circumstances. One area among many current difficulties relates to the need for tribal populations to escape desperate poverty and to obtain regular incomes, and the need to replace structures lacking running water and electricity with adequate and livable housing. Those having difficulty in their present circumstances can look to Laura for words of encouragement—words they can live by 100 years later.

January 14, 2014
Loretta V. Metoxen
Oneida Tribal Historian

Preface

Senator Curtis, I want to ask: What is the objection to keeping an Indian an Indian provided he is a better Indian than he is a white man?

—Laura Cornelius Kellogg to
Senator Charles Curtis, 1916

Laura Cornelius Kellogg's astute and politically loaded question— why not "keep an Indian an Indian"?—evokes, in many ways, her legacy as an Oneida leader and as an American Indian intellectual of the early twentieth century, a time when Native people in the United States faced incredible pressures to assimilate as individuals into American society. The largest barrier to the agenda of assimilation was the common land base that sustained a tribal sense of identity and which represented the most visible sign of Native persistence. Allotment, which broke up the reservations into individual landholdings and opened any "surplus" land to sale and development, was reaching its zenith at this time; a parallel movement followed, signaling the failures of the policy and working on behalf of tribal communities to determine their futures. Native people did not universally agree on the best way to achieve this goal. Some believed that emancipating the Indian from federal supervision (many would say "paternalistic control") would foster self-sufficiency and would alleviate social dysfunction and economic challenges that plagued many reservations; others argued for an increased emphasis on tribal identities, with extensive resources directed toward the reservation to combat the same problems.

When Laura Cornelius Kellogg posed her question to the Senate in 1916, she was also opening a line of critique. One way to interpret her question may be that she was implicitly holding a white identity to a standard that American Indians could not reach, so why not let them remain Indians? Another interpretation (the likelier one, we believe) exposes a sense of pride in Indian identity—why shouldn't an Indian be better than a white man, and in that case, why not let him remain one? This criticism and rejection of the superiority of American values in relation to the assets and potential of Native societies was at the heart of the efforts of many Native reformers and activists of this period. At a time of such intense pressures to reject tribalism and focus on individualism, what gave many of these reformers the confidence to hold on to valuing tribal values and land bases?

Laura Cornelius Kellogg: *Our Democracy and the American Indian* and Other Works brings together these questions—and some answers—about one of the most outspoken, eloquent, and fierce Native women in the first decades of the twentieth century: Laura "Minnie" Cornelius Kellogg, Wisconsin Oneida. A descendent of prominent Oneida leaders, Kellogg was an organizer, author, playwright, performer, and linguist. In an era of government policies aimed at assimilating Indian people, Kellogg advocated for holding the federal government accountable for exercising its trust responsibilities. She worked to achieve a transition from paternalism to self-government, and stood against the further loss of land, which she viewed as the key element keeping Indian nations together and generating economic security and political autonomy for Indian people. At the forefront of an early twentieth-century intertribal "Indian" movement to reclaim traditional leadership positions for Oneidas in Wisconsin and Haudenosaunee people in Canada and the United States, Kellogg tirelessly worked for cultural self-determination when efforts to "Americanize" Native people had reached their peak.

We came to her work through different fields and interests—Kristina through her work on Haudenosaunee land claims and Oneida placemaking, and Cristina through her interest in the Society of American Indians and turn-of-the-twentieth-century Native writers. This book began at the University of Illinois at Urbana-Champaign, where Kristina was a postdoctoral fellow in American Indian studies and Cristina was writing her dissertation in the English department, though the real impetus came after a symposium a few years later. We had the opportunity to present parts of this research at the Society of American Indians (SAI) Centennial Symposium in 2011, organized by Chadwick Allen at Ohio State University, in a panel on "Lesser-Known Figures of the SAI." At that point we realized how little scholars knew about Kellogg, if at all; and, when they did, many questions they asked centered more on her (and her husband's) arrests than on their exoneration; more on Laura's quick temper and sense of style ("Those hats!" or "That fur coat!") than her strategic oratory and use of social spaces; more on her legacy as a former SAI member and less on her legacy as a Wisconsin Oneida. At the same time, the scholarly familiarity with her only published book (that we know of), *Our Democracy and the American Indian* (1920)—including several keynote addresses at the SAI symposium referring to her work—made it clear to us that the time was right for making this "lesser-known" figure of the SAI into a better-known Native public intellectual. We wanted this recovery to include not only the published text from 1920, which is the culmination of her work for over two decades, but also the contexts surrounding, preceding, and following the publication of *Our Democracy*, especially the legacy of her work for contemporary Wisconsin Oneida people.

A controversial figure, alternately criticized and supported by her contemporaries, Kellogg's work has always been claimed by Haudenosaunee people and scholars. In the last decade, interest in Kellogg's work has ranged from philosophy (excerpts from *Our Democracy* were published in *American Philosophies: An Anthology*, 2001); history (excerpts from Kellogg's "Some Facts and Figures on Indian Education" appeared in Frederick Hoxie's *Talking Back to Civilization: Indian Voices from the Progressive Era*, 2001); literature (selections from "Industrial Organization for the Indian" have appeared in Bernd Peyer's *American Indian Nonfiction: An Anthology of Writings, 1760s–1930*, 2007, and her poem, *A Tribute to the Future of My Race*, was reprinted with annotations in Robert Dale Parker's *Changing Is Not Vanishing: A Collection of American Indian Poetry to 1930*,

2011); and Native American and Indigenous studies (David Martinez's *The American Indian Intellectual Tradition: An Anthology of Writings from 1772 to 1972*, 2011).

Aside from (meager) interest in her primary texts, scholars in Iroquois studies and Native American and Indigenous studies have examined Kellogg's contributions to the American Indian intellectual tradition and have reclaimed her as an innovative and prescient thinker, especially for her arguments for the reservation and tribal self-sufficiency. Her work speaks not only to members of her own tribe and the Six Nations Confederacy, but also more broadly, to Native people in the United States and Canada. Her emphasis on the social and economic potential of the reservation, of home and the domestic space, asserted a gendered authority in the debates over the best ways to address the so-called "Indian problem." Kellogg's plan for self-government detailed in *Our Democracy and the American Indian* had four crucial elements: the development of industries connected to viable markets, the use of labor rather than currency as the principal means of exchange, community planning, and governments based on consensus. Kellogg's innovative paradigm drew on a variety of epistemologies, most importantly that of the Six Nations Confederacy, which she argued was the model for the US Constitution and western-style democracies. Her model for Indian self-government acknowledged a common wish among American Indians to remain with their people.

A few scholars have explored Kellogg's life, work, and legacy, including Laurence M. Hauptman (in his foundational article, "Designing Woman: Minnie Kellogg, Iroquois Leader," 1985), Patricia Stovey, Beth Piatote, and a handful of others. Scholarly attention to Kellogg's work has centered on her ideas of reservation self-sufficiency and governance through economic development, her contributions to (and dismissal from) the Society of American Indians (Tom Holm and Hazel Hertzberg), as well as her legacy for contemporary Indigenous feminists and Oneida communities (Patricia P. Hilden and Kristina Ackley). We build on these conversations and offer here a first collection of her materials that seeks not only to reintroduce the text of

Our Democracy and the American Indian into circulation—a text out of print for almost one hundred years—but also to illuminate other texts and contexts informing her work, from poetry and stories, to speeches and congressional testimonies—which particularly showcase her intelligence and quick wit—to media coverage and contemporary reclamations in the Wisconsin Oneida community.

We present here some of our answers to questions about her life and work that we have been asking over the last decade, and hope that our findings will inspire scholars and archivists to continue the search for her lost work. A biography of Laura Cornelius Kellogg is very necessary and timely, and we hope this book will inspire colleagues to keep looking. We know she wrote more—perhaps even a novel (*Ray of Light* or *Wynnogene*)—and still know very little about her two years in Europe, with the exception of several newspaper accounts and a letter she sent to the American ambassador in London requesting to be presented to the court of the King of England. As we were completing a first draft of this manuscript, a scholar in Asian American studies had just recovered over eighty new writings by one of Kellogg's contemporaries, Edith Maude Eaton (Sui Sin Far), a Chinese American writer and journalist who wrote in the United States and Canada. This gives us hope that many other of Kellogg's works are awaiting in remote archives in the United States and Canada. This book, therefore, is only the beginning of the work that remains to be done.

✦

Comprising 152 small pages, *Our Democracy and the American Indian: A Comprehensive Presentation of the Indian Situation as It Is Today* was published in 1920 by the Burton Publishing Company in Kansas City, Missouri, and it sold for $2 a copy. The 1920 edition also includes selections from a document Kellogg refers to throughout the book: "The Report to the Joint Commission of Congress to Investigate Indian Affairs" (1915). Rather than reprinting this document, which is available now in print (but was not widely available in 1920), we have decided to include other documents in addition to the full text and annotations of *Our Democracy and the American Indian*, such as: early stories the aspiring writer published in the early

1910s, speeches and congressional testimonies, and a list of newspaper articles from the era. (We are unable to reprint them here, but many of them are available in US databases of digitized newspapers.) We have not been able to find her manuscripts, except for a few letters here and there; we have reconstructed a timeline of her life and work from letters and documents in the SAI papers, the Carlos Montezuma Papers, Department of the Interior Correspondence, the Barnard College Archives, and many newspaper accounts, as well as with assistance from the Oneida Nation in Wisconsin Cultural Heritage Department.

Throughout the Introduction and annotations, we use the terms "Native" and "Indigenous" to refer to a broader, intertribal and transnational, Indigenous identity. When we refer to Kellogg's words or those of her contemporaries, we use the term "Indian." We also try to use specific tribal names and national identities whenever possible. We use "Haudenosaunee" (alternately spelled Hotinonshonni) to refer to the contemporary designation of the confederacy of Seneca, Cayuga, Onondaga, Oneida, Mohawk, and Tuscarora peoples who have traditionally affiliated under the Great Law. Some other names by which the confederacy is known are Iroquois and Six Nations Confederacy, which are the terms that Kellogg used. We have corrected obvious spelling errors, as they were most likely typographical errors in the original text, but have kept most of the text as it was. Throughout this edition of Kellogg's *Our Democracy and the American Indian* and her other writings, testimonies, and speeches, we provide annotations of what we believe to be less familiar names, places, and concepts. The texts are arranged by genre, rather than chronology, to give the reader a better sense of the different ways in which Kellogg communicated her ideas. While she undoubtedly adapted her ideas to meet the different needs of her audiences, there is a consistency in her message throughout her book, short stories, poem, speeches, and testimonies.

August 29, 2014
Kristina Ackley and Cristina Stanciu

Acknowledgments

Kristina Ackley

A huge *Yaw^ko* goes to a number of people, without whose timely and thoughtful assistance this book would never have been completed. First and foremost, I should acknowledge that Cristina has been the essential motivator and inspiration for this project, tackling tasks big and small. From our first meeting at the University of Illinois at Urbana-Champaign, I have been continually impressed by her intellect and generous spirit, and I deeply value our friendship.

My interest in Laura "Minnie" Cornelius Kellogg was first sparked by work I did many years ago for the Oneida Nation in Wisconsin Land Claims Commission. Patty Ninham-Hoeft, the late Marla Antone, and Jennifer Stevens were very helpful and supportive of my many questions and queries. Tonya Shenandoah and the late Jake and Geralda Thompson shared their perspectives on the place of Kellogg's ideas in the broader Oneida Nation. The late John M. Mohawk and Oren Lyons advised my early research while I was a graduate student at SUNY–Buffalo, and the faculty and staff of the American Indian Studies Program provided a collegial and enriching experience during my fellowship at the University of Illinois at Urbana-Champaign (particularly Fred E. Hoxie, who commented on my work, and Anthony Clark and his student Robin Amado, who assisted in the earlier stages of this project). The manuscript was given significant momentum by the 2011 Society of American Indian Symposium at Ohio State University, where Cristina and I served on a panel with Renya Ramirez. We are both grateful to all the symposium participants for their interest in Kellogg's work. The symposium resulted in a special issue of *SAIL/ AIQ*, edited by Chadwick Allen and Beth Piatote, who provided guidance and support on sections of the Introduction. My understanding of Kellogg and her intellectual legacy has been informed tremendously by the work of Laurence Hauptman and Tom Holm; both have been unfailingly generous with their time.

A Faculty Foundation grant from The Evergreen State College (TESC) supported this work, and I am deeply grateful to all my colleagues in Native American Programs, all my teaching partners over the years, and to the TESC staff who assisted this project, particularly John McLain in academic grants, and the outstanding support staff team of Pam Udovich and Julie Rahn. I need to give an especially heart-felt thank you to the staff of the Oneida Nation in Wisconsin, including Nic Reynolds, Tyler Webster, Sara Summers-Luedtke, Judith Jourdan, Anita Barber, and Dawn Walschinski. They provided me with documents, patiently answered my many questions, and provided permissions for the many images in the book. Randy Cornelius and Bob Brown provided translation work and discussions of concepts and meanings of the Oneida language that I hope I was able to do justice. In terms of evaluating Kellogg's legacy for the Oneida Nation in Wisconsin, I benefitted immeasurably from conversations with Oneida scholars Loretta V. Metoxen, C. F. W. Wheelock, Susan G. Daniels, Marge Stevens, L. Gordon McLester, Doug Kiel, and Renee Zakhar. Arlen Speights brought his many talents to this project—reading and commenting on several drafts and restoring the photo for the cover. I am so fortunate to have him in my life.

Cristina Stanciu

I came across Laura Cornelius Kellogg's work in graduate school at the University of Illinois at Urbana-Champaign, and I remember my initial frustration with the scarcity of scholarly and newspaper articles about her (not to mention a biography of Kellogg, which is still sorely needed in the field.) This project grew alongside my other work on Native and new immigrant writing in the first decades of the twentieth century, and I am thrilled to have worked with the most patient, supportive, inquisitive, and brilliant co-editor. Kristina Ackley, I will cherish our regular phone conversations from coast to coast (Richmond, Virginia to Olympia, Washington), the many lists, hundreds (thousands?) of emails, our little victories and frustrations, as well as our unwavering determination to bring Laura Kellogg's work in print.

Many people and institutions deserve recognition for helping along the way. Robert Dale Parker, my mentor at Illinois, has supported this project from its inception to its conclusion, and his generosity may take a few lifetimes to repay. At the University of Illinois at Urbana-Champaign, an army of scholars in the American Indian Studies Program have offered guidance at various stages: LeAnne Howe, Robert Warrior, Jodi Byrd, Matthew Gilbert, Frederick Hoxie, John McKinn, and Debbie Reese. In the English Department, two former graduate directors, William J. Maxwell and Stephanie Foote, helped fund early research trips. At Michigan State University, the late Susan Krouse in the American Indian Studies Program was a superb interlocutor. I met Larry Hauptman in the summer of 2013 by accident in the National Archives, after he had answered many questions by phone and email long before this chance encounter; his work on Kellogg remains groundbreaking in the field.

Many thanks also to the English department at Virginia Commonwealth University (VCU), my home institution, for their continued support (my colleagues, my chair, Katherine Bassard, and the best staff any department could hope for: Margret Schuler, Ginny Schmitz, and Derek Van Buskirk). I would also like to acknowledge the support of my VCU colleagues, particularly Catherine Ingrassia, Marcel Cornis-Pope, Bryant Mangum, Katherine S. Nash, Jennifer Rhee, Kimberly Brown, David Golumbia, John Glover, and Gregory Smithers. Thanks also to Santos Ramos, my smart and tireless research assistant at VCU. Bogdan Stanciu has juggled parenting, image editing, and cheerleading in gracious ways, and I could never find the right words to thank him.

Kristina Ackley and Cristina Stanciu

We would both like to thank the following scholars for their support and assistance at various stages of this project: A. LaVonne Ruoff, K. Tsianina Lomawaima, Chadwick Allen, Jeanie O'Brien, Jackie Rand, Brenda Child, Brian Hosmer, Phil Round, John Troutman,

P. Jane Hafen, Ned Blackhawk, David Martinez, Theresa McCarthy, Susan Hill, Mary Jane McCallum, Kevin White, and Rick Monture. We also thank the following institutions: the staff at the Newberry Library in Chicago, particularly Scott M. Stevens and John Aubry, for their guidance and generosity; the staff at the National Archives in Washington, DC; the Missouri Valley Special Collections; the Kansas City Historical Society; the registrar, archives, and special collections at Barnard College (especially Hillary Thorsen and Shannon O'Neill); the Onondaga County Public Library (especially librarian Kimberly Kleinhans); the Stanford University Archives (Aimée Morgan); the University of Wisconsin–Madison Archives (Cathy Jacob); the Missouri Valley Special Collections (Katie Sowder); the Wisconsin Historical Society (Lisa R. Marine); the Southwest Museum of the American Indian and the Autry National Center (Marilyn Van Winkle).

It was a pleasure to work with Deanna McCay, Mona Hamlin, Jennika Baines, Christopher Vecsey, Kelly L. Balenske, our talented copy-editor Bruce Volbeda, the staff at Syracuse University Press, and the anonymous reviewers. For permission to reprint parts of previously published articles, we thank the University of Nebraska Press. We are both very grateful to the Oneida Nation of Wisconsin and their continued support of this project. As we were completing the final draft of this manuscript, we received the sad news that Kristina's grandmother, Alice M. Torres, had passed away. Alice was extremely proud to have lived her entire life on the Wisconsin Oneida Reservation, deeply valued the power of education, and always said that the Oneidas were a strong people who overcame great obstacles. Part of her legacy is her family—at the time of her death she had 87 direct descendants (children, grandchildren, and great-grandchildren). We hope that Laura Cornelius Kellogg's words will inspire and inform those already familiar with her work, as well as a new generation of readers. We dedicate this book to our parents and children, and to the Oneida community.

December 1, 2014

Chronology

September 10, 1880   Born on the Oneida Indian Reservation (Seymour, Wisconsin), near Green Bay, Wisconsin, the daughter of Adam Poe and Cecilia Bread Cornelius. US Indian Census Rolls of 1925 report Kellogg's birth year as 1879, but genealogical records held by the Oneida Nation in Wisconsin Cultural Heritage Department report her birth date as September 20, 1880. The database of genealogical materials of the Oneida Cultural Heritage Department is comprised of tribal enrollment records and, in Kellogg's case, family birthdates recorded in the nearby Church of the Holy Apostles.[1]

1887–1933   Nearly 100 percent of the 65,000-acre reservation in Wisconsin was allotted following the Dawes General Allotment Act of 1887. Over 90 percent of land was lost as a direct result of this legislation, the Burke Act of 1906, and the Federal Competency Commission of 1917.

1898   Graduated with honors from Grafton Hall in Fond du Lac, Wisconsin.

May 1903   Spoke at the eviction of Indians from Warner Ranch Hot Springs; was called "Indian Joan of Arc" in southern California newspapers.

1902–1904   Was instructor at the Sherman Institute, Riverside Government Indian School, California.

January–May 1905   Attended Stanford University.

Fall 1906– **Spring 1907**	Attended Barnard College, Columbia University, as a special student. At Barnard, she appeared in an undergraduate play and was elected to the Undergraduate Election Committee. Published the story "Overalls and Tenderfoot" in *The Barnard Bear.*
Spring 1908	Attended the Normal School at the University of Wisconsin–Madison; was a member of the tennis club (played for the seniors' team in the spring of 1908).
1908–1910	Traveled to Europe, where she visited Great Britain, France, and Germany.
May 1910	Confronted Buffalo Bill in New York City about the Indian stereotypes he promoted and from which he profited.
October 1910	Her father passed away; she was called home to Oneida.
April–October 1911	Member, Temporary Executive Committee, American Indian Association/Society of American Indians (SAI).
1911	Presented her response to Edgar A. Bancroft's address "The Indian" at the unveiling of Lorado Taft's "Black Hawk" statue at Eagles' Nest Bluff, Oregon, Illinois, on July 1.
October 1911	Member of the Executive Committee of the Society of American Indians (SAI).
April 22, 1912	Married Orrin Joseph Kellogg in Stevens Point, Wisconsin. Born in Davenport, Iowa, Kellogg was an attorney living in Minneapolis, Minnesota.
October 1912– **October 1913**	Vice-President, Education Division, Society of American Indians.
June 5, 1913	Testified before the Senate Committee on Indian Affairs on an Indian appropriation bill. Advocated

for funding for the Lolomi industrial village plan. Argued strongly for a protected autonomy and continued relationship with federal government.

October 11, 1913   Arrested in Pawhuska, Oklahoma.

December 24, 1913   Her adopted son, Robert Kellogg, was born in Oneida, Wisconsin.

1916   Arrested in Colorado.

May 2, 1916   Testified before the Senate Committee on Indian Affairs. Called for a congressional "scientific investigation" to uncover the incompetence of the Indian Bureau. Presented her proposal for industrial development and for instituting a policy of self-help to "continue the common ownership of the tribe."

August 7, 1917   Provided testimony to the Federal Competency Commission about ending trust period on allotments at Oneida Reservation in Wisconsin. She gave the testimony in Oneida and had it translated into English.

1919   Newspapers report her trip to the League of Nations.

1919   The federal government closed the Oneida Boarding School.

1919   The United States filed successful suit in district court, *U.S. v. Boylan*, 256 F. 468 (N.D.N.Y. 1919), which recovered the last thirty-two acres of the Oneida Reservation in New York State.

1919–1922   Involved in the Everett Commission; hired Edward Everett to pursue Six Nations lands claim.

1920   Published *Our Democracy and the American Indian*. The court of appeals affirmed *U.S. v. Boylan* (256 F. 468 (N.D.N.Y. 1919), aff'd, 265 F. 165 (2d Cir. 1920)).

1921–1924	Tried unsuccessfully to buy former Oneida Boarding School for her Lolomi plan for economic self-sufficiency. The Catholic Diocese of Green Bay bought the school in 1924. The tribe was successful in efforts to reclaim the site, which they bought back in 1984. Known today as the Norbert Hill, Sr. Center, it is the location of the current tribal government and high school.
November 1922	Her mother, Cecilia Bread Cornelius, passed away. Cecilia Bread Cornelius, who was the youngest daughter of Daniel Bread, was survived by four children (Chester Poe, Alice Cornelius, Laura Kellogg, and Frank Ford Cornelius) and two grandchildren (Mildred and Cecilia).
1922–1924	Started raising money in Haudenosaunee communities (also urban communities in Wisconsin and the Stockbridge-Munsee and Brothertown tribal nations) for the Six Nations land claim. Told members of the "Six Nations Club" that if they gave money to support the litigation, they would share in a monetary claim. It was these activities that led to charges of fraud and the later removal of Haudenosaunee political and spiritual leader Tadodaho (George Thomas) at Onondaga, New York, in 1924.
November 1922	Attended a meeting of the Indian Welfare League in Albany, New York.
June 26, 1925	Suit filed in *Deere et al. v. State of New York et al.* 22 F. 2d 851 (1927). Kellogg worked with James Deere (St. Regis Mohawk) to initiate litigation on behalf of himself, the tribe, and the Iroquois Confederacy to eject the state of New York, the St. Lawrence River Power Company, and others from land reserved to the plaintiffs in the 1784 Treaty of Fort Stanwix. Though the case was dismissed in 1927 (and upheld in *Deere v. St. Lawrence River*

Power Co. et al. 32 F.2d 550 (2d Cir. 1929), Kellogg and others established an Iroquois (Haudenosaunee) land rights strategy that relied on treaty rights and the idea that no single Iroquois nation had the authority to cede or sell land.[2]

October 10, 1925 Took part in a ceremony to condole Oneida Chiefs at Oneida, Wisconsin. The ceremony was part of a larger effort to revitalize the traditional, political, and spiritual leadership, based on clan affiliation and a relationship with the Iroquois Confederacy. From the time of the Oneidas' arrival in Wisconsin in 1821, there was a steady move away from hereditary leadership and toward an elected one. The 1925 ceremony was part of a broader movement to reestablish the Oneida Longhouse; in 2005, it culminated in the travel of members of the Oneida Longhouse to the Tonawanda Seneca in New York State to receive strands of wampum, which were part of the *Katsistowan*^ or "Big Fire."

May 4, 1926 Testified before the Senate Committee on Indian Affairs (regarding development of oil and gas mining leases on Indian reservations) in support of the Indian Defense League.

October 1927 Arrested in Canada with Orrin J. Kellogg and Wilson K. Cornelius. The charges were related to fundraising for Six Nations land claim.

March 1, 1929 Testified before the Senate Subcommittee on Indian Affairs (regarding survey of conditions of the Indians of the United States), as part of a larger contingent of Haudenosaunee leaders from New York State. Responded sharply to the Bureau of Indian Affairs' criticisms about her work in Native communities, advocating for a continued "protected autonomy" status and a continued relationship with federal government.

1930	Corresponded with J. N. B. Hewitt of the Smithsonian about compiling an Oneida (or Six Nations) dictionary; Hewitt discouraged her.
1934	The Indian Reorganization Act passed.
July 1935	Her husband, Orrin J. Kellogg, passed away at the Kelloggs' residence in Wisconsin at the age of 54.
1936	The Oneidas adopted the Oneida Constitution, which established the tribal governing bodies (the Oneida Business Committee and the General Tribal Council); one of their goals was to recover the land lost during the allotment period.
Summer 1937	As its executive secretary, Laura Cornelius Kellogg convened the Grand Council of the Iroquois Confederacy at Hogansburg, New York, home of the Saint Regis Mohawk Tribe.

Sources date Kellogg's death as either 1947 (in New York) or 1949 (in Wisconsin). The details of her life just prior to her death are not clear, but it is likely that she struggled financially.[3]

Laura Cornelius Kellogg

Introduction

Laura Cornelius Kellogg:
Haudenosaunee Thinker, Native Activist, American Writer

Cristina Stanciu and Kristina Ackley

Scanning through a recent edition of the Wisconsin Oneida tribal newspaper, *Kalihwisaks* ("she looks for the news"), we read stories that cover a variety of issues: the tribe's passage of a judiciary law that will implement a new court system, photos of a youth powwow, warnings about the public health risk of influenza, maps of a proposed community events recreational area. Letters to the editor critique recent decisions by the tribal leadership, advertisements call the readers' attention to local businesses, and the numerous birth, wedding, and death announcements document the life of the Wisconsin Oneida community.[1] The bi-weekly newspaper, sent free of charge to all tribal members, is a material representation of a continuing and highly visible Oneida culture, which resists stubbornly the dominant colonial narrative of the vanishing Indian.

The Wisconsin Oneida are engaged in ongoing conversations about how to make their community sustainable, exploring ways to exercise self-governance and tribal sovereignty politically, economically, and culturally. How to best provide for the next Seven Generations is a question asked often in the *Kalihwisaks* and other tribal forums; and, while tribal members don't seem to take their community for granted, there is nonetheless an assurance of tribal continuance and persistence that permeates these tribal discourses. This atmosphere contrasts sharply with discussions in the past, particularly in the early twentieth century, when the community's continued existence was precarious.

Oneida Tribal Historian Loretta Metoxen refers to the early twentieth century as "the time when we almost lost it all,"[2] and although
the community today draws on its many strengths, it is sobering to
recount the challenges the Wisconsin Oneidas have faced. The threats
were many: land loss, unemployment, frayed social ties, and competing visions of tribal and US citizenship.

The Oneidas continued to exercise sovereignty during one of the
most intensely assimilationist eras in recent times. Laura Cornelius
Kellogg, the Oneida leader, was an integral part of a broader movement that contested the erasure of Oneida identity and self-governance. A well-known, yet contested figure both within and outside
the Wisconsin Oneida community, Kellogg mirrors in many ways the
resiliency and endurance of the Oneida nation. A combative idealist
who continually searched for ways to implement her ideas, Kellogg
and her legacy belong within a larger framework of Oneida values and
beliefs about tradition, modernity, locality, and connection.

◆

Laura Miriam ("Minnie") Cornelius Kellogg was born on the Oneida
reservation in Wisconsin in 1880, daughter of Adam Poe and Cecilia
Bread Cornelius. She came from a long line of Oneida tribal leaders;
her grandfather, Daniel Bread (Dehowyadilou, "Great Eagle"), was a
well-known "Pine Chief" (civil leader)—a friend of Henry Clay and
Daniel Webster—who helped find land for his people after the Oneidas were forcibly removed from New York State to Wisconsin in the
early nineteenth century.[3]

The Oneidas, today spread across three communities (located in
New York State, Wisconsin, and Ontario), have an active land claim in
present-day New York State, stemming from several late eighteenth-
and early nineteenth-century treaties with the federal government, as
well as treaties with New York State. Congress passed a law in 1790
precluding states from entering into treaties with tribes, but New York
State ignored that provision, pressuring Oneidas to sign agreements
that led to a loss of millions of acres of Oneida land in New York State.
In 1821, a large group of Oneidas left New York State and settled
in Wisconsin. Later, another group went to Ontario, while another

group remained in New York, where many Oneidas lived with the Onondaga Nation. The three communities remain separate in terms of land base and governments, although many Oneidas consider all three to be part of a broader Oneida nation.[4]

The Oneidas' uprooting from New York to Wisconsin in the 1820s and 1830s, along with tribal disunity, led to severe changes in Oneida politics.[5] The enormous loss of land caused by relocation and, later, by the Dawes Act (1887), shrunk the Wisconsin Oneida land base to less than ninety acres by 1934.[6]

Most importantly, Kellogg came from a long line of strong Haudenosaunee women; among Six Nations' peoples, women held great political and social powers, not only providing tribal sustenance with their control of cleared lands for agriculture but also choosing the representatives of the Six Nations Confederacy Council. Reflecting on the importance Haudenosaunee women placed on maintaining social bonds and political relationships, Kellogg worked to strengthen relationships with Haudenosaunee people. She understood that the Oneida Nation was inextricably linked to the Six Nations Confederacy in New York State. She argued for an Oneida political subjectivity, a vision whereby Native people would articulate and determine their own beliefs in tribal spaces. This vision was informed by Kellogg's citizenship as a Wisconsin Oneida, her steadfast belief in the possibility and viability of working with the US federal government, and her grand vision of Native autonomous places. Kellogg's genealogy is important for understanding her political and aesthetic views; like Daniel Bread's activism, her political action and later work on the Oneida land claims were informed by traditional tribal values and a favorable view of "modern" adaptation to economic and political changes.

A founding member of the Society of American Indians (SAI) executive committee and a vice-president of the education division between 1911 and 1913, she testified before the Senate Committee on Indian Affairs on several occasions in the 1910s and 1920s. Local newspapers reported her plans to appear before the League of Nations in 1919, and she was described as "a woman who would shine in any society."[7] She traveled extensively, not only throughout the United

States and Canadian reservations and reserves, but also throughout cities in North America and Europe. She developed her ideas on Indian labor, education, and economic sovereignty in her only published book, *Our Democracy and the American Indian: A Comprehensive Presentation of the Indian Situation as It Is Today* (1920). Kellogg fought tirelessly for the implementation of her model of the industrial village (her "Lolomi" plan of industrialization and federal incorporation) and faced enormous challenges on the Wisconsin Oneida reservation and from other Iroquois nations as she attempted to "resurrect . . . the structure and operation of the eighteenth-century League of the Iroquois" in the 1920s and 1930s.[8] Allegations of mismanagement of funds haunted her throughout her later professional life, but her work and legacy are important for the contemporary Oneida community, as well as for scholars recovering her work as an aspiring writer, orator, performer, and Oneida lands claims activist.[9] As an author, activist, and public figure, Kellogg promoted the persistence and creation of places that were uniquely Oneida. As we shall see, she envisioned sustainable places with a deep sense of meaning to community members, extending the possibilities of her Indian industrial village model for other Native communities. Against all odds, Laura Cornelius Kellogg voiced her frustrations with American capitalism, federal Indian policy, and the widespread misrepresentation of American Indians.[10]

◆

> She is a woman who would shine in any society: it is said that she is destined to take the place in literature Zitkala-Ša seemed about to achieve.
>
> *Los Angeles Times,* March 1904

Laura Cornelius Kellogg was an Oneida activist, orator, linguist, performer, and reformer of Indian policy, a founding member of the Society of American Indians, as well as an author of fiction, poetry, speeches, and essays. As the national newspapers took note, there was much to admire in Bonnin's and Kellogg's work as Indigenous women activists at a time when women's rights and citizenship were prominent issues on the national scene.[11] Nevertheless, although they diverged on some issues, Kellogg's radicalism and political work is more reminiscent of Carlos Montezuma than perhaps any other SAI member. Like Montezuma, she helped found the SAI, was a fervent and acerbic advocate for Indigenous rights, and was often at odds with the Office of Indian Affairs; like Montezuma, Kellogg was controversial, exoticized, and misinterpreted in the popular press; and although she differed from Montezuma in her views on education—she strictly opposed the off-reservation boarding school model—Kellogg shared the Yavapai doctor's ambition and determination to change the lives of Indian people for the better. In 1912, she married Orrin Kellogg, a lawyer from Minneapolis and an important ally in Kellogg's activist work. He did not often take the public stage, although he was hired as a lawyer and adviser by many of the tribal nations that Kellogg worked with and thus worked closely on many of the same issues.[12]

A public speaker with electrifying charisma who was often stereotyped as an "Indian princess" in the popular press, Kellogg drew on Haudenosaunee and non-Native traditions and discourses to support her life's work to transform Indian reservations into cooperative, self-governing communities, and to offer practical solutions for achieving Indigenous autonomy through economic sovereignty. Reading her surviving work alongside her public speeches and oratory, and in the light of internal SAI tensions and factions, competing representations in the popular press, and her cultural work through the 1920s and beyond helps us see how this controversial and fierce public Indian intellectual woman fought for Indigenous economic self-determination, education, and the recuperation of Oneida land. Her versatility and negotiation of several audiences (local, national, and international), her occasional transgressions and irreverence point to Kellogg's determination to find an Indigenous voice of her own as she also became the voice of the Oneidas on the national scene. Her surviving published literary work, along with her public speeches and addresses to Congress and at SAI meetings, as well as her work at Oneida, Wisconsin, offer a useful archive to understand one of the most controversial "citizen Indians" at the beginning of the twentieth century. Ultimately, Kellogg's daring enterprise of diverging from the expected path of "new Indian" leaders came at an enormous personal cost as she sought to envision a future for the Oneidas in Wisconsin.

In the first decade of the twentieth century, Kellogg's record suggested a bright future. In 1898, when she graduated with honors from Grafton Hall (in Fond du Lac, Wisconsin), national newspapers took notice of her, announcing that she had already compiled a grammar of the Oneida language.[13] Her literary ambitions led to the publication of two stories in *The Church's Mission to the Oneidas* in 1902. One year later she professed that "Literature shall be my life work, and its aim shall be to benefit my people."[14] Later that same year she published her only surviving poem, *A Tribute to the Future of My Race*, a poem she recited during the commencement exercises at Sherman Institute in Riverside, California, where she was instructor between 1902 and 1904. Kellogg, whom historian Laurence Hauptman considers "one of the most important and tragic figures in recent American Indian history," has a controversial legacy despite her recognized accomplishments on the Oneida reservation and in the national political and cultural arenas.[15] Despite the many controversies surrounding her public persona—including the often-cited episodes of her arrests—Kellogg was recognized for being one of the best Oneida speakers of her generation and a linguist who spoke Oneida, Mohawk, and English equally well. She attended several prestigious universities (Stanford University, Barnard College, and the University of Wisconsin), and lived in Europe to round out her education and to learn about social and economic models she would later try to implement at Oneida (especially the German model of industrial villages).[16]

She was read in the company of her more famous peer writer and activist Zitkala-Ša, and was described by the *Los Angeles Times* in 1904 as "one of the most interesting Indian women in the United States," praise that brought Kellogg to national attention as an Indian public intellectual.[17]

In 1898, the year she graduated with honors from Grafton Hall (a private school in Fond du Lac, Wisconsin), national newspapers praised her accomplishments: "she is a good Latin and Greek scholar

1. Laura Miriam Cornelius, 1902. Photo Source: *The Church's Mission to the Oneidas.*

and has compiled a grammar of the Oneida language," announced *The Detroit Free Press*; "Minnie Cornelius, an ambitious Oneida Indian girl, was graduated from Grafton Hall. . . . She speaks five languages fluently," announced *The Indiana Democrat*.[18] The world was ready for Laura "Minnie" Cornelius.

2. Grafton Hall, Fond du Lac, Wisconsin, ca. 1905. Courtesy of the Wisconsin Historical Society (image #WHi-31084).

The Washington Post placed her in the select company of other "New Indian Women"—in an article subtitled "Bright Daughters of Chiefs Who Have Many Accomplishments"—alongside E. Pauline Johnson, Inshta Theambra, Eugenie Vincent, Maud Echo Hawk, Jane E. Waloron, Go-Wan-Go Mohawk, and Gretchen Lyons. Striking examples of their intellectual vigor are shown in what the new Indian women have accomplished in art, literature, and education, and in their higher standing generally."[19]

The writer for *The Post* was not exaggerating; in an intense interview for *The New York Tribune* in 1903, "Laura Miriam Cornelius" [Kellogg] spelled out her plans "for the uplifting of her race." Throughout her career she would continue to advocate for "the Indian point of view": "White men and women have written cleverly of us, but from a white man's point of view. I hope to give the Indian side of American life." An image of the "Indian girl" as an aspiring writer accompanied the interview.

If the interview recorded her words accurately, Kellogg offered— as early as 1903—a glimpse into her long-lasting views on education, the sustainability of the reservation, and the future of Indian people: "Perhaps it seems strange to an outsider, for I know the ideas that prevail in regards to Indian life, but to do something great when I grew up was impressed upon me from my cradle by my parents, and I have known no other ambition."[20] This ambition would follow Kellogg throughout her life.

"The Old Indian Adjusted to New Conditions": Modernity and Tradition

Though Kellogg was an exceptional individual, she was no aberration, and we can locate many of her ideas and practices alongside an enduring political ideology and practice held by the members of the Wisconsin Oneida community. Though she was a divisive, often combative figure who polarized her community, she was also very much a product of it. Kellogg took pride in her upbringing on the reservation as well as in her education in non-Native schools. Kellogg was passionate about Native rights, framing them within an understanding of the political and legal relationship with the federal government that protected their unique status and inherent rights to lands. Exercising these rights was central in her lifelong efforts in the restoration of the Oneida Nation.[21]

At the same time, she was perhaps an anomaly among most of her contemporaries. At the inaugural meeting of the Society of American Indians (SAI) in 1911, she proclaimed, "I am not the new Indian; I am the old Indian adjusted to new conditions."[22] She saw the reservation as a potential place of opportunity, in direct opposition to a general consensus at the time that assimilation and a breakup of the reservation represented the best path for success. In a speech at the SAI annual meeting, she argued explicitly for the value of an "Indian" identity that relied on the knowledge of her elders:

> There are old Indians who have never seen the inside of a classroom whom I consider far more educated than the young Indian with his knowledge of Latin and algebra. There is something behind the superb dignity and composure of the old bringing up; there is something in the discipline of the Red Man which has given him a place in the literature and art of this country, there to remain separate and distinct in his proud, active bearing against all time, against all change.[23]

This emphasis on the value of the knowledge of elders and "the old bringing up" was central to Kellogg's arguments that the reservation was a place of potential for all Native people, particularly the Haudenosaunee. She balanced these long-standing beliefs with an embrace of change, as she placed her knowledge of traditions and community values firmly into modernity in order to assert her position as an Oneida woman. Fairly brimming with ideas about community empowerment that ran counter to the dominant push for assimilation, she worked to create places where the Wisconsin Oneida would have a stronger voice in a newly reconstituted Oneida Nation. By linking the Wisconsin Oneida to a larger sense of indigeneity, to a space that was marked as "Six Nations" (Haudenosaunee), she sought to re-cast Oneida, Wisconsin, as a place for industry, a place for tradition balanced with modernity.

In advocating for the reservation as a place of refuge for Native people, Kellogg went against much of the prevailing sentiment of Indian reformers in the early twentieth century. Many of her colleagues in the SAI, and prominent Oneidas such as Dennison Wheelock, were suspicious of her work to reframe the reservation as a place of opportunity and community. One of Kellogg's key insights was that tribes needed resources to create resources. Lack of economic opportunities fueled social dysfunction on the reservation, she argued, and Native nations could be vibrant places only if they had the economic base to support its members.

Kellogg may have also seen her work as a way to create a place for Haudenosaunee women, continuing the work of previous generations of Oneida women who were clan mothers and protectors of the nation's culture.[24] Throughout her life, Kellogg worked to create and plan physical spaces that nurtured Haudenosaunee beliefs and philosophies. She would develop her ideas about these spaces in her plan for "modern villages for Indians," first in a speech she gave at the SAI meeting in 1911 and, later, in her book, *Our Democracy and the American Indian* (1920). Kellogg ultimately dedicated her life to put this plan into practice.

The "Joan of Arc of Indians"

In May 1903, a dramatic scene unfolded at a place known as Warner's Ranch in northern San Diego County, California. It was a collision between those who believed in the original title of the Cupeños and their rights to the land, and those who sought to displace the Cupeños. The setting was tense—while the Cupeños had never ceded the land under Spanish, Mexican, or US colonial rule, the US Supreme Court had ruled that they had waited too long to press for their land rights. As a result, a non-Native was ruled the rightful owner, and he subsequently sued to have the Cupeños evicted. Many non-Natives were sympathetic to the Cupeños (also called "Copahs" by area newspapers). News coverage stressed the possibility of violent resistance. Many of the Cupeño men were reportedly armed, and news stories told of a foreboding "wailing" that was coming from the houses of the Cupeños as the removal date approached.[25]

Among the outsiders who had come to witness the removal was the young Laura "Minnie" Cornelius [Kellogg], who was teaching at the Sherman Indian Institute in nearby Riverside, and was subsequently welcomed into a meeting of the Cupeños. She rolled up her sleeves and donned the cowboy hat, well-adjusted to her new surroundings (figure 3). California newspapers dubbed her "the Indian Joan of Arc" for her conciliatory speech in what became popularly known as "the eviction of the [Southern California] Warner Ranch Indians."[26] According to newspaper accounts, she single-handedly and narrowly averted bloodshed:

> An Indian maiden prevented an uprising of the Copahs and caused them to submit peaceably to removal from Agua Caliente, on the Warner Ranch. . . . It was the tact of Laura M. Cornelius, a full-blood Oneida Indian girl that, at a critical time in a tribal council of the Copahs, turned their thoughts from resistance to compliance with the order to move. She did not argue with them; she told them no harrowing tales of the consequences of going on the warpath, but in simple language, spoken in their own tongue, she told those heartsick, discouraged aborigines the story of her own people. She called it a message from the children of the rising sun to the children of the setting sun.[27]

This performance, the newspaper argued, was sufficiently powerful to sway a number of people present. It is unclear exactly what she said, as no full record of the speech exists, but it is likely that she first presented her thoughts in Oneida, and then translated them for the Cupeños, who after all, did not speak the same language, regardless of what the newspaper erroneously believed was a common language. The speech and the resulting news coverage illustrated how a young Laura "Minnie" Cornelius presented a message about place and Native people and resiliency. Over the next two decades, she

3. Laura Cornelius in Southern California, 1902. Courtesy of the Braun Research Library, Autry National Center of the American West, Los Angeles (photo #1348).

consistently worked to secure her place as an Oneida woman in the early twentieth century, confronting a colonial government that sought to displace and erase Native presence. In doing so, she worked to create rhetorical spaces built on relationships, particularly with the federal government and other Haudenosaunee (also known as Six Nations and Iroquois) people.

"An Indian Girl and Glad of It"

Although Kellogg did not study at any government boarding schools, unlike many of her Native peers, she was an instructor at Sherman Indian School in California for almost two years before she resigned so that she could study law at Stanford University. Although her Stanford sojourn was brief (January–May 1905), newspapers in California took notice of her: "[She] will be the first Indian girl lawyer," the *Los Angeles Times* announced, "to teach her people their rights." Kellogg did not go on to become "the first Indian girl lawyer" right away, but she continued to study law and social work. An intriguing physical description accompanied this provocative caption:

4. Laura Cornelius in Southern California, 1903. Courtesy of the Braun Research
Library, Autry National Center of the American West,
Los Angeles (photo #1349).

"You would know her for an Indian instantly, *though* she is pretty and svelte and stylish, and talks with the finished grace of a trained society woman"[28] [emphasis added]. A stylish Indian woman was perhaps too much for this reporter, whose expectations of what "an Indian" should look like reflected contemporaneous views on Indian representation; yet he was not the first—or last—to remark on her physical qualities, style, and grace.

She transferred to Barnard College in the fall of 1906 to continue her study of law (and remained at Barnard until May 1907, focusing her studies on social work). The newspapers in New York City announced that Cornelius would start studying at Barnard, describing her as "unmistakably Indian in features and build," "tall, lithe, wiry of frame. Her complexion is olive without color; her abundant hair, worn parted, and drawn loosely back from her face in a heavy coil behind, is glossy and black; her eyes, very dark brown, are soft and kindly, rather than beadlike and glittering, after the popular notion that Indian eyes should be like" (see figure 5).

Although such descriptions exoticized her, her behavior and comments surprised the reporter, just as her stylish photo may have surprised the readers: "Say 'Indian' to Miss Laura M. Cornelius and verbally she is off. On such occasions she is the despair of the average shorthand writer." Her witty responses ultimately defied expectations:

> "I would not be anything but an Indian," she declares, proudly. "I am not weaned from my people and never will be. More schooling than usually falls to the lot of an Indian woman and more contact with Caucasian artificiality and insincerity have graduated me into what might be called *a polite Indian*, and

5. *Miss Laura M. Cornelius.*
Source: *The Sun*, 1906.

the process, I sometimes think, has taken a lot out of me[29] [emphasis added].

Laura Cornelius did not stay "a polite Indian" for the rest of her life, and this interview marks a shift in her public rhetoric; when she professes to have become a "polite Indian," she maintains her irreverence, especially when she comments on Indian misrepresentation and the public's ignorance about Indian life: "They don't know us; they don't know what it means to be killed alive." Although she had declared her interest in becoming a writer only a few years before, in 1906 she decided on deeds over words: "At one time I had a marvelous ambition to write; but the more I live the more I know that words, words, words are futile. I want to do, not to preach." Very critical of reservation life, which lacked "industry," she concluded: "It must be changed or we will die."[30]

The 1910s marked Laura Cornelius Kellogg's maturing decade. Between late 1908 and 1910, during her European sojourn, she made a vivid impression on British society: "Wherever she has gone, society has simply 'ovated' her; and, were she to remain in England long, she would doubtless be the leader of a circle all her own."[31] Europe was ready for "Princess Neoskalita" (figure 6). Competing representations and self-representations marked her stay in Europe. American and Australasian newspapers described her as a socialite in London:

6. *Laura Cornelius: A Redskin Princess.* Source: *Review of Reviews for Australasia*, 1909.

"A Redskin Princess" and "Princess Neoskalita" became the common descriptions. Although still exoticized and said to be "danc[ing] in the courts of Europe to obtain funds to help red men to a higher civilization,"[32] she was reported to be in Europe to study "the art, social lore, music and literature of the French and English and the system of town planning in Germany . . . [for] elevating her people." As the writer for *The Galveston Daily News* concluded his correspondence, she may well have been "a social toast in the city."[33] In 1909, *The Review of Reviews for Australasia* called her "the only racial representative of Minnehaha now in London,"[34] which may support the claim that she performed in Europe (given that Minnie Devereux, or "Minnie Ha-ha," was the only Indian actress European audiences may have been familiar with), but the evidence we have at this point is inconclusive. Laura Cornelius was known in Europe as "Princess Neoskalita," who lived in a "cosy London flat" according to newspaper reports. Having just arrived from Paris, "dressed in becoming English tailor-made costume, she spoke with enthusiasm of the flattering reception she had received from the most exclusive set in London society." Nevertheless, her goal was to study "English institutions and modes of thought."[35] Her lucid interviews show that, although she enjoyed the most select aristocratic company—fitting for the "chieftainess of the Oneida Iroquois nation"—she wanted to build cultural capital, forge connections, and plan ahead: "it is her intention to begin a movement in America to reorganize Indian affairs."[36] Her plan to "reorganize Indian affairs" stayed with her throughout her life.

A student of law, political science, and social work, Laura Cornelius attended prestigious institutions in the United States and Europe. Although she attended Stanford University, Barnard College, and the University of Wisconsin, she never graduated. A portrait of her in academic regalia appeared in a Madison, Wisconsin, newspaper in 1908 (figure 7), revealing that she may have had the best intentions to graduate, but they were thwarted, perhaps, by different opportunities and a trip to Europe in 1908.

Nonetheless, her education at "Sap Kettle," as she would put it in an interview later in the 1910s,[37] would remain essential for her: "I am

7. *Miss Laura M. Cornelius, Indian Student at the University.* Wisconsin newspaper clipping, ca. 1908. Courtesy of the Oneida Nation Museum.

confident that I learned as much from these untutored Indian men as I ever learned from all the universities which I attended in this country or in Europe."[38] In 1908, while in England, in a letter to the US Department of the Interior, she demanded that the federal government make arrangements to have the American ambassador present her at the royal court of England.[39] In 1910, she confronted Buffalo Bill in New York and, very critical of his stereotypical performances, explained to him that not all Indians in the United States were Plains Indians. Taking Buffalo Bill to task, she told him: "I don't belong to any tribe. . . . I am of the Six Nations of New York. We weren't tribes. We were called the Six Nations because we long ago had left the tribal state of society when the Europeans found us."[40] Although she made her literary plans secondary to her fight for Oneida land, she may have written at least one novel; newspapers in 1909 and 1910 reported her work on a novel (which we haven't found yet)—although the reporter did not consider it "serious work" of the "[Indian] princess":

> Apart from her more serious work, the princess has written a novel illustrating the ideas, the manners, and the customs of the aborigines of North America, being the first Red Indian to write such a work of fiction. The title of her book is "Wynnogene," or "A Ray of Light," and the scene is laid in America fifty years before Columbus crossed the Atlantic.[41]

In 1909, her literary plans were still clear, albeit deferred: "Later, *when my people are happier*, I hope to show that the quality of the Indian imagination has a place among the literatures of nations"[42] [emphasis added].

Although Laura Cornelius devoted most of her life to political and activist work for the Six Nations land claims, she was a passionate writer and, had she had the leisure and disposition, she might have rivaled fellow Native women's literary work (recall the earlier comparison with Gertrude Bonnin by the *Los Angeles Times* reporter). From her correspondence with Carlos Montezuma in 1914, we learn that she had a play coming out on Broadway in December of that year.[43] The editors of her only published book, *Our Democracy and the American Indian*, presented her in 1920 as "author," "lecturer," and "playwright." Although no manuscripts of the titles listed by editors survive (*The Lost Empire, The Trail of the Morning Star*, and *Eagle Eye*), we know that she registered an "Indian play in one Act," *The Trail of the Morning Star*, with the copyright office in 1916, using a rather surprising name—"Princess E-gah-tah-yen [i.e., Mrs. O. J. Kellogg]."[44] In 1916, *The Edgefield Advertiser* and *The Day Book* used this name to refer to the "Indian Princess's" work in Washington, DC, in articles with provocative titles: "To Solve Indian Problem: Oneida Princess Is Championing Bill for Autonomous Government of Her Race" and "Indian Princess Is Active Lobbyist in Capital," respectively. The journalist for *The Edgefield Advertiser* quoted her on her new name:

> Egahtahyen is the name by which Mrs. O. J. Kellogg, an Oneida Indian princess, is fondly called by the people of her race for whose advancement she is always struggling. She is in Washington, D.C., at present, working in support of a bill by which the Indians will be provided with a protected autonomous government. . . . The Cherokees gave me my name of Egahtahyen, and it means "The Dawn," which they think I bring to them.[45]

The *Syracuse Journal* also chimed in, explaining that "Egahtahyen, generally known as Mrs. O. J. Kellogg, the Indian princess of the Oneida, is in Washington, D.C., where she has gone to work on behalf of the bill to provide the Indians with protective autonomous government, soon to be introduced by Senator Lane of Oregon." After "Princess Neoskalita," a persona she cultivated—or was cultivated for her—during her European tour, "Princess Egahtahyen" was back in the American spotlight. Did she internalize the "princess" category that the American and international newspapers had described her by, or was this a new way for Kellogg to present her various public personas, to use this category to her advantage by seizing the public's attention? Perhaps we'll never know; but we do know that she wanted to attract attention. Whether through hats, dress, names, or words, Laura Cornelius Kellogg wanted to be seen and heard.[46]

The Writer: Against the Vanishing Indian Trope

Laura Cornelius's early writings reflected her interest in Oneida storytelling. Although she wrote in English, with a clear sense of literary conventions, she grounded her stories in Oneida history. Before her work received national attention, she published two stories in *The Church's Mission to the Oneidas*: "The Legend of the Bean" and "The Sacrifice of the White Dog." Both stories present brief aspects of Haudenosaunee cosmology to a primarily non-Native audience, from whom the Episcopal Church was soliciting funds. The Oneidas had removed to Wisconsin in part because of the promises and support of the missionaries such as Eleazar Williams, and many of Kellogg's contemporaries regularly attended the Episcopal church (founded as Hobart Church, later changed to Church of the Holy Apostles), founded in 1825. Oneidas also sent their children to the church's mission school. Jack Campisi argues that the Oneidas did not practice the Longhouse spiritual and political system once they arrived in Wisconsin, and instead were a "Christian society." At the time of Campisi's research in the early 1970s, Oneida members of the Longhouse began publicly practicing ceremonies and advocated for community recognition, culminating with the Wisconsin Oneidas receiving part of the *Katsistowan^* in 2005, an essential ceremony that confers Haudenosaunee spiritual and political legitimacy. Laura Cornelius was obviously aware of some of the ceremonies and stories of the Longhouse traditions, and she chose to present them in a publication that was written to appeal to potential donors to the Episcopal Church.[47]

Although the editor of *The Church's Mission to the Oneidas* referred to her stories as "legends"—"We are indebted to Miss Cornelius' graphic pen for the following Oneida Legends"—he recognized her talent as a writer in his praise of her "graphic pen." *The Legend of the Bean* is an etiological story, explaining the emergence of the new plant among the Oneidas. Told in the first person, the story recounts an old oral story the writer "begged" of her grandmother, who had carried the story through many generations. It begins formulaically in the "long ago." After learning how a "pretty green vine" emerged to create this "strange product," the narrator tells of an old woman who tasted it, risking her life "for the benefit of my friends, my home, my race" (112) The community adopts this new product, and the narrator's grandmother ends the story praising the old woman's act of courage: "This brave old woman lived to see her six sons grow in wisdom and virtue and become great Chiefs of the tribe" (112). These multiple levels of mediation, rendered through the voices of Oneida women of several generations, suggest that the story from "the long ago" survives as it is passed on through generations. The story also points to the meeting ground of the Oneida oral tradition and the translation and rendition of the story into English, which facilitates the meeting of old and new epistemologies and storytelling strategies.

The Sacrifice of the White Dog shows the emerging writer's increasing awareness of her imagined audience: "Oh that the expanse of time were less, and the camp fire burning, to make my story glow with interest to the reader" (113). As she elicits her audience's attention through a faux-apologetic rhetorical device, she prefaces her story with a limitation: "But my pen paints poorly." This lack, however, appears to signal the expected reader's inability to decipher the cultural landscape of the story, because of translingual difference and the generic reader's inability to understand what the writer calls "the old Oneida vocabulary which so well my tale would tell." Cornelius, therefore, turns the seeming apology—a strategy many American women writers also used to appeal to broader audiences—into an occasion for cross-cultural translation of an old Iroquois sacrificial ritual (of a white dog, described as "the emblem of innocence"). The story ends with an intriguing spectrum of patriotic colors: "the white dog, the emblem of innocence; the red, of victory over enemy; and the blue, heaven's color, the sign mark of the Divine Spirit, which guided them to the worship of the Great Spirit."[48] In an interview a year later, she explained her method: "I have travelled long distances and to the remotest corners of the reserve to get from the oldest residents these quaint fancies of our tribe. I go to many persons for the same story, in order to compare their versions. These I take down in the Indian vernacular, from which I make literal translations, and later do them over into good English." Cornelius also opined on Indian humor: "There is a great deal of racial humor quite new to Indian literature, because no one who cannot understand the everyday communion of these people has been able to catch this flavor."[49]

In her next story, published during her time at Barnard College, she would try to capture just that. Her story *Overalls and Tenderfoot*, published in *The Barnard Bear*, is about a "Western girl" who travels out West to Yosemite National Park without a chaperone and is repeatedly scrutinized by middle-class white women who find her behavior outrageous.[50] In some ways, Laura's picture at Barnard emulates the character she describes (figure 8).

Laura Cornelius [Kellogg] wrote the poem *A Tribute to the Future of My Race* (1903) while teaching at the Sherman Institute in Riverside, California. *A Tribute* was reprinted in a Carlisle Indian Industrial School newspaper, *The Red Man and Helper*, accompanied by this note: "The following was read at the Sherman Institute, Riverside, California, recently by the author, a talented Indian maiden, well known to many at Carlisle. The occasion was the graduating exercises of the Indian school, where Miss Cornelius is instructor."[51] Only five years earlier, her graduation address from Grafton Hall was an essay entitled "The Romans of America," where she "traced the analogy between the Iroquois Confederacy, or Six Nations, and the ancient Roman Empire."[52] Her interest in this analogy as a marker of Indigenous sovereignty, notwithstanding military conquest, also informs her only surviving poem. *A Tribute to the Future of My Race*, a nod to Henry Wadsworth Longfellow's *The Song of Hiawatha*—from which she borrows not only the meter, but also full lines—is an intriguing and surprising poem. The title is forward-looking,

8. Laura Cornelius as a student at Barnard College, 1907. Courtesy of the Barnard Archives and Special Collections, New York.

suggestive of continuity, survival, and "the future."[53] Read in the context of its initial address, the poem celebrates the "future of the [Indian] race" represented by the graduating class of 1904. Nonetheless, there is more to Kellogg's poem than a reductive endorsement of federal Indian policy. Her views on education differed tellingly from those promoted by Carlisle and other off-reservation boarding schools, as her activist and political work show: "There are old Indians who have never seen the inside of a class room whom I consider far [more] educated than the young Indian with his knowledge of Latin or Algebra."[54]

How do we reconcile the aim to maintain a federal-Indian relationship with the critique of its uneven power? How do we read the speaker's incantation in mid-poem that "our glorious America / Be the world's salvation—haven" (lines 82–83) when we know the dramatic (and traumatic) consequences similar messianic lines that her poem invokes have had on some Indian students in boarding schools? Ultimately, what are the implications of Cornelius' surmise toward the end of the poem, "Yea, the hearts' right hand we give them, / Blue-eyed Royalty American" (lines 143–44)?

One way to begin to answer these questions is to consider that the celebratory and patriotic images are a necessary part of Cornelius' poem, given the poem's occasion; at the same time, the speaker's direct address to Indian students, in well-crafted lines, lies at the heart of the poem, conveying the idea of necessary adaptation and survival through education. The poem begins with a negation, meanders through historic images of colonization and dispossession, and culminates in an unpredictable ending on a note of loss, necessary adaptation (including assimilationist practices like education), and survival: "Theirs, our native land forever, / Ours their presence and their teachings. / Ours the noblest and the best" (lines 145–47). The beginning positions the speaker as an Oneida orator greeting her audience:

But from the Northern of Wisconsin,
From the land of the Oneidas,
From the Chieftain clan Cornelius,

From the friendly Iroquois
Comes the greeting of the wampum
And a tribute, humble, simple. (lines 5–10)

The emphasis on the "humble" and "simple" "tribute" the speaker prepares to deliver presupposes a friendly relation with the audience; but to know the story "of the future of a nation," the speaker has to descend into a troubled past of an "infant, warrior people," when they had "a whole continent their own!" (line 55), moving swiftly through a series of questions about the students' ancestors and suggestive images of traditional education: "Ah, who were they? All barbarians? Were they men / Without legend or tradition?" (lines 56–57). The speaker ends by reminding the Native students that they "spring from noble warrior blood, / As brave as Saxon, Roman, Greek" and by suggesting reconciliation, extending "the wampum strand," a symbol of "friendship" and "gratitude" (lines 123–24 and 139–40): "*Theirs, our native land forever,* / Ours, their presence and their teachings. / Ours, the noblest and the best" (lines 143–47; our emphasis). The poem ends in an apparent surrender of "hearts' right hand" to the "blue-eyed Royalty American," but the key image of the lost Indian land lingers after the poem's last lines. The speaker reclaims Indian agency particularly in the poem's last line, a direct address to Indian students across the country: "Ours, the noblest and the best." This optimistic view is part of Cornelius Kellogg's versatile, performative public persona, which often negotiated the competing demands of her audiences.

Laura's invitation to speak at the unveiling of Lorado Taft's statue of Black Hawk in Oregon, Illinois, July 1911, was a timely occasion to meditate on contemporaneous representations of Indian people—this time in sculpture. Laura Cornelius and Charles A. Eastman were tasked to respond to the designated orator Edgar A. Bancroft's speech, which was a direct rendition of the nineteenth-century rhetoric of the "vanishing Indian," full of references to "the primitive peoples" and "[the] true child of nature"—and different from "our great Christian Anglo-Saxon Race."[55] The two Native orators had the daunting task of responding publicly to the white supremacist relegation of "the

Indian" to an everlasting bronze statue, but respond they did. Eastman started by acknowledging the virtues of "civilization" but went
on to point out the greater influence his "untutored" tribe had on
him, saying that he was not a heathen and sanctioning the civilizing
work that Bancroft extolled in his speech. Like Eastman, Cornelius
started her speech by lamenting the disappearance of Indian people
who were killed before they could commemorate what they could
have celebrated if they were still alive: "The race is not here to-day.
The race is not here, to rejoice with me for this great moment" (167,
current edition). She turned to the absence of Indian leaders and orators to rewrite the trope of the "vanishing Indian"—a trope familiar
to her audiences. Like her poem, *A Tribute to the Future of My Race*,
her speech is also heavily punctuated by lines from Longfellow's epic
The Song of Hiawatha (1855), which has also generated a series of
immortalizations in stone. Well-versed in European Fine Arts, Kellogg
glosses over the long-term implications of the statue but takes the
time to speak about American art, with an awareness of the aesthetic
implications the statue will carry throughout time:

> Rightly is its subject the American Indian. He who knows the
> throes of Gethsemane. He who knows the blood-sweat of
> anguish. He who has sounded the very depths of a national
> tragedy. [. . .] He who, like the Greek, belonged to a hero
> age they could not comprehend. Yet when all is done, calmly
> he draws his simple robe about him and stands there mute and
> upright, looking boldly back upon it all, even as the eagle faces
> the glaring sun. Looking back to the East. (170)

Laura Cornelius's sarcasm and implied criticism of Indian
removal—especially as she describes the American Indian "looking
back to the East," to the lost homes—are telling especially as she
ponders the American Indian as the subject of this new American art
form. Her appreciation of the new artistic medium collides with her
implied critique of colonialism and her call for justice: "today it is to
the mind of the artist we must turn to for justice to the American

Indian" (171). This momentary sliding into her activist persona—
an opposite persona to her public performer persona—creates the
momentum for further evaluation and self-evaluation: "But I am not
here to unearth the long story of infamies. [. . .] Rather I have
come here to thank you for the Indian" (171). The end of her speech
returns to the muteness of the statue; she moves from thanking the
audience to concluding that the statue, though mute, may be a lesson
in history rather than an object of passive admiration: "Perhaps it is
worth a national tragedy to go down to posterity an inspiration to all
men" (172). The sense of national tragedy that she describes at the
end of her speech on the unveiling of the "Black Hawk Statue" would
continue to influence her work beyond the SAI.

Laura Cornelius Kellogg and the Society of American Indians

In the published proceedings of the first meeting of the Society
of American Indians (SAI), a portrait of "Miss Laura Cornelius,"
dressed in an elegant Edwardian suit and wearing an imposing hat,
precedes her published talk. The picture is set against a faded stu-
dio background; she holds a paper in her hands and looks toward
the camera with confidence (figure 9). Previous and future images
of Kellogg, with or without a hat, convey the same sense of resolve
and determination—an image she helped create as part of her public
persona performing for a variety of audiences locally, nationally, and
internationally. And while many of her writings have been lost, her
inquisitive eyes—and often her vast repertoire of hat ensembles and
fashionable suits—along with her public speeches, interviews, letters,
and testimonies in Congress throughout the 1910s and 1920s, help
revise and reconstruct her intricate legacy.[56]

If poetry allowed Laura Cornelius Kellogg the rare occasion to
meditate on an optimistic future for her "race," her political and activist writings open another window into her concern with how that
future could take shape. As Tom Holm has argued persuasively, when
Kellogg helped found the SAI in 1911, she "thought that she could
not only enhance the position of Indian women but also undo the
damages done by the vanishing policy to Native American societies."[57]

9. Laura Cornelius at the first meeting of the SAI, 1911. Source: *Report of the Executive Council on the Proceedings of the First Annual Conference of the Society of American Indians*, 1912, p. 43.

Refusing to see herself as a "new Indian" was her way of withstanding the rhetoric of the vanishing policy. And although she wore the "sober citizen dress" throughout her public life, elegant suits and imposing hats, she found the idea of "the new Indian" a "fake" and was not shy to share that view with an applauding SAI audience.

She presented her preliminary ideas about Indigenous economic self-determination at the first SAI meeting in 1911. In her talk, *Industrial Organization for the Indian*, she proposed a radical transformation of Indian reservations into "industrial villages" that would withstand the encroachments of the market economy and would use local, tribal resources that would also provide employment for returned Indian students by developing industrial tribal economies.[58] This vision appealed to Kellogg since it placed tribal economies at the center of Indigenous self-governance; at the same time, tribal economies in her vision were no longer static, isolated in remote parts of the country, but active players in modernity's new industrial demands. At the center of her vision was Indian labor for the Indian: "He must labor—and he must labor to the best advantage for himself and not the exploiter." To this end, she starts by accepting that the Indian "cannot copy *everything* the white man does," acknowledging the limits of such imitations; she argues that through cooperation, reservation resources can strengthen the ties between community members and those estranged (i.e., students attending off-reservation boarding schools), which in turn can "reorganize the opportunities of the Indian *at home*." Kellogg's plan is also an endorsement of corporate capitalism and industrialization in her emphasis on Indian competition and struggle: "I believe in struggle and in competition with the outside world. I am one who knows at firsthand what the knocks in it are."[59]

More to the point, her vision of an Indian industrial village relies on a combination of the "foreign Garden City" (an industrial experiment in New York) with "the Mormon idea of communistic cooperation": "In this institution every man draws his proportion performed. Each man in it shall own lands, but the work and the advantages are communistic. The Mormons to-day are the richest people per capita

10. *Some of the Indian Members of the First Conference.* Kellogg is seated, fifth from the left. Source: *Report of the Executive Council on the Proceedings of the First Annual Conference of the Society of American Indians,* 1912, p. 2.

in the world." Kellogg specifies that each tribe would make the best of its available local resources (farming, dairy, arts, or crafts, etc.). Reversing the significance of capital in the competitive market, she posits that Indian villages could follow "the Mormon idea of making men the capital of the community." Kellogg sums up her short speech by showing how the model of the Indian "[i]ndustrial village" may, in fact, "teach the white man."[60] Kellogg's speech did not generate much interest among SAI members; yet, historian Hazel Herzberg considers it "perhaps the most interesting paper" at the first meeting of the SAI.[61] Kellogg's vision of the industrial village was just beginning to take shape, and was ahead of its time in foreshadowing the Indian New Deal.

Kellogg had an opportunity to present her views on Indian education at the Society of American Indians' second meeting in 1912, in a talk later published in the first issue of the society's journal and titled *Some Facts and Figures on Indian Education*.[62] Looking back on over twenty-five years of federally funded Indian education, Kellogg explores the meanings of education to "our race," tracing the contradictions of misused government funds and their consequences for Native children.[63] She points out the importance of Indian self-determination in the process of education and sees the future of Indian education as a meeting ground of tribal knowledges and epistemologies with "Caucasian" education.[64] Kellogg expounds: "We want education, yes, we want to know all the educated Caucasian knows[,] but we want our self-respect while we are getting his knowledge." Echoing Franz Boas, whose work she encountered while studying at Barnard, Kellogg invokes the "power of abstraction in the Indian mind" and describes the merits of Indian oratory in its "profound thought, literary merit and logic." Ultimately, she criticizes the irresponsibility of Indian Office personnel in handling resources appropriately and suggests future directions for congressional appropriations, which she says should include funds for Indian students' health care, a transition from off-reservation schools to local public schools "where feasible," and appropriations for Indian students pursuing higher education: "Our future is in the hands of the educational system of today. Those of us who have come thus far know how our youth have longed to reach the summit of the mountain. Let us not forget our own yearnings and the prayers of our ambitious young for opportunity. Let us climb the highest mountain, without looking back till we have reached the top."[65] She ends her speech on an optimistic note but reminds the audience members how crucial education is for Indian self-determination.

Kellogg's views on education, economic sovereignty, and Americanization diverged from many of her SAI peers, but it was ultimately her arrest in 1913 that triggered her dismissal from the SAI, "an injustice and humiliation she never forgave."[66] Laura Cornelius Kellogg and her husband, Orrin Kellogg (whom she married in 1912), were arrested in Oklahoma and were charged "with having obtained money under false pretenses and impersonating United States officials."[67] Although they were not found guilty, this episode marked the break of the Kelloggs' affiliation with the SAI, which had never been very strong.[68] Her name did not appear in the membership list after 1913. This episode did not intimidate her. Besides continuing to work on her Lolomi plan, she continued to advocate for women's rights throughout the United States, giving speeches, lectures, and interviews. In 1915, *The Washington Herald* published an interview in which she supports women's suffrage: "It is a cause of astonishment to us that you white women are only now, in this twentieth century, claiming what has been the Indian woman's privilege as far back as history traces."[69] Irreverent, provocative, and determined, Laura Cornelius Kellogg embodied white women's ideal of "the new woman." More tellingly, in Patricia Stovey's words, she "was not one to leave a room, a meeting, or a community without notice."[70]

Laura Cornelius Kellogg continued her work on the Lolomi plan, although her years after the SAI are not well documented in national or Wisconsin newspapers. In 1919, however, she was back in the Oneida area when the federal government closed the Oneida school. In 1914, she lived in Washington, DC. *The Washington Post* quoted her address to Secretary Lane, in which she pleaded for attention: "We are a people far removed from serfdom. Before we will be

11. *Laura Kellogg, Daughter of Long Line of Indian Chiefs, Laughs at the Old Idea of Downtrodden Squaw. Washington Herald*, 1915.

vagabonds begging at the door of a sham civilization we will know why our own way cannot be given a fair trial." As the newspapers at the time reported, Kellogg justified the advantage of her Indigenous model of economic sovereignty over government intervention:

> because it provides individualizing schools instead of government boarding schools; modern model homes and villages instead of the ugly insanitary reservation home; from a demoralizing social chaos to one of organized effort, with incentive and reward for right doing; from an attitude of arrogant superiority toward the race as now evidenced by the Indian service to one of sympathy and interest by real teachers.[71]

In her testimony in the US Senate that same year, Kellogg declares her unwavering determination to continue the fight against the Bureau of Indian Affairs: "We are not going to be indefinitely the puppets of another race, and that is exactly what we have to look forward to[—]nothing but pauperism." Critiquing bureaucratic indolence, she concludes forcefully: "We will not be under the yoke of a government that is unjust, that is as flimsy, that is as hopeless, and that is as ruinous as the present one."[72] Her emphasis on collective agency, rather than her individual voice, rendered her capacity to voice the Oneidas' concerns on the national political stage and, by extension, other unheard Native communities' voices.

◆

Kellogg's vision of an Indian industrial organization that could withstand the pressures of the American industrial capital sustained her interest over the next decade, and ultimately took shape in her only published book, *Our Democracy and the American Indian: A Presentation of the Indian Situation as It Is Today*.[73] Kellogg had rehearsed and fine-tuned many of the ideas at the core of this book throughout the 1910s—from her speeches at the SAI meetings, to congressional testimonies, private[74] and public talks—and the reception of the

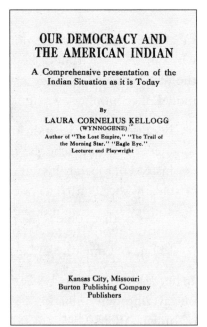

12. Title page, first edition, *Our Democracy and the American Indian* (Burton Publishing, 1920).

book was utterly positive. In his review of *Our Democracy*, Warren K. Moorehead praised the writer's accomplishments: "Mrs. Kellogg has written a remarkable book. It is certainly [high] time that someone familiar with Indian affairs presented in concrete form a remedy for the existing evils. We have had much sentiment, but little of value in the way of constructive policy." Moorehead, who was himself an author of a "plea for Justice" for American Indians (*The American Indian in the United States*), was also an acerbic critic of Indian policy: "It is common knowledge in Washington that our management of Indian affairs has been a disgrace and a scandal for eighty years." While acknowledging her project's limitations, he found Kellogg's Lolomi model worth pursuing:

> Briefly, the assets of tribes and individuals would be pooled in a general organization acting under federal authority. The Indians would be enrolled as members of this cooperative body and would be entitled to one vote each, regardless of the number of shares held. A central authority would administer generally, but local communities would be in charge of their affairs. The author makes a point of how this would safeguard the Indian from the horde of white grafters now the bane of Indian existence. Indians would be free from many present ills. Their property, if held in common, would be sufficient for education, health and commercial development expenses. The huge sums paid white people . . . would be paid the Indian themselves.

Moorehead ends his review by appealing to the "good Americans" who want to see "a square deal for the Indian" to read the book.[75]

Kellogg structures the book around four interconnected strands of argument that come together in her revised model of the "Lolomi Program of Self-Government," which theorizes a democratic model of Indian self-governance for "modern times." In the first two sections, the writer-orator addresses her two imagined audiences, "The American People" and "The American Indian." The opening chapter offers a history lesson to her non-Native readers about the Haudenosaunee confederacy: "The idea of the League of Nations and Democracy originated on the American Continent about 600 years ago. It came from an American Indian." Next, she invokes Benjamin Franklin's view on the Iroquois Confederacy (as scripted in the Iroquois Constitution): "Tradition says Franklin brought his hand down on the table and said, 'That's the greatest wisdom I have heard among nations of men.'"[76] Her address to "the American people" ends with a series of excruciating questions:

> But what shall I say to you now, America of my Americans? [. . .] Shall I fawn upon you with nauseating flattery, because you are rich and powerful? [. . .] Have you not pauperized and debauched a whole people? [. . .] Have you not overcome with your foul diseases that physical excellence in the race which even the Greek did not surpass? Have not 98 per cent of your treaties with the Indian been "scraps of paper"? [. . .] Shall the American Indian who first conceived the democracy of this continent call for liberty in vain?[77]

Kellogg's radicalism, mildly veiled in her previous addresses to American audiences (such as her speech at the unveiling of the Blackhawk statue), explodes at the end of the first chapter, where she calls on her (mainly) white readership to acknowledge the contradictions between American democratic principles (which she attributes to the Iroquois Constitution) and their enactment toward American Indians.

In her second chapter, "To the American Indian," Kellogg addresses her fellow Indians, calling on their responsibility "to wake up" and "refuse to allow" white Americans to represent them: "There comes a time when men must measure themselves by the things they have not done." She urges her "Red brothers" to cast off their indifference and to act as responsible members of Indian communities: "Our aged starve, while the young generation is intimidated into cowardice and vice, and we are 'dubbed' a race of beggars before the world. [. . .] What a spectacle we are—we of this generation!" Kellogg's acerbic criticism of Indian employees of the federal government is unambiguous in her targeting "the Indian Bureau School of Sycophants" or "warehouse Indians" who contribute to nothing more than tribal factionalism and misrepresentation of Indian needs and rights, charges she would continue to make in testimonies before Congress. She ends her address to her Indian peers by invoking a "fraternity" of Indian people coming together to withstand government control, demoralization, and "a reign of terror," a radical "fraternity" whose "spirit cannot be broken by a million years of persecution" and "to whom death is sweet if that is the price." Envisioning a collective resistance of Indian nations against both misrepresentation and poverty,[78] Kellogg thus prepares her readers for the collective model of economic self-determination that she offers in the last two chapters, where she describes the "Lolomi program of self-government."

Kellogg theorizes and exemplifies a democratic model of Indian self-governance that enables Indian participation in modern economic self-determination, thus resisting a future of poverty. The "Lolomi" economic program encapsulates Kellogg's vision of an Indian industrial village premised on both Indigenous and non-Indigenous worldviews that sought adaptation and self-determination of Indian nations facing the encroachments of capitalism, what Kellogg calls "the commercial age."[79] Noting both the corruption of US government officials responsible for implementing Indian policy and the indifference of the American people to Indian nations as participants in modernity, Kellogg sets her model of Indian self-government against the policy and practice of the Office of Indian Affairs, calling the mission of the Lolomi "an order of protected self-government by means of a Federal incorporation into industrial communities." Moreover, grounding the Lolomi in her training in social work, she argues for the protection of Indian economic and social interest. The Lolomi is, therefore, a democratic political and economic model: in the industrial Indian village, each member has only one vote regardless of his shares; the Lolomi does away with both the "indefiniteness of taxation" and the semi-citizenship status imposed on Indian people; it recognizes the Indians' lack of credit and promotes the notion of using Indian property economically, on a cooperative basis; the system of salaries is fixed for all community work and community members are held accountable for their actions.[80]

Kellogg's closing chapter of *Our Democracy and the American Indian*, "How the Lolomi Handles the Social Side of the Problem," considers the interdependence of the economic and the social to make the Lolomi a viable model. Taking a sociological approach to the environment of the Indian reservation ("lack of sanitation, of proper educational facilities, organized effort, means of transportation, proper shelter, proper food, knowledge, incentive and reward for effort"), Kellogg sees one of Lolomi's immediate tasks as creating a "new environment and a real home." To this end, she acknowledges the crucial role of Indian women, "the most responsible element of the Indian population." At the same time, she sees the future of the Indian industrial village resting on good housing, good sanitation systems, modern hospitals supervised by the Public Health Service, elimination of distance, as well as local Indian control of educational facilities. Two of the most radical arguments Kellogg makes in this chapter plead for the elimination of US government boarding schools and the Office of Indian Affairs. Expressing unwavering confidence in the future of Indian education and self-government, Kellogg's *Our Democracy* concludes on an optimistic yet sarcastic note, collapsing the distance between American capitalism and Indian economic self-determination: "It looks like a long way between Wall Street and the Reservations, but it is not very far."[81]

Kellogg's optimism in "the Lolomi" stemmed from her belief that it could, in fact, offer Native people across the United States a tangible way out of poverty and reliance on federal aid, while at the same time reinforcing tribal notions of cooperation and appropriate use of natural resources. Kellogg also believed that, with a real chance at economic self-sufficiency, Indian nations could revive and cultivate belief in tribal values. Reviving tribal social structures, which implied considering the role of kinship ties in tribal and federal politics for the individual and the community, also made room for applying tribal epistemology (often referred to as "tribal ways") to contemporaneous social and economic problems, as well as problems of the representation of Indian people. Kellogg's optimistic and radical rhetoric in *Our Democracy*—which many of her peers did not share in the 1920s and which had serious implications for the Six Nations over the next decades—is a marker of her advocacy for Indigenous rights "to the American people," her imagined audience in the near and remote future.

The Lolomi Industrial Community and Oneida Placemaking

The central concept in *Our Democracy and the American Indian* is economic empowerment through an Indian industrial village plan, or what Kellogg called "Lolomi."[82] Kellogg's ideas about relying on tribal knowledge and the community as the unit best equipped to meet the needs of the people were not solely based on Oneida beliefs. During her European tour she took a particular interest in German town planning, especially garden cities and industrial villages. Kellogg saw the model as a possibility for Oneida economic self-sufficiency and tribal sovereignty. In a news article, she stressed the economic possibility of her vision for what would become Lolomi:

> Nothing will be done in the way of regenerating the American Indian, she said, unless each individual Indian is touched with regard to his bread and butter. Unless something is definitely and quickly done for Indians, she foresees a great danger of the Indian becoming a pauper and public burden. . . . [T]he Princess expressed her desire to meet a capitalist, capable of recognizing the great advantage of helping, by his patronage of the movement, the building up of the scattered Indians into a cohesive nation.[83]

In *Our Democracy*, Kellogg confidently called for a solution based on economic development, emphasizing the words BUSINESS and ECONOMIC. She clearly drew on other ideas in planning and social welfare, arguing that Lolomi would bring both needed economic resources to the reservation as well as a sense of beauty to the community; she believed that both would reinforce pride and an Oneida sense of place. Kellogg placed Lolomi in close proximity to the non-Native world. Keenly aware of her audience, she stressed Lolomi as an Oneida place, a refuge from urban, non-Native decay even while it was still linked to it. In chapter four of *Our Democracy*, "How the

Lolomi Handles the Social Side of the Problem," Kellogg places much of the blame for destitute Oneidas not on individual or tribal failings, but on their environment. Oneida people came from cohesive and valued belief systems, she argued: "from my infancy I had been taught what we Oneidas had contributed to American liberty and civilization." In contrast, the contemporary reservation was an environment tainted by non-Native paternalism, even worse than non-Native places due to geographic isolation: "Why[,] the [urban] slums are not so destitute! At least they are within walking distance of something better." She appealed to the social conscience of non-Natives who might read the book: "Within a few miles of the most comfortable evening lamp is someone dying from the evils of the environment, evils like tuberculosis, that great indicator of the lack of nourishment and sanitation." By calling attention to the plight of reservations by linking them explicitly to places where non-Natives lived, Kellogg sought to displace non-Natives from their comfort of ignorance of Indian problems and hoped to win support for Lolomi, for her vision of a place that would be based on Oneida values and beliefs.

Kellogg called for placemaking that was based on density, arguing that "incorporation into industrial communities means the development of industry, and that in turn means the concentration of population" in what she called the village model: "All Indians understand village organization in a primitive way and want it. Their gregariousness and the monotony of their surroundings make them seek neighboring towns now."[84] She stressed the connections Oneidas had to urban places, as did all Native people. In her placemaking attempts, she balanced a number of seeming binaries: urban/rural, modern/traditional, educated/uneducated. *Our Democracy* urges readers to try to understand the ways Native people complicated these terms, straddling boundaries, recognizing the value of some aspects of these identities while rejecting others. Native people clearly understood the non-Native impulse to place them within set categories, even as their actions and beliefs transcended them. In this sense, Kellogg articulated what many Oneidas already knew—that in order to persist as tribal people and as Native nations, they needed sustainable places for both industry and ideas. Only by having both, she believed, could they exercise self-sufficiency, or autonomy.

Kellogg clearly believed that her ideas, while strengthening Oneida traditions and culture, were also a "modern" solution, based on her academic research. She strongly promoted the aesthetics of the modern villages, arguing that Native people were "above all a social being," and she was "positive that a village grouping would take away his desire to go to the white man's city and fill himself up with whiskey." A *Los Angeles Times* article in 1909 quoted her saying that "[t]he Indians who are sufficiently prosperous to make home attractive are not the people who are seen on the streets, she said. Their social life should be organized. So long as they are far apart they spend most of the time visiting one another."[85]

Aware of her audience, she envisioned that there would be some Oneidas who might not wish to reside full time at the village. Perhaps soothing fears that Native density would mean less freedom of movement, Kellogg situated Lolomi within a global community, one in which members shared a common idea of protecting places where someone could replenish and nourish an Oneida identity. She argued that, "it is not the wish of the Lolomi to detain those who wish to live in Paris or New York . . . [any] more than the modern corporations require their investors to remain in a certain place."[86]

In seeking to create Lolomi, a modern Indian village that was both self-sustaining and beautiful, Kellogg contributed to an idea of Oneida placemaking, attaching to the proposed industrial village the meanings of Oneida and Haudenosaunee identity and connection. These communities were envisioned as sustainable places with a deep sense of meaning to the community members, and while contemporary urban planners and designers might attach the term placemaking to the idea of public places, we would instead substitute tribal, or Indigenous, for "public" in this discussion of placemaking. These tribal, Indigenous spaces are both a process and philosophy—one that values tribal sovereignty and an Indigenous sense of place based on the landscape and the cultural traditions of the people: "the old Indians who have never seen the inside of the classroom." It is fundamentally a collective vision, for while she advocated it as an individual, Kellogg clearly sought to link Lolomi and the modern Oneida Indian village to a broader Haudenosaunee Confederacy.

"A Civic Centre for All": The Oneida Boarding School

Kellogg also wished to cement her place and legacy in her home community. In *The New York Tribune* she confidently stated, "[T]o do something great when I grew up was impressed upon me from my cradle by my parents, and I have known no other ambition. . . . What I have done up to this time has been in competition with the white world, and I have succeeded according to their standards, so that I want no one to say of what I do, 'That is good . . . for an Indian.'"[87]

Although Kellogg was well-traveled and educated away from the reservation, she considered her home to be Oneida, Wisconsin, and it was here that she directed her most long-lasting and substantive

13. Oneida Boarding School, ca. 1910. Courtesy of the Oneida Nation Museum.

efforts.[88] The Wisconsin Oneida had long placed a high value on education and in the mid- to late nineteenth century many Oneida children were sent to off-reservation boarding schools such as Carlisle Indian School, Hampton Institute, and Flandreau Indian School. They also wished to have schools closer to home, and as soon as the reservation boundaries were established in 1838, the Wisconsin Oneida advocated for one to be built there. They thus had a longer history of using education for their own ends, ultimately complicating the assimilationist aim of the schools. Federal officials, spurred on by the urgings of local Episcopal priest Father Edward Goodnough, proposed the Government Industrial School, or the Oneida Boarding School, as part of an inducement for support for allotment, part of a broader assimilation policy aimed at breaking up the reservation by assigning parcels of land to individual Oneidas. Land allotted would eventually be taxed, and any land left over would be declared "surplus" and opened up for non-Native settlement.[89]

A tract of land was reserved near the center of the Oneida reservation for a school and, at its opening in 1893, the number of applicants exceeded the school's capacity. By 1899 the federal government reported the nearly 100-acre boarding school had 134 students and five staff.[90] In a history of the school published by the Episcopal

14. Oneida Boarding School, ca. 1910. Courtesy of the Oneida Nation Museum.

Diocese, *The Church's Mission to the Oneidas*, the writer reported that in 1902 "the capacity is two hundred and twenty-five pupils, and is valued at about $65,000."[91] There were seven brick and twelve frame buildings, with steam heat and electricity in some of them. It was centrally located on Duck Creek near the railroad station and Episcopal Church. Oneida children were educated at the school in curriculum the Episcopal Church described as "both literary and industrial" (see figures 13 and 15).[92] The school had a strong symbolic as well as practical function. Many of the recorded memories of the school are mixed, but what was not in dispute was that it was an important building and place for the Oneida people.[93] It was a visible sign of the relationship between the federal government and the tribe.

In 1910 the Bureau of Indian Affairs recommended that the school be closed, arguing that cost of schooling should be borne by the Oneidas as part of their responsibility as citizens. Many Oneidas

15. Oneida children learning to darn socks at the Oneida Boarding School, ca. 1910. Courtesy of the Oneida Nation Museum.

were concerned, wishing that the school remain open. In 1914 tribal members asked for the Superintendent to look into the advisability of changing the Oneida Boarding School into a day school, noting that there were 160 students enrolled at the school and twenty-four employees. The school was often enrolled over capacity by Oneida parents who valued education, and it was a safety net for some families who would send their children there as financial need dictated. Correspondence on the issue makes it clear that the federal government wanted to be free of the responsibility of the boarding school, while the Oneidas wanted it to stay open.

Federal government efforts to begin closing and selling the Oneida Boarding School began in earnest in 1919, and Oneida tribal members began a spirited opposition. In June 23, 1914, Martha B. Hill wrote to the Commissioner of Indian Affairs protesting the closing of the school and requested that the school run about five or six years longer. In 1914, Reginald H. Weller wrote to the federal government and stated that there were 160 Oneidas at the Boarding School, some day students and some residing.[94] Kellogg was actively involved in these efforts while working in what were referred to as "Oneida council" meetings and in her leadership in the Oneida National Council.[95] She consistently sought to keep the property in tribal hands, as it would be a showcase for her ideas of Lolomi. She encountered opposition from both inside and outside the reservation, but she was also able to build a great deal of support. Even those who were against the idea of re-purposing the school for an industrial center thought that perhaps the land could be sold to the state of Wisconsin in order to open a public day school, ensuring that Oneida children could continue to attend the school. Very few supported the idea of selling the land and school to outsiders.[96] Nevertheless, in 1920 the property was surveyed in anticipation of its eventual sale.[97]

In 1920, Kellogg wrote to the Department of the Interior on behalf of the Oneida Business Committee, expressing a wish to buy the school. An excerpt from the letter makes it clear that the group she represented saw the building as a centralized place and potential marker of Oneida identity and important to the Oneidas, regardless of

the differences in the community: "We are interested in the incorporation of some industries as a means of supporting a centralized public
school for our children. . . . We feel that since the Oneidas belong to
four different (religious) denominations, this property, which is naturally a civic center for all the people, should not be turned over to any
one sectarian interest."[98]

Kellogg arranged for a committee made up of prominent local
non-Natives to inspect the property and to interview Oneida tribal
members. She wanted to gain support for using the school property
as an industrial center. The committee, focusing on a successful farm
and herd of cattle in particular, supported Kellogg and the Oneida
Business Committee in their efforts to lay claim to the place. Committee members also recommended establishing a canning factory, noting
the proximity of the railroad and the centrality of the location. They
were also impressed by Kellogg's idea of Lolomi: "The Committee
also wishes to state that it has been much interested in learning of the
plan of the proposed Lolomi Industrial Community for the Oneidas,
and feels that if it can be successfully organized and executed, it would
be provide the Indians with a protection from exploitation which they

16. Oneida Boarding School, *Going Home Day*, ca. 1910. Courtesy of the
Oneida Nation Museum.

very much need, and be a stimulus to the social and industrial development of the community."[99]

The superintendent at the nearby Keshena Indian Agency was generally supportive of the efforts to keep the Oneida boarding school within tribal hands.[100] In 1921, after several council meetings of the Oneidas, Kellogg requested to buy the land for the tribe.[101] Her group then began the difficult process of securing the necessary funds. Correspondence shows that the group was successful in raising a five percent deposit, but ultimately they were unable to raise the money for the rest of the sale. Kellogg acted as spokeswoman for the group of interested Oneidas and was the public face, gathering support from various local businessmen and elected government officials.[102] The two-year negotiation process between the Oneida Business Committee and the federal government was amicable, with the school eventually reduced to no students and only a small staff to keep the building and farm maintained. Though several extensions were granted by the federal government, the group was unable to raise the funds and thus defaulted on their deposit in January 1923.[103]

Kellogg's letters make it clear that she was speaking on behalf of others, particularly as they refer to tribal council meetings that were held in which her ideas gained support. However, since the plan for the school was based on her idea of Lolomi, and because she was the spokesperson, she was the face of the failure to buy the school.[104] The school was again put up for a bidding process in April 1924 and, this time, the highest bid was the Murphy Land and Investment Company, which immediately transferred title to the Catholic Diocese of Green Bay.[105]

The sale of the Oneida Boarding School property to the Catholic Diocese would seem to have ended any claims that the Oneidas might have had to the property. However, Oneida tribal members, with Kellogg representing many of them, continued to believe, and more importantly, to act as though the place belonged to the Oneidas. The Oneida Business Committee became the Oneida National Committee, in order to represent the work that the group was doing with all three Oneida communities in Wisconsin, Canada, and New York.[106] This group actively contested the sale of the school. They wrote to the head of the Catholic Diocese advising him that the land was held under communal properties and therefore could not be sold by the federal government.[107] They continued to try to get the land back, and in April 1926 fifteen people refused checks from the sale of the school, insisting that the sale was invalid because the tribe had not agreed to it.[108]

In fighting the sale of the Oneida Boarding School, Kellogg articulated a long-standing Oneida intellectual tradition that is based on the importance of places built on relationships. The Oneidas' efforts to claim the school were interrupted when it was sold to the Catholic Diocese of Green Bay. The buildings and campus continued to be an important place to the Oneida in subsequent years, however. After buying the school, the Catholic Diocese first operated an orphanage and school, known as Guardian Angels. Guardian Angels cared for both Native and non-Native children. In 1954 the orphanage and

17. Former Oneida Boarding School grounds after sale to Catholic Diocese, ca. 1956. Courtesy of the Oneida Nation Museum. Many of the buildings were part of the original school campus (the large building on the left). It begins the transition to Sacred Heart Seminary (owned by the Catholic Diocese) and what will eventually become the Norbert Hill, Sr. Center (bought by the Oneida Nation in Wisconsin in 1984).

school was closed and the Catholic Diocese operated the Sacred Heart Seminary, which educated Catholic priests (figure 17). During this time, the place, located within Oneida reservation boundaries, continued to occupy a central role in Wisconsin Oneida identity. Oneidas worked and resided there, and, eventually, in 1976 the tribe opened an education office in the building, leasing space from the Catholic Diocese. Efforts to buy the school on behalf of the Oneida Nation in Wisconsin resumed, and in 1984, the Oneidas were successful when the Catholic Diocese sold the buildings to the Oneida tribe. Some tribal members considered the initial sale fraudulent and thus resented having to buy back the school, but its return was widely celebrated. Today known as the Norbert Hill, Sr. Center, the former Oneida Boarding School site houses three key tribal institutions: the tribal council, the education department, and the tribal high school.[109]

Kellogg's Political Legacy: Membership in the Six Nations Club and Reclaiming a Homeland

The sale of the Oneida Boarding School in 1924 did not dissuade Kellogg from her plans to create a sustainable place for Oneida people. If anything, she became more outspoken and direct in her criticism of the federal government and tried to hold it accountable for upholding the trust relationship with Native people. She called for the federal government to honor its promises, namely by upholding federal treaties which protected Haudenosaunee rights to the land. As a member of the Wisconsin Oneida, Kellogg was well aware of the pressures for land that had forced the Oneidas to leave New York State, and she repeated community narratives that spoke about being cheated out of a homeland through treaties that were concluded without proper tribal or federal approval. Land claims became increasingly important to Kellogg and to those with whom she worked in the early twentieth century. Securing ties to the land, or at minimum collecting damages for illegal treaties, would provide a way for Oneidas and other Haudenosaunee people to become self-supporting.

Kellogg had long been aware of outstanding Oneida land claims, as she told a reporter in 1923: "In my childhood, I remember having heard the old folks frequently refer to the great inheritance, the big claim they had left in New York State. . . . But like many another poor relation that is heir with many others to a large estate, we had not the means at our disposal to fight for our heritage."[110] The ruling *United States v. Boylan* in 1920 became one more tool by which Kellogg hoped to fight for Oneida land rights. In *Boylan*, the court found that despite the removal of the majority of Oneidas from their homeland, the New York Oneida still remained a federally recognized tribe and, therefore, New York State courts had no jurisdiction in disposing of the their property without the consent of the United States.[111] This decision confirmed a view among many members of the three Oneida communities that litigation was the best means for the return of land. Kellogg and others aggressively pursued this avenue, seeing the courts as their best way to secure a land base to support their ideas for industrial villages. In doing so, she joined other Native activists who sought the return of their land, particularly as a way to challenge the US policy of allotment.[112] As envisioned by Kellogg and other Haudenosaunee people, a legal strategy that relied on the trust responsibility of the federal government was charted that subsequent generations would follow, though Kellogg wouldn't live to see just how successful this strategy would be in the later twentieth century.[113]

In 1920 Kellogg and her group, the Six Nations Club, presented her ideas to the Six Nations Confederacy Council at Onondaga and gained the support of the head of the confederacy, Tadodaho (George Thomas). In this meeting she called for financial support for advancing the claim in federal courts. The group conceived of a highly controversial way of funding the litigation: they collected money directly from members in every Haudenosaunee community, not only in New York but also in Canada, Oklahoma, and Wisconsin.[114] In this way, her group relied on a business model of identifying investors to fund the litigation of the claim; these "investors" would then share in any reward, as members of the Six Nations Confederacy (figure 18). Those who protested and refused to pay did so mainly because they did not think the litigation would succeed, and they believed (correctly) that they would share in any claim regardless of any money they had contributed. Though initially trusted by many people, the fundraising ultimately cast Kellogg in an unfavorable light.

With the money collected, the group would hire lawyers who would gain for the Haudenosaunee a sizeable restored territory and an economic base. They appealed to members not only from Oneida communities, but from all of the Six Nations. Kellogg was sure that with a large land base, the Haudenosaunee could again assert their sovereignty in ways unequaled in the nineteenth and twentieth centuries. A central part of this plan would reposition the Wisconsin Oneida as full members of the Haudenosaunee. She underscored this idea when she set up her headquarters for the land claim at Onondaga territory in New York, the seat of the Six Nations Confederacy.[115] She did not distinguish between an Oneida and a Six Nations land claim. The group obtained funds from Haudenosaunee people by appealing to both their dreams of a large financial award and by emphasizing a renewed sense of pride in their continued existence as culturally distinct tribal members. Savvy Haudenosaunee political leaders as well as American courts and congressmen affirmed for many their belief in a continued tribal sovereignty and political will that had endured in spite of colonialism. With this continued existence came a responsibility.

Kellogg emphasized this idea when she spoke specifically to other Native people in *Our Democracy and the American Indian*, reminding them that simply existing was not enough: "If I did not believe there were enough left of my red clan to make it worthwhile to say the last word, I should not speak. If I did not believe enough of you remain staunch to our ancestral standards of truth, to stand the ugly facts that concern us now, I should not speak."[116] At a pivotal time when the continued existence of Native people was in no way assured, Kellogg and others sought to solidify the financial support of the Oneida and other Haudenosaunee in order to regain the homeland. She argued for a Haudenosaunee sovereignty that was based on treaties and a nation-to-nation relationship of the Six Nations Confederacy.

Through her efforts in many Haudenosaunee communities, Kellogg did more than solicit funds for the land claim effort. She also articulated a vision for Haudenosaunee unity and collaboration. She

18. Receipt given to supporters of the fundraising efforts of the Six Nations Confederacy, 1924. Copy in Kristina Ackley's possession.

had an expansive definition of who was included as Haudenosaunee, including in her talks potential members outside New York State, such as the Wisconsin Oneida, the Stockbridge-Munsee and Brothertown tribes in Wisconsin, the Cayuga of Oklahoma, and Six Nations members in Canada. On October 10, 1922, the *Fond du Lac Reporter* recounted a meeting: "Addressing an audience of more than two hundred Indians, members of the Stockbridge, Brothertown and Oneida tribes, at Quinney [Wisconsin], Sunday afternoon, Mrs. Laura Cornelius Kellogg made an impassioned appeal for unity among tribes in order that they may present a united front in their demands for their rights in New York State."[117]

Federal officials reacted to the fundraising with alarm and suspicion. They monitored her activities and solicited statements from Oneidas and other Six Nations tribal members arguing that that the fundraising was illegal and putting a significant hardship on individuals.

Stories were told, and continue to be repeated today, that many families lost significant amounts of money and that some Oneidas were left penniless after they gave money to the Six Nations Clubs.[118] Opposing groups of Oneidas began a concerted effort to stop the fundraising and undermine Kellogg's authority and her call for increased unity among the Haudenosaunee through a land claim.

In this context, we can also view the ceremonies in 1925 to raise Oneida chiefs in Wisconsin as a way to assert control over who could speak for the Wisconsin Oneidas. Membership in the traditional political system would unify all Oneida people rather than place or geography. In her efforts to revive the Chiefs' Council and Longhouse in Wisconsin, Kellogg tied Oneida traditionalism to the aboriginal homeland in ways that still manifest in contemporary Oneida politics.[119] Land claims became an important way to assert sovereignty. The belief in holding the federal government accountable for ensuring Haudenosaunee land rights was an important avenue the activists used in their attempts to regain their homeland. By recognizing how important the land and treaty rights were in forming a broader Wisconsin Oneida and Haudenosaunee identity, she ensured that a

19. Photo of Kellogg (third from right) and Oneida chiefs, 1925. Courtesy of the Oneida Nation Museum.

consideration of the land and a continued relationship with the federal government would be inextricably linked to Oneida rights and responsibilities.

"Protected Autonomy": Holding the Federal Government Accountable

While Kellogg was a tireless critic of the federal government, resisting the overt control that officials sought to impose on Native people, she also worked to uphold the trust relationship that Oneidas had with the federal government. She did so, viewing the relationship as the best way in which to secure a land base for industrial villages. The federal trust relationship was often contested. Kellogg and the Oneida National Committee clearly wanted the federal government to honor their trust responsibility, but they rejected a dependent, subservient position to the United States. The Oneida repeatedly called on the treaties they had signed with the federal government to affirm and protect their rights. In so doing, they joined countless other Native people who called on the United States to uphold treaties, but the Wisconsin Oneidas show a particular diligence and conviction. They called for federal protection while continuing to exercising tribal governance and authority, such as when traditional Oneida chiefs were condoled in a ceremony in 1925 (figures 19 and 20).[120]

In 1928, the Senate passed Resolution 79, which authorized the Committee on Indian Affairs to undertake a survey of the conditions of Native people in the United States. A subcommittee was directed to hold hearings to better understand the legal status of tribes and evaluate the administration of the Bureau of Indian Affairs.[121] In March 1929, Kellogg and other Haudenosaunee leaders traveled to Washington, DC, to give testimony before the committee on the status of New York Indians. Their testimony demonstrated how well they understood the obligations the federal government had to protect them from outside interests that coveted their land and sought to undermine tribal authority. They framed their testimony on the idea of the reservation as a place of self-empowerment and opportunity,

20. Photo of Oneida women, 1925. From left to right: Dinah Schuyler, Christine Skenandore, Alice Cornelius, Margaret Summers Cooper, Ida Skenandore Baird, and Laura Cornelius Kellogg. Courtesy of the Oneida Nation Museum.

still hoping to achieve the Lolomi village that Kellogg had worked for in her home community in Wisconsin.

Their audience was not sympathetic, and members of the Senate subcommittee at the outset asserted that the federal government did not have any authority over Indians in New York State, relying on testimony from the Bureau of Indian Affairs that the Indians in New York were "practically independent" because they had resisted administration by the federal government.[122] Assistant Commissioner of Indian Affairs Edgar B. Merritt argued that the Iroquois in New York State were largely responsible for themselves, yet he acknowledged that treaties had been signed with the federal government, a situation he likened to a "twilight zone."[123] To the tribal leaders, the problem lay less with murky jurisdiction than with the federal government not exercising its trust responsibility in Haudenosaunee disputes with private businesses and the State of New York.

Livingston Crouse, an Onondaga leader, highlighted this problem, recounting his own experience trying unsuccessfully to bring a wrongful death suit against a Syracuse street car company on behalf of his sister's estate. New York State courts refused to hear his case against a private business, on the grounds that the state had no authority over him, while the federal government declined to take up the case on his behalf. He was met with incredulity, with both Senator Burton Wheeler of Montana and Senator Elmer Thomas of Oklahoma challenging his account (Senator Wheeler dismissively said, "I cannot conceive of a court holding that"), and inferring that the problem lay with the Indians themselves. Crouse forcefully defended himself and his understanding of the federal/tribal relationship, arguing, "Well, it is a question of jurisdiction. We cannot get anything from the State. Then, where does the Indian stand? Where does he get his protection? That is what we are here for. Am I an Indian or am I a white man? Tell me that."[124]

Clearly, Crouse knew that he was Onondaga. He called on the federal government to acknowledge that the tribe's insistence on governing themselves collectively did not mean that the federal government could abdicate its trust responsibility. His testimony was supported by Kellogg and her husband, Orrin. Orrin Kellogg defined the need for the committee as one of protection from outside forces he darkly said had used "powerful political means and propaganda to oust them from their rights." He was careful to note that the Native people in New York had continuous, active tribal governments, stating: "[T]he Six Nations, while they offer a tenacious resistance, are not properly protected. They are a people who have wonderful traditions, who are organized, and who have a superior legal status peculiar to Indian relations[—]one which they have faithfully kept, and one which entitles them to the highest protection in the land, the protection of the United States Government."[125]

The tone of the hearings exposed deep-seated resentments and distrust between Kellogg and Assistant Commissioner Merritt. Kellogg had a long history of criticizing the Bureau of Indian Affairs and the parasitic control that she felt limited both individual Native people and the collective potential of the reservation. She alluded to this contentious relationship in a letter she wrote to Senator Irvine Lenroot (Wisconsin), asking for his support for cooperative industry at Oneida. She hoped to gain allies in the Senate, for she said she had "criticized this hopeless Administration in the Press so unmercifully that the Indian Office would balk at anything I wanted."[126] *Our Democracy and the American Indian* lists a number of complaints against the bureau, and calls out for Native people to reject stifling federal control and assert their own authority. Ever the activist, Kellogg investigated bureau misconduct on tribal reservations other than her own, lobbied elected officials for changes, and initiated litigation to redress injustices. To support these activities, Kellogg actively engaged in fundraising, and it is likely that these funds financially compensated her and others she worked with. Sometimes she and others held written contracts that clearly outlined this relationship, and other times it was less clear to outsiders. This led to controversy in Oneida Wisconsin, as some tribal members and federal officials questioned the group's fundraising. All of this contributed to Kellogg's combative nature as she testified.

In a wide-ranging and defiant testimony, Kellogg then called for the federal government to be held accountable for their inaction in New York State, listing many of the issues that would have increasing importance in the years to come—the problems of leasing to non-Natives in Salamanca, New York; the difficulties of jurisdiction when tribal land was bisected by the US-Canada border; the danger of Cayuga termination. She linked the Wisconsin Oneida to the Iroquois Confederacy through the Oneida National Committee, through which both she and her husband were retained as paid advisor and attorney, respectively. It was these paid positions, and the group's fundraising, that opened her up to criticism from Assistant Commissioner Merritt, who questioned the ethics and legality of the committee, portraying the group as preying on their fellow Indians. He testified that the bureau had "information in our files which shows that they have gone so far as to require these poor helpless Indians to sell their chickens in order to pay for them." He testified that Kellogg and her husband had been arrested for their activities, but under further questioning admitted that they had been exonerated.[127]

Kellogg met Merritt's concern for Native people with derision. She argued that her fellow tribal members were sophisticated in their understanding of their rights, and shrewd in hiring someone to fight for them. She called for Congress to support their broader effort of a "reconstruction program," whereby the Six Nations would incorporate a village at Onondaga to address both fiscal and social concerns of tribal members. Kellogg was clearly referring to her plan of Lolomi, which she said would eventually create a trust that "all the Indians of the United States" would benefit from. Far from taking advantage of Native people, the Oneida National Committee was filling a void left by the inaction of the federal government to uphold their rights, Kellogg asserted. She ridiculed the hypocrisy that the federal government needed to protect tribal members from the Oneida National Committee, but not from private businesses or New York State. At times eloquent, and certainly aware of the effects of her performance in front of the Senate subcommittee, Kellogg defended herself and the Oneida National Committee from Merritt's accusations, and also defined Lolomi in terms of self-help:

> A propaganda was started on the ground that here were these thieves, who were filling their pockets with money, because we had instituted the policy of self-help, having discovered this protected autonomy though an action in the court. . . . We are sick, all the Indians of the United States, of our being forced into that status practically by the action of the Bureau [of Indian Affairs], or everlastingly being submerged like penitentiary wards of the United States Government. We called our original people together, the chiefs of the great confederacy, and we said, "We will take inventory. Let us see what we are able to do."[128]

In casting Lolomi as a plan by which Native people would be self-supporting financially, Kellogg presented Six Nations people as capable and active in directing their lives, provided the federal government

acknowledged their unique political status (the "protected autonomy") that they needed to safeguard their collectively held lands. Far
from needing protection from the Oneida National Committee, Six
Nations people who contributed to funds that paid not only the Kelloggs but also the New York law firm of Wise, Whitney, and Parker
were thoughtfully asserting their rights in creating places that would
eventually benefit all Native Americans, she and others argued.

During the hearing, Kellogg made a show of trying to restrain
herself from attacking the Bureau, at times relying on her seemingly
unruffled husband to interject calming words during her testimony
(brief statements that seem scripted, given that she paused and turned
her attention to him at specific points). After Meritt's comment about
the "poor, helpless Indians" selling their chickens, Kellogg sarcastically
responded that she was "very much concerned about those poor chickens Mr. Meritt referred to."[129] She argued that much of the accusations against the Oneida National Committee and their Lolomi village
plan were the result of bureau sabotage and self-serving Native people, whom she painted as agents of the federal government who were
brought out to legitimate the work of assimilation ("they put on fine
clothes because they have fine jobs"). Particularly outraged by Meritt bringing up the arrests of members of the Oneida National Committee, Kellogg contemptuously dismissed him as one of the bureau's
"anaemic, slimy-fingered, hothouse fellows." Shrewdly recognizing
the political space as theater, when she was asked if she had concluded
her statement, Kellogg retorted: "I have not concluded it. I have rested
it now. I am never through, so far as the Bureau is concerned."[130]

"Dreamers and Doers": Laura Cornelius Kellogg's
Legacy for the Oneida Community and Beyond

Haudenosaunee people as well as outside scholars have tended
to stress the dissension that surrounded Kellogg for much of her life,
arguing that she "helped factionalize every Iroquois reservation."[131]
One serious example of the disunity among Haudenosaunee people
was the removal of George Thomas as Tadodaho, the political and
spiritual leader of the confederacy. Thomas had supported Kellogg's

work and she worked unsuccessfully to have him reinstated. (Both are pictured in figure 21.) Nonetheless, she constructed relationships among Haudenosaunee people that endured as cultural, politically, and spiritually distinct. In order to view her work in this way, we must reevaluate differences in the Oneida communities, particularly in light of how many contemporary Oneida simultaneously deny Kellogg a place as an important historical leader and yet still adhere to many of her ideas about the land claim, the importance of economic development, and the continued emphasis on a relationship with the federal government.

Kellogg envisioned the homeland as an open space rather than a bounded one when she mapped how the Wisconsin Oneida would participate in the recovery of the Oneida Nation territory. Continually reconciling dissension in the Wisconsin Oneida community became an accepted way of political life, for if difference was continual, it was also

21. *Federal Court Upholds Jones Chief of Six Nations. Syracuse Herald*, August 1929. From upper left, clockwise: Joshua Jones, George Thomas, Laura Cornelius Kellogg, and Judge Frederick H. Bryant.

repeatedly mediated within the community. The Wisconsin Oneida continued to exist as a political, social, and cultural entity throughout the most intensely assimilative period of the early to mid-twentieth century. Throughout her efforts, Kellogg tirelessly promoted the clan system and traditional form of government, and her supporters carefully recorded tribal members and their clan affiliations. This record had particular value later in the twentieth century, when there was an attempt in Wisconsin to revitalize the clans and members continued Kellogg's efforts of travel and promoting the land claim and the link between Wisconsin and New York. They used the records to trace the clans of tribal members who did not know them and a long-term effect was its contribution to a partial resurrection of the clan system that emphasized a Haudenosaunee identity, genealogical ties and kinship, rekindling an Oneida identity that defies colonial erasure and control, and lays claim to a decolonized space that emphasizes Oneida social relationships and kinship. Though a majority of contemporary Wisconsin Oneida do not adhere to it, some still use the clan system today. One visible, though perhaps superficial, use of the clans outside the Longhouse at Oneida, Wisconsin, is the automobile license plates that indicate the driver's clan. Today they are visible all over the reservation. Issued by the Oneida government in Wisconsin, the license plates are a marker of Oneida sovereignty as well as cultural pride. This renewed emphasis on the clan system is an intriguing social development that can be linked to a renewed sense of affiliation with other Haudenosaunee people.

Kellogg's ideas were already reclaimed by some members in 1984, in *Shenandoah*, a Wisconsin Oneida newsletter: "Minnie Kellogg's fight for our people was to save our school and land and to allow that we enter the League of Nations, as an independent Nation. This effort is continuing as we enter the present United Nations. We are entering as *Onyoteʔa:ka*, Ho-de-n-sau-ne, member of the Confederacy."[132] The newsletter proudly spoke of the way in which the Wisconsin Oneida were linked to the Six Nations Confederacy and therefore could make a united stand with them to protest the injustices done to Indigenous people.

Today, some Wisconsin Oneidas are reclaiming Kellogg's ideas while still recognizing her complicated legacy. In 2010, the Oneida Nation in Wisconsin Social Services building was the site of several performances focused on Oneida history and culture. Sponsored by the Green Bay branch of the American Association of University Women, the "Dreamers and Doers" events honored several leaders, and the main recipient for that year was Oneida tribal member Maria Hinton, a noted linguist and leader who co-founded the Oneida tribal school. An important part of this annual event is the "Dreamers and Doers" tour. Over several nights, attendees travelled to various historical sites where the honored women were from and were given a social and political context of several Oneida community leaders and their relevance and place in history. Participants, both tribal and non-Native, were then treated to performances where Wisconsin Oneida tribal members brought to life honored women of the late nineteenth and early twentieth century. Audience members could ask questions while the performer, still in character, responded. On the "Dreamers and Doers" tour in 2010, Judith L. Jourdan portrayed Laura Cornelius Kellogg as a Dreamer. In a performance that stressed her confidence, some might even say arrogance, Jourdan skillfully portrayed Kellogg as someone to be reckoned with, much as she was during her testimony before the Senate in 1929.[133]

Performances like Judith Jourdan's gathered Oneidas together to pay respect to individuals who had contributed to their understanding of what it means to be Oneida, creating moments of Oneida identity and connection, both fleeting and enduring. Audience members asked questions about Kellogg's work and were asked to think about what implications her work for the land claim might hold for the Wisconsin community. "What might the reservation look like without Kellogg and the others," audience members were asked that night.

Work at the national level, particularly with the Society of American Indians, provided Kellogg an important opportunity to work through her ideas and dreams about Native places, particularly the industrial village plan. She then moved beyond the SAI in her work with her home community to balance modernity with tradition, in modern Oneida placemaking. She was very much a dreamer, but she was also a "doer," and her legacy lives on in the ways the Oneida reservation continues to be a place of business and industry, self-governance, and an ongoing autonomous relationship with the federal government. Her strategy of maintaining connections to the Oneida homeland through personal connections, litigation, and lobbying continues. Kellogg had a wish "to do something great," as she told *The New York Tribune* in 1903, and the reenactments of her life and ideas have helped to ensure that she could deliver on that promise, as contemporary tribal members recognize the many contributions she has made.

◆

Laura Cornelius Kellogg continues to fascinate Wisconsin Oneidas today. At various times, she has been alternately presented as a tragic, frustrating, compelling, forward-thinking visionary. During her life-time, her work polarized the community, continuing to inform the ways people remember her work. Good, bad, conflicted—regardless of how people feel about her—Laura Cornelius Kellogg has endured in Oneida memory. As scholars in Native American and Indigenous studies also recover her work, her ideas continue to be timely. Reading her work is instructive for understanding the ways in which an Indig-enous intellectual maintained a sense of self and community at a time when others advocated the dissolution of reservations and the end of the trust relationship with the federal government. How did Kellogg remain steadfast to her beliefs? Shrewd, undaunted, and untiring, she did so with a barely contained rage at the injustices that fueled much of her work.

Irreverent, radical, provocative, and determined, Laura Cornelius Kellogg embodied the suffragists' ideal of "the new woman." In addi-tion to her oratorical skills, she used her social capital and calculated fashion statements to attract public attention, so she could be heard speaking about her life's work: her plan of Indian self-government and sovereignty. A passionate leader, a fighter, an outspoken public Indian figure, Laura Cornelius Kellogg had vision for the future of Indian self-determination, which was ahead of its time. Sometimes described as "an Indian Booker T. Washington" in the popular press,[134] she was determined to recover the Six Nations' land, to build a viable economic system on tribal lands across the United States, and to reform Indian education. Equally loved and distrusted by fellow SAI members and Oneida and Six Nations people during her lifetime, Kellogg continued to fight tirelessly for Oneida lands throughout the 1920s and 1930s, pursuing her plan of making the Oneida nation a place where indigeneity and community coexisted with the new demands of modernity. Recovering Kellogg's work and reclaiming her legacy for Haudenosaunee and American audiences more broadly will ultimately help us place her in an Indigenous intellectual tradition that has so long overlooked her.

Our Democracy and the American Indian:
A Comprehensive Presentation of
the Indian Situation as It Is Today

Publishers' Introduction, 1920 Edition

For four centuries the white man has put off the day of reckoning with the American Indian. Whatever may have been our intention in our relations with the Red man, one thing is certain: our policy has been a haphazard anomaly, not consistent with our principles of Government, not consistent with our Christian civilization. We treated with him as a separate sovereignty, we violated the treaty when it served our convenience, and made him a ward. From this experiment, this backward step, we juggled him on to the fee-simple title, to our final form of land-holding, through a cumbersome period of Trust not prescribed by our constitution. From a state of enviable freedom we coerced him into a state of tutelage without any real training, but we had taken away his personal liberty.

He was a high type of primitive. We have him in our literature, in our arts. We have caught a glimpse of him here and there, as he really was, unaided, or unhampered by our civilization. All he has inspired suggests depths in him we have not fathomed. With his training of silent endurance, we have not known the throes of his degradation, we have not known his heart-throb. With the helplessness of plundered fortunes, ethnic barriers, and the bitterness of a proud spirit, he has almost passed from our midst without having compelled us to any reckoning—almost.

At last comes a cry from him we cannot put away from our minds. In it is the desperate note of a final appeal. This time we cannot partially understand him. This time we cannot escape from our responsibility, for the truth revealed in it is startling enough to destroy any degree of indifference. And it comes, like the historic heroism of Pocahontas, from a woman.

Laura Cornelius Kellogg is a real daughter of the race, as we like to think of the Indian, the tall lithe figure of the forest type, whose quickness of body and mind never deserted him in the hour of need. Representing the ancient lines of leadership in the Iroquois Councils, she bears the marks of the patrician which defy all the patronage. But she is more than that. She loves to champion a helpless people[;] to her it is a sacred right and she is flamingly sincere.

This book she has written has been condensed from twenty years of cruel struggle and unusual privileges. The material presented is collected from personal experiences and official documents. Seldom is one privileged to know life at first hand ranging from the primitive world of the Indian tribes to the royal circles of England, and our metropolitan life. Such has been the eventful life of this young Indian woman.

Chapter I is a dramatic statement of the Indian's case against the white man. Chapter II is a merciless condemnation of the present-generation Indian's shortcomings. Breathing through this part of the book is the consuming fire of a righteous wrath.

Lastly, the LOLOMI plan is presented in cold detail, not a theoretical dream but a practical plan based on real values, with the singleness of purpose of bringing new life to a whole people.

It has come at an appropriate time. With hundreds vexing the public with unsolved problems, here is a problem with a real solution, a constructive proposition, not a whining complaint. Whatever may be said of an inexperienced author's first book, one thing is certain, we are made to feel through this one, the undaunted spirit of an indestructible race.

THE PUBLISHERS.
[Burton Publishing Company,
Kansas City, 1920]

Chapter Synopses, 1920 Edition

CHAPTER I, "To the American People"

The Origin of the League of Nations—Our Democracy—The Birth of the Leader—The Long Trail—Sagoyewhata, the Awakener—The Message of Peace and Love—The Iroquois Confederacy—The League of the Five Nations—The Great Island of the Peaceful Empire—The First Defeat—Its Effect on Civilization—The Sixth Nation—Franklin and the Indian's Philosophy of Government—The Great Democratic Principles—The Colonists and the Oneidas—My Country—The First Seed of Civilization—My America—We Must Face the Facts—What of My People?—"Scraps of Paper."

CHAPTER II, "To the American Indian"

My Red Clan—Our Ancestral Standard—The Tragedy Nearly Ended—Our Burning Shame—Classes Among Us—Men Must Measure Themselves—What Our Children Have Suffered—Our Aged—We of This Generation—The Verdict of the Blanket Indian—The Fraternity—Some Have Succeeded—Where Are the Sons of the Race?—I Hear a Cry from the Vastness of the Wilderness.

CHAPTER III, "The Lolomi Program of Self-Government"

Lolomi—Real Independence—In Modern Times—Nobility of Nature—Our Philosophy of Life—The Human Equation—Lowering the Red Man's Inheritance—The Sweets and Bitters of this Civilization—My Forefathers—The Old Iroquois Civilization—The Oneidas' Contribution to American Liberty and Civilization—Attitude of the Indian Service—Real Facts in the Situation—Business—Work Must Be a Pleasure, Not Servile—Peaceful and Pleasant Homes—Real Education—The Economic Structure—The Lolomi Policy—The Indian Bureau—Indian Agents—Philanthropists—Congressional Investigation—Only Two Scientific Investigations Ever Made—State of Corruption in Politics—Indifference of the American People—Petty

Politics Practiced by the Bureau—The Sycophant—"Jobs" in the Service—Dissipation of Property—Piecemeal Legislation—Legalizing Loot—Federal Incorporation—How the Lolomi Settles All Questions—The Bureaucrat's Argument—The Type of Man Needed.

CHAPTER IV, "How the Lolomi Handles the Social Side of the Question"

The Red Man's Income, Credit, Physiology and Morals—Environment—The Reservation—Succeeding in Spite of the Agent—Representatives of the Great Trusts—The Indian Home—The Original Village Life—The Indian Woman—Effects of Good Housing—The Awakening—Education—Another Suppressed Document—Mental Ability of the Indian Child—The Destruction of Individuality—Capacity of the Race Mind—My Discoveries.

Our Democracy and the American Indian: A Presentation of the Indian Situation as It Is Today
• • • • • •

Lovingly dedicated to Chief Red Bird of the Night Hawk Cherokees, who preserved his people from demoralization, and who was the first to accept the Lolomi.

(This dedication appeared in the original edition of
Our Democracy and the American Indian, 1920.)

CHAPTER ONE

To the American People

The idea of the League of Nations[1] and Democracy originated on the American Continent about 600 years ago. It came from an American Indian.

At a time when the jungles of wilderness in what is now the Empire State, and the region of the Great Lakes resounded with the war-whoop of enemy tribes, and the great stock of the Iroquois were living bloody days, a son was born to the Turtle clan.[2] He had been predicted by the seers. His parents had been selected for him by the clan and its Council leadership. In those primitive days, the greatest interest in the life of the Iroquois was the production of the physically perfect and fearless man. This time the seers said to his mother: "A leader to all the Iroquois and to all the tribes of this Great Island is to come soon. Prepare for him." And when he was born the Council sent a runner to all the tribes of the Iroquois to announce him. They watched him grow. They watched his eye, they watched his body. Physically he was of that type of man of whom Kipling has since written: "He trod the ling like a buck in spring, and he looked like a lance at rest."[3]

Almost too early he excelled in the games; almost too soon he changed his voice, and the old chiefs shook their heads with grave concern over his matchless courage and ambitions, and his youth. Already the Long Trail called to him, the Long Trail, that more than severe Epictetan[4] school of the American Indian, which said to the young man at puberty, "Go, find yourself in the Great Silence, and do not come back without achievement."

When he went away, they sent the prophet to his mother to tell her the smokes promised his return. And when Sagoyewhata,[5] the Awakener of the people, had finished all his lessons, and the last fast was upon him, he put his ear close to Mother Earth, and begged for the message of the Great Spirit. It was the message of peace and love to his fellow-man. It was the message of organization, confederacy, government, order, [and] progress.

Sagoyewhata went home, and after many councils, the Iroquois Confederacy,[6] the League of the Five Nations, was launched. When the organization was completed they adopted the King of Birds as the national emblem. The nations called themselves *ongwe-onwe*, which means real people, as distinguished from *odwaganha*, which means savages.[7]

Once cohered, they marked out the territory of each separate nation, and created the policy that the home of the Nations was not to be the ground of wars. They began offensive warfare, taking in the peaceful tribes and their conquests, and of all these they exacted the learning of the Iroquois language, and tribute for their protection. They expanded westward to the Ohio Valley, they conquered and held certain strips southward as far as the Carolinas. They dreamed of finally allying themselves with the Aztecs and subduing the Great Island into a peaceful empire.

Once only they were whipped after this; that was by the French General[8] who did not know their position. It was the first time they had met modern ammunition. Later, because of this, when the contest between the French and English arose, for the possession of this continent, the Five Nations allied themselves with the Anglo-Saxon. They constituted the balance of power which was necessary to win the continent for the English.

The great note in the Iroquois constitution was confederation upon qualification. As proof of this, the Tuscaroras[9] later came into the League as the Sixth Nation, though they were years trying to get in.

When Franklin and the other writers of the Constitution of the United States sat at Albany, they sent for a delegation of the Five Nations to come before them. And when they were asked to explain their constitution their head chief took the wampum,[10] that sacred strand, the touch of which was necessary to give oath.

"This strand is the record of the Galiwhago,"[11] he said, "these five figures of men holding hands means that in times of peace each

Nation is free unto itself like a man. But when the eagle, which scans the heights and the valleys over the home of the Nations, gives the cry, then are they, one heart, one head, one man."

Tradition says Franklin brought his hand down on the table and said: "That's the greatest wisdom I have heard among the nations of men." And so, historically, he admitted elsewhere that the idea of a separate states government within the Federal [government] was an inspiration he received from the Five Nations. And this is the fact that makes the Constitution of the United States different from another in history.

The great democratic principles behind the United States are freedom and equal opportunity to each nation, under the protection of a Confederate Government. Without these bases for a commonwealth, Liberty is impossible. Without the spirit which promoted the first Awakener[12] of the People to lay the foundations of American liberty, democracy is dead.

When the Colonists were struggling for liberty, the Oneidas of the Six Nations remained true to the dream of Sagoyewhata, and they sent every fighting man they had to the front.

And so I love my country. I love her every stream and rock and tree. To me there is hope in the thundering strength of her mountains. There is solace in the sweet ways of her valleys. And I love the ideals which made her a republic. I love the ideals of her enlightenment, just as my fathers, who planted the first seed of civilization in the land—just as my fathers who first dreamed of democracy on this continent—just as my fathers who bled for the liberty of the land. In noblesse oblige I could not do less.

But what shall I say to you now, Americans of my America? Shall I make soft speeches here for the acts of a Nation in which an individual would forever have forfeited liberty? Shall I fawn upon you with nauseating flattery, because you are rich and powerful? Have we departed so far from the truths of our fathers that we cannot now face the facts? Have you so soon forgotten the spectacle you have created of my people, whose shortcomings were that they were rich and primitive— the spectacle indeed of Belgium and Russia in the United States? You, the Christian Nation of the world! Just look over the land, and count the billions that have gone to erect your temples of worship, your edifices of stone and mortar. Why the price of your stained windows alone would have settled whole tribes in comfort forever! The husks of doctrine your pulpits offer the hungry soul—there is no corn in them. The American Indian cannot understand—Aye—have you not robbed my people of a real god for your million "golden calves"[13] of hypocrisy?

Have you not pauperized and debauched a whole people who were not only the richest in possessions, but whose native character has inspired those of your arts and literature which contain national distinction? Have you not overcome with your foul diseases that physical excellence in the race which even the Greek did not surpass?

Have not 98 per cent of your treaties with the Indian been "scraps of paper?"

Are you going to be guilty of these things while you preach from the housetops the self-determination of peoples and the democratization of the whole world?

Shall the American Indian who first conceived the democracy of this continent call for liberty in vain?

CHAPTER TWO

To the American Indian

If I did not believe there were enough left of my Red clan to make it worthwhile to say the last word, I should not speak. If I did not believe enough of you remain staunch to our ancestral standards of truth, to stand the ugly facts that concern us now, I should not speak. If I did not think there remained in you the mettle of men who smiled at death itself, I would not speak the burning word of criticism before the world. If I did not believe the spark can still be struck out of your dormant souls, I should not act. For the drama we have been enacting is a tragedy, nearly ended.

There was a time, my Red brothers, when our racial training taught us that to endure pain was a virtue, when silence meant self-containment and the unflinching endurance of pain the better part of manhood. But that is past. Today our very tolerance of the demoralization and subservience which have been coerced upon us has become our burning shame. To the world, our seeming complacence with the outrages upon us is a mark of our slow awakening, a reflection indeed upon our intelligence, our racial character, our national honor.

And we will take the blame upon ourselves to the extent that we have been too long dazed in the chaos which surrounds us. We have presented no respectable comprehensive measure, which is capable of solving our embarrassment.

We will take the blame upon ourselves for having been simple enough to trust our fate into the hands of incompetent and dishonest government officials too long.

In our fate, like Russia, in our appearance, like Russia, we are a motley throng; and as a throng, there are times when we seem unworthy of the trust we crave. We have no consensus of opinion, no

national judgment, [and] no collective action. We have been systematically used to defeat these things.

As individuals, there are times when we seem to have nothing in
common but oppression. Some of you have been willing to let our
enemy tell you our place in history. Some of you have no appreciation
of the heritage of noble primitive stock, which differed from every
other primitive stock in the world, in its advanced philosophy of life,[14]
its depth of nature, its inherent superiority of character. You have no
real knowledge of these things.

We have a class among us, who constitute the Indian Bureau's
School of Sycophants;[15] with a few notable exceptions, they have been
trained to petty trickery. They are recruited from the low mixtures of
race with the proverbial "little larnin" from the Government school,
they are the most cocksure of theorists that the present order is good
enough. They have not reached the point where they can be factors in
any organization promoting ideals, for they are still the slaves of their
whims and their fancies, their jealousies and their hatreds. These are
the fellows who have their hands at the throat of your opportunity.
These fellows were found when Tecumseh[16] wanted to nationalize the
race, and they have been part and parcel of the policy of centralization ever since. When the Bureau wishes to create factions among the
tribes, the "warehouse Indians" are its executors. Our solidarity will
be threatened by them just so long as you do not wake up and refuse
to allow them to represent you.

There comes a time when men must measure themselves by the
things they have not done. We have reached that time, my Red brothers, when the individual attitude of this race can no longer be indifferent, any more than any self-respecting soul can be indifferent over the
atrocities of Belgium or the wanton outrages of Bolshevism.

Our children have been maimed with disease, malpractice, and
a broken-limbed system of education which carries its own publicity
campaign to deceive the world at our expense.

Our aged starve, while the young generation is intimidated into
cowardice and vice, and we are "dubbed" a race of beggars before the

world, for whom the United States Government has done everything and yet we fail. What a spectacle we are—we of this generation.

Is the verdict of the blanket Indian[17] correct, when he says, "The mind of this generation is like a broken reed, it cannot say no—a smile, and a pat, and our cause is undone!"

There have been times when I thought all one Indian had in common with another were ignorance and oppression. There have been times when I thought there were Indians and Indians ad infinitum. I had not then broken through the fastness of the wilderness, I had not then found the fraternity. The fraternity whose spirit cannot be broken by a million years of persecution, the fraternity who, regardless of ethnic culture or Bureau propaganda cannot be coerced into demoralization. The fraternity whom exile and "a reign of terror" have only strengthened. The fraternity to whom death is sweet if that is the price. My heart has not ached through the mountains in vain. The heroes of my childhood are not all gone from the earth. But, they are not begging a bean of politics with which to drag out a miserable existence. They are not around fawning upon the Paleface. Long ago they analyzed the situation—"no use, we must wait for our turn to die." What is starvation to them?

And there are some of you who have gone out into the new world and without theory or bias leaped into the thing which came your way first. Some of you are Anglo-Americans, some of you are not, in either case you are not credited to the race, for you have succeeded and even "beaten the Paleface at his own game." You have been like a great wind from the mountain tops. The fraternity is still larger than I thought. But you so long have believed nothing can be done, I wonder if you are open to conviction, and when convinced have you energy and patriotism?

Or, has the blood of our clan turned to water that we can be bent and broken into paupers and puppets cringing before the insolent arrogance and arbitrary dictation of political bosses[18] who rise to positions of absolute despots over us?

How long shall our tongues lap the vulgar adulation which can silence the most glaring outrage?

Where are the sons of the race who did not steal, who did not lie? Where are the sons of the race who fell defending their homes, their children, their country?

Where are the sons of the men who bled for Liberty—I hear a cry from the vastness of the wilderness. I see the fires over the tops of the mountains. Bring me the buckskin robe embroidered in the art of the people I love. Bring me the eagle plume that stands for vision and valor. I want to be with the fraternity, for it is very dark before the dawn—and tomorrow, emancipation.

CHAPTER THREE

The Lolomi Program of Self-Government

Years of search brought me the Indian word which means just what I wish to bring to the race. Lolomi is a Hopi term and it means "perfect goodness be upon you."[19]

So long has this race had Siberian exile, that the only order which can in any way atone for crushed spirits, broken hopes, plundered fortunes, wasted lives is one which can obtain, secure, and maintain real independence in modern times. I emphasize the modern times. The Red man had independence once, of a kind that could not be more idyllic. He followed the beautiful water courses and shot rapids in the romantic canoe, in the solemn solitudes of the great forests pursued the chase. Aesthetic even in the greater part of getting his livelihood, he was a brother of the gods and knew little irksome routine. And he was Lord of the richest continent on the globe. The commercial age had not yet cast her lustful eyes upon his pure simplicity. But when she did, she came, and she is here to be reckoned with.

There is not a semblance left of that independence, outside of the refinement in the real Indian. Till he is gone, there will always be a certain nobility of nature, and a fine physique. Independence and leisure, with a fine philosophy of life behind them create fine spirit and fine bones. Whenever I have reminisced upon that Homeric time and have remarked upon the type which that great life bred and nurtured, people have immediately jumped to the conclusion that, after all, I am merely a dreamer with the Lolomi program, that I am indulging my fancy to lead me into paths impossible. Not so. I am merely trying to show the contrast between the man who was an exponent of better days and the man whom modern civilization with all its fallacies and vulgarity has produced. I am merely trying to show how vast the difference between them can be in a short period of time. I am merely arguing that the highest results of an upward movement are obtained when the human equation is given consideration. Like the structures of a beautiful stone wall, someone must conceive it first in the realm of dreams. Then how many arts and what care must be employed to lay each stone with regard to color, line, fitness, durability. A slow process, building up, but it may all be pulled down into a heap in seconds. So it is with the races of men. No, it should not be hard for one who thinks to see how vain is any attempt to reproduce all the peculiar things of beauty in our primitive life. What a sight is before us of the failure of that former independence to convince this age of its rights. How far would any order succeed which did not take this modern day into its calculations? But, on the other hand, how far has any attempt at remedying the present maladies of the race gone, which has swung to the other extreme and not taken the man as its first consideration! The whole trouble has been that of all the philanthropists outside of the race, who have given themselves to the cause, and of those of the race who have ardently longed to do something for their own, there did not happen to be one whose experience was that of the race itself. Not one has lived so close to the old days that he could honestly glory in the Red man's inheritance, and yet know its hardship. No one has tasted the sweets and the bitters of this civilization so that he could give it its true values, not hating it broadcast, not loving it broadcast. I dwell upon this point because I do not see how I could keep from giving back something to the influences and the conditions that have led me to the discovery of what I ardently believe to be the final solution, if any, to the whole Indian situation.

As a child, my aunts and my grandfather and the old people who to a soul have since departed, contributed to this find by the wonderful things they told me of the life they knew. There were epic tales whose kindred spirits I found in *The Iliad*, or *The Anaeid* many years later. There were tales of state in the old Iroquois civilization, which were confirmed by researches long after. From my infancy I had been taught what we Oneidas had contributed to American liberty and civilization. What did it matter then, what wrenchings I might receive after that from the Paleface, I had been preserved from the spirit-breaking Indian schools through my father's wonderful foresight.[20]

My psychology, therefore, had not been shot to pieces by that cheap attitude of the Indian Service, whose one aim was to "civilize" the race youth, by denouncing his parents, his customs, his people wholesale, and filling the vacuum they had created with their vulgar notions of what constituted civilization. I had none of those processes of the Bureaucratic mill in my tender years, to make me into a "pinch-back white man."[21] Had it been imposed upon me, I am certain something would have happened to it then.

I have gone a long way to show that a social order which intends to rebuild a broken people must come from an experience which is big enough to realize the real facts in the situation. It must know at first hand the good things and the shortcomings of the Red man, as well as the good things and the bad of the Paleface and his civilization. It must seek to avoid the evils of both, to combine their higher values, and then to weave them into the hardest-headed kind of BUSINESS. That is it, it must have business. But while its head must be high enough to have its eyes on the horizon, it must have a voice of thunder. It must be abreast with the institutions of the times that succeed. It must gather the fragments of the race, nurture them back to health and spirit, and under the kindest and best trained of guidance, promote them to be producers of the highest efficiency. The school must be carried to the gardens whence comes the maintenance. Work must be a pleasure, not servile and brow-beaten, but it must be done. The reward for effort must come in the possession of peaceful and pleasant homes in attractive surroundings, in maintenance that is stable for all times, in real education, in dividends, in leisure enough for proper recreation, in the security of these things so that the speculator and the politician cease to be our daily night-mares. The structure upon which all these things depend is the ECONOMIC one. This is the task and the preparation of the LOLOMI.[22]

The Lolomi policy is diametrically opposed to Bureaucracy in all things. It carries an order of protected self-government[23] by means of a Federal incorporation into industrial communities.

The first essential [way] in which it differs from the present policy is in the very nature of its origin. The Bureau came into existence with the idea of centralizing all power unto itself. It has succeeded to such an extreme that Russia ten years before the war, when at the height of her despotic power, was not more depleting than the Indian Bureau. Where Russia had one Czar, this Bureau had a hundred and fifty. Its aim was to substitute over the country, in the place of Indian organization by the tribes, Bureau control of property and person, through its Indian agents. With some exceptions these men have become a type of historic criminals. As absolute despots over the Reservations, they had the right to seize children away from their parents, to dispose of all questions pertaining to health and education, to interfere in the private lives of their wards and to incarcerate them without trial. They exceeded these powers in instances where their personal prejudices led them further. They instituted a "reign of terror" and when the tribes rebelled and there was a border outbreak, the Bureau could call upon the United States troops to quell the rebellion.

Philanthropists like the Indian Rights Association of Philadelphia, the Boston Citizenship League and the Board of Indian Commissioners[24] all came into existence to handle the problems that were growing out of such a state of things. These organizations were able to institute Congressional investigations, and to agitate public sentiment concerning the rights of individuals and tribes. Some of the early scandals of this democracy were uncovered by these efforts, and while they have deteriorated into secondary aids, they originally had power and influence. They were instrumental in obtaining alleviative legislation for the time being, but they have been no real force of any permanence against the everlasting power of politics now. The Congressional investigations likewise have fallen into a hopeless rut.

At the beginning of this administration when the advent of Wilson[25] gave us every hope for a new touch in our affairs, a Joint Commission of the Senate and House to Investigate Indian Affairs was created by Congress. I went to Champ Clark,[26] then Speaker of the House, who had the appointing power on the House side and I pleaded with him for a proper personnel on this body. He turned his searching but kind blue eyes on me and said, "Will you tell me what is the use of Indian investigations, what have they ever done for the race?"

"That is why they must do something now" was the only answer I could muster, but I confess I realized the futility of Congressional Investigations then more than ever. I had gone to Washington originally to see how far every cooperation on our part could achieve any benefit and I was bound to exhaust every conservative means toward a final solution. And while I never had any faith in the ability of Congress to make a thorough investigation of affairs about which some National Committeeman wrote, "Indian affairs constitutes the greatest trading post in politics," I did hope something could be got out of it that would be telling. When therefore, I discovered the late Senator Harry Lane of Oregon,[27] and received his audience, and his unwavering devotion to the Cause, I felt gratified and when he as a member of the joint Commission authorized the investigation of the Business Methods of the Indian Bureau by the Bureau of Municipal Research in New York, he made Emancipation for the race possible. (Municipal Research No. 65, Sept. 1915.)

The startling facts disclosed by this cold scientific investigation, by men trained to get to the bottom of things, has given us a document which will stand any test and which is in itself sufficient to overthrow the present order. It is interesting to note that when the report was made to the Joint Commission, it failed to become a public document. However, the Bureau of Municipal Research,[28] not being a ward, could not be treated like an Indian, and it published its own findings as Municipal Research Document No. 65. This is one of two scientific investigations made by this Government in its relations with the Red man. The other, "Contagious and Infectious Diseases Among Indians," Marine Hospital Report, 1914,[29] was made by the Public Health Service during the administration of ex-President Taft, who in that one stroke did more for the race than any President of the United States has ever done. *The New York Herald*'s[30] energetic use of these facts so disclosed saved many lives from trachoma and tuberculosis though it could not remove the danger of them since the environment of the race and their circumstances remain the same.

Outside of these two instances, Indian investigations white-wash, or totally suppress the glaring facts, except such as do not concern the interests or good repute of the political [personnel] of Congressional Committees. As such they merely license corruption.

And men like that "good old man," ex-Senator Teller of Colorado[31] and ex-Senator Lane, have served on these Committees, only to find that they can only give a minority report. Before Senator Teller died, he gave me the message, "so long as politics last, there is no hope for Indian Affairs." Some years later the verdict of Senator Lane was the same. The state of corruption in politics and the indifference of the American people when politics is getting a strangle-hold on this democracy is indeed food for thought. As the years go, Liberty for the Red man seems to become more and more impossible.

I recall the remark of Senator Clapp[32] two years ago. He had been presiding off and on over some Crow hearings before the Senate Indian Affairs Committee. They had been prolonged into whole days and weeks. Suddenly he thundered out, "[T]he Committee will adjourn till tomorrow at ten o'clock if the members have not all died of apoplexy." And I think all of us who had tried to follow the hearings agreed with him (Crow Hearings, S. 2378).[33]

The controversy which had brought the Crows to Washington was an Act introduced in Congress by one of the Montana Senators. It provided for the sale of some sections of the Crow domain, proceeds from which were to be administered to Crow needs which were getting acute. The Crows were divided into factions over the proposed legislation. The people of Montana were likewise divided into people and cattlemen. The people wanted the Crow lands opened up for settlement. As usual, title was to be created for the broken pieces because the Crows needed help. The cattlemen, on the other hand, wanted the ranges kept intact for their herds as they already had leases there. These two interests were ably represented, but the Indians' aid was the Bureau. Incidentally, this arrangement, if carried out, would break up the hold the Bureau had on the reservation, and so it was not willing to have it happen. One of the ablest of the young Crows wanted the lands kept intact and the cattlemen were not slow to seize him for the strengthening of their position. They paid his way to Washington. Some others of the Crow delegation were Carlisle men, who were sent, it was said, by the Commercial Clubs of Montana.

The Indian Affairs Committee had sent for a large Crow delegation with an honest intent, I think, of getting at the facts in the case. After the most patient of hearings I have ever witnessed, no one could arrive at any consensus of opinion outside of the danger of apoplexy to us all. I took pains to go to those members of the tribe who could be approached. The Bureau's delegates were, of course, well-barricaded as usual. In my conversation with the young man who seemed the strongest of them all, I said: "Do you know you are accused of having taken money from the cattlemen to represent their views?" He turned to me frankly and said, "I am not surprised to hear that, and it's no secret that I have taken money for my expenses to come here. But who hasn't among us all? Hasn't the Bureau always given favors to A. and B. and C. and D. and all its hangers on? Haven't the other factions who want this Act passed received money from the Commercial Clubs of Montana? The Bureau sees to it that some of us, who differ with it, do not get here. How then shall we come unless some other money than our tribal funds bring us?[34] And is it not possible for me to have an honest opinion concerning the breaking up of our Reservation? Isn't there any one in Washington who can see the truth in anything?"

The argument of the other one, who wanted the Act passed, was in substance this: "Everything and everybody is juggling with us. The Crows are in need of money which this Act would release. Suppose the white man does come in? What of it? He is going to clamor to come in till he does. This Act is a business proposition to us, not the best perhaps, but we might do worse."

The Carlisle[35] point of view is to break up the Indian reservation—because of the environment. There is no reckoning made as to the loss in this step on the economic side.

Keeping it intact gives a chance for the better day to arrive, while the dismemberment of the Indian domain puts the Indian out into the labor world of the white man, landless.

For my part, between the Bureau and Politics, I fail to find any reason why there should be an Indian left to threaten the Committees of Congress with apoplexy. Why we have not long ago passed away with it ourselves is indeed a question.

The petty politics which the Indian Bureau practices meets the larger politics of state and country around the corner when it promotes the individual interests of both; when it doesn't, they disagree. Against this combination, the sincere individual may beat his head against the stone wall in vain, till he drops. When he becomes too uncomfortable to someone, he may suddenly find his reputation gone, or he is indicted, or he is starving or destroyed.

Individual and collective philanthropy may stop the plunder of millions, temporarily. We have done it—but for what end? In order that the next set of scoundrels whom we do not now know may have it to play upon in the next administration. So far as the Indian is concerned, it matters very little whether the name is Democrat or Republican, politics is everlastingly one and the same thing. I see no hope in the party politics of the United States until the women of the land get the suffrage and form a no-party organization.

And who shall pay us for saving the Indians' property at the risk of our lives? Hardly Congress, hardly the Bureau. The Indian? Sometimes he would like to. That is when he knows about it and some sycophant has not been to him to tell him to beware. It remains for the Indian to be always embarrassed. The Bureau controls his friends and his property and when it does not, how is he to know a speculator from some other kind of deceiver? He does not know any one, not even his own friends.

The Bureau as a school for sycophants has a method of destroying natural leadership in the race which has no equal. With few notable exceptions, this breed of them is recruited from the Indian schools. With such English as they have acquired there they cannot become very dangerous to it, as they command no great respect for their knowledge of anything. They can however "hold jobs" in the Service, which will give them a livelihood, and when it comes time to use them, they will come forward and voice the wants of the tribe at the instigation of the agent or the Commissioner of Indian Affairs. They pack the councils, they outvote the Indian in policies where tribes are supposed to have any prerogatives left. Our Lenins and our Trotskys are no accidents.[36] They have been systematically made. And what can we do to stop the making of them? The power which the United States Government has given to its representative, the Bureau, is so vast Congress itself cannot always curb it. The decisions of a judicial body like the now extinct Joint Commission of Congress can be treated with contempt by the Commissioner of Indian Affairs. He can always find a rule or regulation in the Interior Department, and when he cannot, he will have one made, which will give him the right to carry out their decisions according to his own idea. The force of the Bureau to ameliorate the sentence of its pets, or to heighten the suffering of its enemies, can hardly be estimated. Those Indians of the reservations who have been strong and who have tried to change the conditions of our life have found themselves in trouble, to get out of which has come to be the business of their lives. When we investigated Osage conditions, the powers of Government which used to shadow and threaten us, or arrest and indict us on false charges, would fill another volume but it is not the purpose of this book to give details of any persecution.[37] I merely mention this to show that my facts are not secondhand. There is no liberty of speech on the reservations, and the Bureau has power to stop any propaganda among them. When, therefore, people ask me why we have no leaders, I want to answer by asking, "Why is Kerensky[38] not leading the Russians today?"

When a constitutional authority said, "A bureaucracy is sure to think that its duty is to augment official power, official business, official numbers, rather than to leave free the energies of mankind," I want to add: "The one at Washington does not stop with the making of lariat experts of red tape, and paper government, it is a school of crimes upon a helpless people. For over eighty-five years, under the cover of benevolence, this arm of the United States Government has starved out the man with an idea of Liberty, it has gone to his wife in disguise and broken up the home; it has inoculated his children with tubercular bacilli; it has made the young generation blind with trachoma; it has made the richest people on the globe, a race of vagrants."

The dissipation of poverty is hinted at in the figures which Senator Johnson of South Dakota[39] gave on the floor of the United States Senate two years ago: "The Bureau has dissipated $218,000,000 since 1889, prior to this administration." He means that these figures constitute what can actually be found. What the dissipation of property is under a system which keeps no Balance sheet, as was discovered by the Bureau of Municipal Research, when it investigated "the Business Methods of the Indian Bureau" is beyond anybody's calculation. Under Senator Johnson's figures, the yearly rate of pauperization is over $8,000,000. The vast resources of timber, minerals, water power, lands, now owned by individuals in the United States and which constitutes the wealth of the country belonged to the Indian.

As to Congress, which created the Bureau and which is allowing it to remain, all its energies are consumed acting upon piecemeal legislation that is either remedial of former acts, or the legalizing of loot. As one of the Senators said to me, "there might be some interest in coming here (Indian Affairs Committee) if we knew what we were doing, but here we are acting upon legislation without precedent, and no one is able to tell us the actual facts we ought to know." And who shall be the authority for the facts? Congress cannot make an impartial investigation. It does not want to call to its Service men, who are trained to uncover cold facts. Even if it is not true that all the members of committees are not to be trusted, even so, just let a Senator or a Congressman develop facts which are vital and startling, and what happens? Some National Committeeman will be in Washington to tell that member that he must stop, or face political suicide! And is anybody's career in Congress worth the Indian's justice? Of what concern is this pauper's cause before the supreme greed of the American nation?

Men who are towers of strength from every consideration, like Senator Townsend of Michigan,[40] leave the Indian Affairs Committee "because nothing can be accomplished in it outside of the rut."

In such a state of things as we have now reached with Indian Affairs, there is no hope of securing uniform legislation outside of the Lolomi, unless it is what Dr. Montezuma[41] and his Carlisle followers want—doing away with the Bureau without any substitution whatever, leaving the helpless Indian open to the exploitation of every grafter in the land. When I have remonstrated with these advocates of what I consider a no less dangerous theory than Bureaucracy, and have asked: "and let the Indian lose every last possession he has?," the answer has been: "suppose he does, he'll have to go to work like a white man, and it will be the making of him." I agree with this point of view, that if one of two evils is to be chosen, why then it is better to die a sudden death than to be eaten out slowly by an ugly cancer whose stench reaches up to Heaven. From my point of view, which is influenced by training in social service, any theory or policy which intends to secure the ultimate welfare of the race, must first of all consider how to secure real protection. We have never had protection, why not give it a trial? The first act is to stop this exploitation of assets, of health, of character. We must save those remains of these things on which to build.

It is plain the Indian himself does not know what theory to advance to save himself and his possessions, but he realizes that the concrete thing he wants is to save them.

It is plain the American people do not know what to advocate, but that that element of them who save situations anywhere, would like to see the Indian protected. Many of them know the failings of the government and would like to see a new order but they fear to remove the Federal hawkeye, lest they throw him open to their own millions of highwaymen.[42]

There is only one combination in the whole world which can avoid becoming another Bureau and, at the same time, secure protection. That is a Federal incorporation of a self-governing body. When I have advocated this, I have met with three classes of opinion:

One says, "Why ask the Federal Government, which has already made a botch of Indian affairs, to again have a hand in it? Why not merely get the fee simple to all Indian lands and incorporate the Indian's assets under the laws of the various states?"

Another says, "Incorporate!—why look at the white man's corporations? Even he cannot always cope with the exploitation possible under them. Where would the Indian be?"

A third class says, "Why has this not been done before?"

The Lolomi enjoys answering these questions: As to the first, incorporation under the state laws would mean petty politics. A small population of Indians in a state would have as much chance with state legislatures as a lamb would with a hungry lion. Whole states are eternally clamoring now for Indian possessions. There is no room to speculate what would happen to Indian shareholders under laws influenced by the white constituents of a state.

What, for instance, would prevent a white politician from ingratiating himself in the affections of an influential Indian to whom he could say, "you buy A and B, and C, and D, out and you sell to me. When we get the control of the organization we can advance its development and own the whole business." To go from one scoundrel to another cannot be entertained. There might be found a state where public sentiment would not allow it but it behooves us hereafter to beware. The Lolomi takes no chances.

The second brings up the defects of the modern corporation as it stands. Economic authorities agree that the greatest evil in the constitution of the corporations of the United States is their form of representation.

Now then, to avoid the domination of the rich man over the smaller shareholder, the Lolomi provides "that each member of said corporation shall have only one vote irrespective of the number of shares he or she may hold."

Inasmuch as the idea of incorporating is to save and promote Indian assets, and to educate the race in the forms and responsibilities of self-government, homogeneity is necessary. By this fact the door is positively closed against the white speculator and by the following provision, "that shares of stock shall not be transferred without the consent of all the Board of Directors, and cannot be transferred to any individual but to the corporation only; we close the door on the unscrupulous Indian, for no organization with any vision can leave the latter out of the consideration." One of the pillars in the success of the Mormon communities of the West was homogeneity. All successful organization is based on likeness of kind. I believe where white communities have cooperative organizations that have failed, the fact that they were composed of all kinds of race elements has counted largely.

I wish now to show how the Lolomi settles other questions which have seemed incapable of solution. Just as soon as the assets are pooled, Indian property is of necessity turned into the fee simple title. With that stroke is done away piecemeal legislation enacted without precedent, and out of which proceeds the present exploitation of the ward by politics.

It does away with the indefiniteness of taxation. It does away with the present ban on the development of our natural resources by ourselves. It gives us something to do under direction.

It does away with the status of semi-citizenship (the status of wardship),[43] which is at once unconstitutional and chaotic. This state has invited more evil to the race than any other one thing. Till we secure uniformity in our legal status from which we can gauge standards and check up on them, the burden of legislation for the Indian will remain unpleasant, unreliable, unjust, and everlastingly disgraceful to the statesmanship of the American Nation.

That long circuitous road from the unallotted reservation through the Trust patent to the fee simple title will be cut off and the clerical force which spends its time writing, "your matter is under consideration," will have to make an honest living by cleaning up backyards.

I have previously mentioned the settlement of the question of taxation by incorporation. By any other method of granting the fee simple, the experience of the Red man has been a disastrous one. When the old Indian objected to allotments, he feared to trust himself with that form of property holding he did not understand and could not promote. And he was right. Nowhere else in the United States is property taxed which is denied the right of production.

In one of my sojourns into the wilderness, I came upon one of the old leaders whose eyes were faded from the years of persecution. But he was strong and he still commanded his band of followers.

After some discussion in which he pictured to me, on the sand with a stick, what he would like to see in a model village, he said, "This Lolomi law is written to a certain point but where is it written about how we shall act? What shall we do to govern ourselves?"

And so while he had his Council together, we drew up the Constitution and By-laws for his particular band. This brought about the deepest inquiry.

Before we left it, I said to them, "There is one feature of the Lolomi you may not like. And that is that after the trial period of its existence it will have to pay taxes. Do you think you could take care of the Community's taxes?"

Their chief answered, "In the old days, when our people were one in action, we bore all our burdens together and did not feel them. So again, if we had peace instead of fear in our minds, my braves are anxious to do something. But what is the use, tomorrow we may have to leave our homes." And thus the paralysis of the reservation is but an index of the state of mind.

I need not dwell at length upon the possibilities of combination. Where, for example, the individual Indian has $500 in assets, it is obvious this is no kind of a start to the ostracized, unskilled, uneducated man. The handling of $500 is not even an experience which would teach him a lesson in frugality. Removing the restrictions from it simply means the dissipation of it. But let us take 1,000 or 2,000 of them and pool them, and immediately we have a capitalization big enough to promote an independent industry.

The present method of making citizens by the Department of the Interior is by sending out a Competency Commission, composed of its subordinate officials, who decide when and how an Indian is competent, and upon whose decision this man gets his fee simple title, then his relations with the Government are forever severed. I have been told that those who "shot the last arrow" and "kissed the plow" under the special auspices of the Secretary of the Interior several years ago have all lost their property and are shifting around. This same will happen to most of them and boiled down to the last analysis this is DISSIPATION, and carried out far enough there will be no per capita wealth to combine in a short time.[44] When the present Secretary of the Interior came into office, we had great hope that Indian Affairs would receive his vitalizing touch, and that a new order was in store for us. I made many attempts to see him personally with regard to the Lolomi before going to Congress with it. But he was inaccessible, due, I always thought, to the fact that a now ex-private Secretary was there serving the double task of being a watch dog for the Oil Trust whom I had investigated.

I went so far as to try to get the ear of the National Committeeman from Texas, who is the present Head incumbent of the Bureau. He assured me he could not possibly take me to the Secretary, but that he would be pleased to take what I had to say to the Secretary himself. In order that I might not be guilty of having left one straw unturned, in the wake of conservative measures, I thanked him and proceeded to tell him. I had not gone through my first sentence when he went on after this fashion: "I just want to show you what I receive every day from all parts of the country," and with that he piled into my hands telegrams and letters to him of a flattering kind. I tried to resume the subject of my visit but it was quite impossible.

The Indian appropriation by Congress of ten or twelve million dollars, "for the support and civilization of the Indian," has been the great argument by the Bureaucrat of what this country through the Government is doing for the race. Here again is a deceiving figure. The most the last appropriation passed by Congress prior to our declaration of War, contained of gratuity moneys, was a little over seven million. There is a reimbursable fund "for encouraging industry and self-help" among the tribes which in policy is most pernicious. It authorizes this Bureau to spend so many hundreds of thousands or so many millions of the Indian funds for projects the Bureau and members of Congress may deem fit. For example, the Blackfeet Irrigation project of Montana,[45] a $3,000,000 project is an experiment for which the Blackfeet fund is mortgaged. If this project fails, the

Blackfeet lose the money, no one else, since the national government has protected itself.

I asked the Blackfeet, "who does the work on this project?" and the prompt answer was, "the white men, of course, the constituents of our representatives."

The expense to the government of the maladministration upon the Indian will not show till years later, when the claims of the race will be forthcoming for these Acts of today, which the local constituents of a state are continually bringing upon the Nation.

The aggregate wealth of the race left in the United States was said to be about $50,000,000,000 nine years ago. Most of this was undeveloped. This would make the per capita wealth about $1,600. Of course, these figures are misleading, for there are tribes who have very little left, while there are those who have considerable. But even where members of a tribe have a per capita wealth of $200, there is still something to combine, but the present methods of dismembering the Indian domain and then creating individual titles out of it, piecemeal, for the Paleface, and the rate at which the fee simple is being handed out under the guise of competency, as proved by the Curtis Act, is a matter of caution. The time left for saving property by combination is not long.

The Lolomi in its program of development recognizes several necessary first steps. Among them is the race's lack of credit.[46] No race of men under the sun who have no credit, and no environment in which to labor, and no freedom for initiative can acquire the beginnings of business. The most humble immigrant who comes to the United States with his possessions upon his back, can go out to the remotest parts of our country and go into debt for a home and the necessary equipment for a farm, all upon his racial reputation. The Indian has a reputation for indolence which discriminates him against the world of business. That reputation comes through the fact that the farms of the reservation have been allotted with a great noise about making him into a farmer, and that after so many years of this attempt, they present the most dismal aspect. No one seems to have known that the real nature and the real object of Bureaucracy is to make inefficient and dependent men and women.

Leaving out the question of deserts, for the sake of argument, what other possible way of promoting Indian property is there outside of combination? What other possible way of getting credit is there outside of creating a body by law which shall be responsible according to the business regulations of the land? What other possible way is there of preserving what the Indian has left, and still not interfering with the order in which we live? I challenge anyone to present that way.

I do not excuse all the members of the race from indolence, but knowing what timber remains, I would govern the indolent and promote the industrious.

There have come to my notice innumerable instances of what I am about to relate: A young Omaha came to me six years ago. I had been to his reservation and I knew about him. He had built up on his inherited estate a well-improved farm. This land was better than his allotment which was several miles away. He had gone into debt to a speculating white man for his equipment. This man had taken into account the young man's energy and intelligence and honesty, and had taken a chance in giving him $5,000 for improvements. Looking over the implements and stock, one could readily see where this money had gone. He had figured out that by selling the allotment and buying an extra piece of land adjoining his inherited estate he would be able to get out of this debt, and thereby stop the interest, and would have a fine farm in one piece. But, because of the prejudice of the local agent against him, he could not persuade the latter to his point of view. So he came to Washington and begged of me to take the photos of his farm and stock and to go to the Secretary of the Interior and show him just what he wanted to have done. He added, "of course, if you cannot get his ear and this goes back through the same channels of the agent and his coterie, there is no hope for me." I went to the Secretary. I got together a concise statement and took the photos. The Secretary listened to me kindly, but to show how utterly impossible it is for individual matters to receive his personal attention, this went back to the very channels instituted to handle these questions and the Omaha, after being juggled further for a year had to do the things he did not want to do. I often wonder when something is credited to the head of the Interior Department whether he ever saw it or heard of it. The body of minute details which encumber the offices of the United States Government make it a physical impossibility for individual justice unless the pressure becomes so acute that there can be no indifference about it. This fact makes it impossible for us to put any hope in the personnel of an office any longer. The hopelessness of going higher up for justice is known by the subordinates, and so, often too, the ambitious Indian recognizes the fact and the result is that he wants to stand in with the agent.

I have made it my business to know if there are any yearnings in the hearts of the people who are going to make the Lolomi a success or a failure. I have gone farther, I must know if all the timber is not dead. I have gone to the contractors of many large business projects who employed Indians and asked them all the same question, "Why do you hire a lot of lazy Indians to do your work?" To a man they have responded in substance this: "I know no lazy Indians. I have tried every class of labor in the United States and I'll put none ahead of the Indian. The faithfulness of the Red man to details, his honesty in labor and his quiet dignity and intelligence makes him indispensable to the world outside of the Bureau."

One of the boasts of the Indian Office is that no class of household labor compares with the girls they have trained in the Indian school. I want to say here that it is because they have trained the girl who might have become an instructor or manager of some business into being the servant of the race which has oppressed her people. My objection to turning the Indian into the white man's world of labor, after he has been stripped of his assets, as the Carlisle theorists would do, is that a man who is capable of something better is coerced into the hopelessness of the landless laborer.

Having settled the question of credit, the Lolomi now takes up the matter of supplying the individuals of the community. Again I turn to the Mormons for example.

When the Mormons arrived in the deserts of Utah, a persecuted people, the first institution they put up was a cooperative store. They had no money with which to capitalize, however, and they had to find some other way out, so they capitalized on labor. They kept on the books of the Cooperative store the schedule of wages and balances. They gave every man credit for a year in advance and after his necessities had been deducted from his earnings, they found out much about the members of their community. Some had a good balance left to be credited to shares of stock. Some came out even, a few fell behind. These last could not remain.

One of the most perplexing questions which confronts our populations is how to secure the necessaries of life without paying three prices for it. This cooperative store will do away with the exploitation practiced at present by the local merchants.

One other question is one which has often been asked of me: "How can you take care of the equalization of burdens? There are bound to be some more efficient than others, some more frugal, some more worthy. How can your institution distribute reward according to merit?" The failure to do this is one of the great drawbacks to Indian Communism or any other Communism which has not been modernized.

The system of salaries and wages is fixed for all community work. Every man and woman fits into the place where he or she can do the most effective work. Already everyone knows what each particular class of work pays. That is established and cannot be partial. Beyond this there is a community of effort and behind this is the industrial school for the adult.

The background for the Lolomi is the out-of-door pursuits. It may be agriculture, it may be horticulture, it may be herding in the main, but there must always remain the garden of the home, out of which the living for the individual family must largely come.

Large area farming is not attractive to the race. It is not attractive to any man when he is poor. This part passes over to the burden of the corporation and, where a single man struggled hitherto with poor machinery and poor horses, the corporation has the best of improved machinery. I could never see any virtue in grinding a man's energies on drudgeries which exist as a result of deficit. I would make the place where human beings earn their bread as attractive as possible, so that work would become a pleasure where each one wanted to give his best.

In choosing the business of the organization, there are other things to be taken into the reckoning besides soil. One is the natural bent of the group. Those Indians like the Navajos, for example, who are at the height of the pastoral stage, should not be expected to do scientific farming in the place of herding. But these are all matters of detail.

So far as business accountability is concerned, I want this borne in mind, there is no other organ which can save the Indian. This alone can separate personal liberty from property, and while we have a legal restriction on the dissipation of his property, we have freed his energies. We have guarded him against the scheming individual, white or Indian, against Bureaucracy, against politics, against himself.

Incorporation presupposes a state of self-government in which to succeed. If the corporations of the United States, which have brought a new era of development into the world, were tied to Bureaus, they would be obliged to consult for every next move, or if politics every four years changed their heads, the business of the greatest industrial country in the world would long ago have gone to smash, and the red-blooded men of organizing genius would have sought another flag.

The type of man it takes to run large affairs is not one bred in a state of subservience. "In a state of fixity where there are no fields of opportunities for independent and private initiative and enterprise by individuals or associations of individuals, the spirit which demands self-government is selectively bred out and kept bred out of a nation."[47]

The time has come for the final settlement between the American and American.[48] Shall it become necessary for us to beg a Supreme Court of Justice of the League of Nations to settle the most disgraceful and low-browed state of affairs ever enacted in a democracy?

CHAPTER FOUR

How the Lolomi Handles the Social Side of the Problem

So interdependent are the business and social problems of the Red man, they cannot be separated in his life. Lacking a stable income or credit on the business side, the task of the social survey is to see how these things affect his health, his psychology, his morals, his efficiency, his opportunities.

The setting in which all these things are fixed is the environment in which he has his properties, and where he is obliged to live because of them. The reservation has come to be synonymous with squalor, indolence, disease, vice. Where can anyone begin anything in surroundings where there is such a lack of sanitation, of proper educational facilities, organized effort, means of transportation, proper shelter, proper food, knowledge, incentive and reward for effort? Why, the slums are not so destitute! At least they are within walking distance of something better. And this dismal harpy-faced squalor sits on top of fine soil, fine ranges, timber and minerals, or deserts. And these people who endure all this still have a nominal wealth into the billions. One surveys the scene with the heartache and indignation such as only Siberia[49] must know.

Now and then we can see a fine house, fine stock, fine barns. To them the agent points with great pride as examples of what he can do when there is any response to his educative efforts. But, wait a moment! That is quite misleading. Let us find out if the man who owns those things does not own them in spite of the agent, or is he one of his pets, who for carrying out the designs of the despot, has been rewarded out of the tribal herds. There are solitary successes even in Reservations, from either sheer superiority of the man who is able to ward off with one strong arm, while he toils with the other, or there are those who look like ready money because they have divided the spoils off their people with the agent and his coterie, among whom may be found, representatives of the Oil trust, of the Beef trust, of the Lumber trust, of the Water trust, of the Coal trust.[50] And the Bureau[51] can always produce photographs of these successes that make our complaints look like Mexican money, till the trained investigator comes along and asks, "What per cent of the population do these men represent?" Even then you better have been on that Reservation.

The matter of the Indian home and its setting has perplexed all who would like to do something for the race. The absence of any receptacle for any kind of welfare campaign is the first thing one meets (Contagious and Infectious Diseases Among Indians, Marine Hospital Report, 1914).[52]

Where the home structures have been modernized with the same slovenliness which characterizes the Bureau's touch, do these individual dwellings belong to any regulated system of sanitation? Is it not the great despair of the field matrons that there is no ventilation, no closets, no shelves, no light, no system in the building, no water system, no sewage? I have known some of the most heroic workers in the Service[53] in this particular class who work against terrible odds; of course, I have known of many whose special talent lies in drawing the check at the end of the month.

As I travel over the country and see the beautiful spots of our beloved native land and compare them to the dismal hopelessness of the Indian's home, I wonder if anyone can ever know the heaviness of our environment upon us. Within a few miles of the most comfortable evening lamp is someone dying from the evils of the environment, evils like tuberculosis, that great indicator of the lack of nourishment and sanitation. Our highest types do not survive this life. Before they are all gone, I wonder if this country will ever see the situation as it really is!

The lack of security of possession is another large factor in backwardness. I have found many an able housewife who threw up her hands in desperation and said, "What's the use? Where is the end of our harassment? For whom am I fixing my home?" The class of white men who come to live around us when the Bureau has succeeded in making "citizens," is everything and anything. Our Indian population is interspersed with all kinds of influences. Most of the people, however, are the much exploited poor whom the speculator has induced to come. Some of them move away in canvas wagons after a year or two of untold hardships.

A Cherokee woman remarked to me, "I want to move from Talequah."[54] I looked at her in surprise for her home was a beautiful one and she loved Talequah dearly. "What do you mean?" I asked.

"I want to go to Arkansas," she went on, "I am sure there can be no bad people left in Arkansas. I am sure they have all moved down here to Oklahoma."

It is a fact that the richer, the more beautiful, the original home of the Red man, the greater the greed in those who come to live next to him.

In the investigation of Osage which I helped to make in 1913, we found seventeen different kinds of offenses committed against this group. They were conspiracy to defraud, fraud, unjust discrimination against the Indian by the Bureau, damages, usurious interest (some were paying as high as a 1,000 per cent), threat and assault, coercion, bribery, false imprisonment, malpractice by physicians, misrepresentation and interference, violation of contract, etc.[55]

Malpractice came from an arrangement where the sick wards of the Bureau were committed into the hands of unskilled physicians, and the big surgeons denied these cases because the unskilled ones belonged to the "preferred" set of grafters around the agency.

A story is told of how a certain physician and speculator went about with the thumb of an old Osage Indian in his pocket, after the Osage he had attended was dead. It was the practice of the Government of late years to get signatures of Indians who cannot write, sealed with the thumb mark. The Osage had considerable property which would become alienable upon his death. After his death, the records suddenly appeared with papers thumb-marked over to this doctor. But it would take many volumes to tell all that happened to the Osages. The most interesting fact which that investigation disclosed was that the officials of the Government were in collusion with men of the large interests to defraud the Indian.[56]

So among the tasks of the Lolomi not least is that of making a new environment and a real home.

Incorporation into industrial communities means the development of industry, and that in turn means the concentration of population. Originally, village life was known to all Indians. Even with the Iroquois civilization, where agriculture was the pursuit, the village was still the center. All Indians understand village organization in a primitive way and want it. Their gregariousness and the monotony of their surroundings make them seek the neighboring towns now.

The enthusiasm of the Indian women over the Lolomi—those who know of it—is one of the most hopeful things I have met. I see in their vain efforts to make the home attractive where they are, that the love of the beautiful in the race still remains, though dormant under persecution.

As I know the Indian women of the land; they are the most responsible element of the Indian population.[57] I have not found that they have lost their native character and purity. While whole tribes are gone with demoralization, and while some tribes never had a high position for womankind, due to a difference in ethnic culture, it is not true of the race. It was to the rigid control of the social order by the Indian women that we owe the physical excellence of the race. And behind that physical excellence was the moral purity which characterized this primitive stock. It is an anthropological law that no race can be long-lived whose women practice promiscuity.[58] Our mothers of the clans taught the maiden to despise the familiar man no less than the sick man and the coward, with the result that these types were not eligible for marriage and had no place in the social order. I should like to see the race restore itself to some of its traditional philosophy. I should like to see the sentiment back again which was ashamed of sickness, and low morals. I count upon the readiness of the Indian women of the country to respond to opportunity. Their hunger for the better things of life I have known intimately, and their straightforward common sense makes them a calculable factor in regeneration. If they had decent homes, five years of the proper educational campaign among them would wipe out all the present evils of the Indian environment. It is so easily done; why not give it a chance?

With good housing will come the sanitary systems of water, light, heat, sewage, only possible with concentration. Instead of a hut with a dirt-floor and no screens, and water hauled in a bucket from a half a mile away, and got out of an open hole in the ground, there is the town, with its substantial homes and its abundant supply of water and every means of sanitation.

Until the village comes there can be no segregation of the sick from the well, and no method of control over disease. It is the plan of the Lolomi to install modern hospitals and to put them under the auspices of the Public Health Service.

The elimination of distance makes possible the control of the educational facilities and the means of recreation.

Perhaps though, the indirect good results of incorporation will play just as big a part as these things. There is nothing, for instance, that will classify the race with more accuracy and speed. It is not the wish of the Lolomi to detain those who wish to live in Paris or New York, no more than the modern corporations require their investors to remain in a certain place. There are members of the race who draw their funds from California or Europe. Why should they not draw their dividends from the same places? The Lolomi is intended for those who have lost their youth and their opportunity. At least half of the present generation knows they have been cheated out of these things by the Government school, but their awakening comes after experiencing the hardships and mistakes which might have been avoided had they only known. The blasted hopes of the young, who are yet too old to begin school careers again, is one of the ways in which we bleed daily. The Lolomi carries the school to the field or the home where the maintenance is made. Not being dictated to by politics, it will secure only the sympathetic instructors who know what they are about and whose service terminates when they cannot produce the desired results.

The natural elimination of the sycophant will cleanse the atmosphere.[59] He will suddenly find it is pleasanter to take his share of the tribal funds or properties and move away, just as the whipping, or shooting eliminated him in times when the tribes had their own way of doing things.

We now come to the most harassed phase of our life: education. Between the poles of two classes of theorists, we dangle once more. One believed for so many centuries that the Indian was incapable of the higher education. We proved so many demonstrations to the contrary, we said so many uncomfortable things about Indian schools and their instructing personnel that the House Committee on Indian Affairs suddenly conceived of the idea of having the present methods of Indian education investigated at the beginning of the Democratic administration. So the Efficiency Committee set out to find the facts. I am told their report is one of the suppressed documents of our democracy. How startling their findings must have been that the public could not be trusted to know, we can imagine, since we do know some of the things they could not help finding. It was upon this report that the present Commissioner of Indian Affairs[60] started his vigorous campaign of revising methods. Since then, the curriculum has had considerable shaking and the new theory is that the Indian child is capable of cramming more wonders than any class of children. I have been told that the verdict of some University people on the new plan was that "it is a physical impossibility for any child to comply with it." Be that as it may, we seem doomed to the everlasting whims and fancies of those who love us. We suspect the new curriculum came from a conference of the classroom teachers of the Service and the supervisors, among whom are men of large educational ideas, as for example Supt. E. A. Allen of Keshena.[61]

However, since this method of patch-up-the-crazy-quilt does not change some of the vital facts and factors, perhaps I may be permitted to still hang on to my convictions about Indian education.

In the first place, institutionalism, which is now righteously deplored by the modern educator, still remains in the Government

Boarding School. And whether these schools carry a partial High School curriculum or not, the fact remains that the indiscriminate herding of children during the tender years of adolescence in these places is injurious. These are the years when they belong to the natural environment of the home. In speaking of our differences of opinion with regard to phases of Indian education, General Pratt[62] himself admitted that the Boarding school system was wrong. "It was my intention if I had had Carlisle longer," said he, "to have made it into a mere station for a larger outing system."

The destruction of individuality, that quality of our citizenhood the developing of which this country boasts, is an actual process on the Indian youth, whether one wants to be conscious of it or not. Secondly, the atmosphere of subservience in an Indian school, which any outsider can feel upon entering the corps of the Service, has its injurious effects. Indian school products, after they reach the self-conscious age, have no independence of thought. The Indian school has produced not one independent thinker known to the outside world. There are those who become so by the time they get old, but the Indian school did not give them the English to express themselves. And just so long as this Service lasts, just so long will it be impossible to change this atmosphere. The personnel of the Service which remains is, for the most part, those who have lost their footing in any other world. Themselves warped by the everlasting suppression of the despotism, and for so many years cut off from the proper recreation and interests which should have been their due, they too are self-conscious of their ostracism. The fresh air has never reached their commonplace attitude that the race they serve or vice versa is a servile one.

When I was a girl, my first inquiry was, "What is the capacity of the race mind?" For, of course, if our plight was due to our own inferiority of mind, our reforms must be influenced by the fact. At that time, the theory that the Indian child should not be educated beyond the sixth grade was being vigorously promoted by the Bureau. To the end that I might make this investigation for myself, I went into the Service as a classroom teacher.[63]

My discoveries were quite impressive and encouraging. Among the representatives of 36 different tribes, of all stages of ethnic culture, I found ready response. The powers of imitation, imagination, and abstraction exceeded those of the Paleface children with whom I had gone to school in the little district school outside the Reservation. Their refinement, likewise, far surpassed that of these whites.

My list of beautiful types from whom one might expect futures, so far as their natural endowments went, easily constituted one-fifth of the school population. The early years of adolescence showed these children very highly sensitive, quick and artistic. But one need not remain very long on the grounds of any Indian school to feel the depression, the atmosphere which scorns their racial characteristics. After a while they come under the influence of it. Then they find themselves neither one thing nor the other, neither white nor Indian. This kind of education, G. Stanley Hall has so aptly called, [is] "making a pinch-back white man of the Indian."[64]

Secondly, the commonplace level of the instruction credited to the industrial training has presented no great skill, and no finish among those who have been detained there long enough to have acquired the skill that would command them a livelihood in the outside world. We could forgive many things if, when the Government starts out to make a Paleface out of the Indian, it made an independent one. This is not the case. The number of grownup ambitious men who venture out for themselves only to find they have yet to serve an apprenticeship in their trades they were supposed to know, is too great. It is an actual fact, then, that the time of youth with the race has been mostly spent in drudgery, for no institution of several hundred inmates can possibly avoid the work of keeping it up. Indeed, the shops come in for a small part of the student's energies when all the dish-washing, the sweeping, the scrubbing, and the making of several hundred beds, to say nothing of the laundry work, have been done. I had occasion to note the havoc the work of taking care of a government school made upon the time and the vitality of children and I am not surprised when a Supervisor of schools resigns because nothing is done though he has repeatedly called the Bureau's attention to the fact that the Indian schools were violating the child-labor laws of the states.[65]

The division of the school population into morning and afternoon details for the classrooms allowed every child to go to school a half day. Every so often the schedules were reversed, and it was deplored by all the classroom teachers that the afternoon classes came to the schoolroom with such fatigue [that] they could not do the work of the morning classes.

The lack of anything like a uniform standard in the efficiency of the instructing personnel is another of the deplorable things we meet. The larger part of the Indian Service is constituted of old fossils who came in long before the Civil Service regulations, though not much can be said for that either, since many times the superior individual who had other qualifications than it exacted has been debarred by it. But the fact is that most of the people in the Service are political appointees. I know of no institution in the land that would put up with so many specimens as are gathered together to enlighten the Indian. The attitude of some of the most hopelessly ignorant of them, with regard to the position of the race, makes them positively obnoxious. They exact servility of the children and this goes a long way toward the discouragement of the man.

On the other hand, the superior individuals in the Service find themselves unwelcome at every turn, and their ideas of doing things received with scorn.

I know of no cripple in the world so pathetic as he whose youth has been stolen under the grand semblance of getting an education, detained the same number of years at it as his white brother, but getting about a fourth of what the public school carries to the white child. He comes to an alien world of books, the medium of which has yet to be acquired, and when acquired, is a mongrel pidgin English, which commands no respect from any one!

And yet, the grade schools of the Indian have been mistaken for universities over the country!

I was lunching one day in New York, when my kind hostess tried to give me a chance at the Indian situation. I had no sooner started, when a woman across the table remarked, "of course, we all know the Indian has had his chance and he has not made good."

This remark is typical of a certain kind of American mind. I looked at this person and wondered where her limousine and her diamonds came from. It looks like a long way between Wall Street and the Reservations, but it is not very far.

Other Writings

Short Stories and Poems

• • • • • •

The Legend of the Bean
(1902)

In a brown tepee, nestling cozily in a mass of summer foliage, and shaded from the hot June sun by magnificent old trees, under whose spreading branches, the rich, black sod fed many a flower and fern, lived in years gone by one who had seen many moons wax and wane among her people. Nearby her dwelling a babbling brook wound on its way, and the birds overhead sang fearlessly their many notes of gladness. The air was full of dewy fragrance, and the sun shed a radiance upon the morning mist as I drew near the snug little dwelling, the home of my grandmother; and, sitting down beside her, [I] begged for an old story. She thought briefly, and perhaps the silken tassel of the corn which she had planted at the side of her home made her think of the story which she told me:

"Long ago,[1] when my mother was a young woman, she had a home like mine, where nature bloomed abundantly. She loved to hear the birds sing and could name each kind by its song. One day she was awakened by a strange and beautiful melody and, stealing softly to the spot from whence the sound came, she saw a pretty green vine whirling in the air above a corn stalk. Suddenly, it stopped singing, and descending, lightly twisted itself around the shock. On it were little buds, promising bright red blossoms. These matured and withered, and brought forth long green pods filled with round flat seeds,

"The Legend of the Bean," published in *The Church's Mission to the Oneidas*, 2nd ed., ed. Frank Wesley Merrill (Oneida Indian Reservation, Wisconsin; Fond du Lac, WI: P. B. Haber, 1902), 55–56.

which hardened and browned.² She picked them one day, and when the Chiefs were met in Council she brought to them the strange product and said:

'Fathers and Elders, I beg a privilege; I am the daughter of the Chief who shot the arrow into our enemies' midst, which killed their leader. Give me leave for utterance. I will speak briefly. I have a message from Lalonyhawagon,³ the Ruler of the Heavens, the friend of our own Tribe.'

'Speak thou mayest, fair daughter,' said the Chiefs. She told the story of the bean, and, producing it, said: 'Not without meaning did it sing. It is the sign from Lalonyhawagon to test the courage of our tribe, and to know whether we are worthy of his friendship. Should it be good, other tribes will buy it, and ours would be the glory of interpreting aright the wishes of the Great Spirit.'

The Chiefs were aroused and asked, 'Who will be the one to test the product?'

Then an old woman came forward and bravely answered, 'I will risk my life for the benefit of my friends, my home, and my race.'

She cooked and ate it and found it very good. And so from that day the bean became an ingredient in the mixing of corn bread, because it first grew upon the corn, and its song still lingers amid the silky fringes of the ripening corn, and those who listen hear again the message of the Great Spirit. This brave old woman lived to see her six sons grow in wisdom and virtue and become great Chiefs of the tribe."

The Sacrifice of the White Dog
(1902)

Oh that the expanse of time were less, and the camp fire burning, to make my story glow with interest to my reader. But my pen paints poorly, and you understand not the old Oneida vocabulary, which so well my tale would tell. Briefly but barely I must tell my legend. It is of a curious rite and ceremony. When the Oneidas were still warm in the nest of the Iroquois, they went along with the Six Nations to their annual sacrifice of the White Dog.[4] With patient care they seek for a white dog—without spot or blemish he must be. Then was he killed without the shedding of a drop of his blood. His body, after the white man had introduced those decorative articles, was adorned with blue and red ribbons—originally it was the gorgeous autumn leaves of the forest that decked the offering. When the decorating was done, the people came together and formed in procession behind the bearers, singing weird offertory hymns, for they were worshipping that divine spirit, Lalonyhawagon. On an altar of brush they laid the body to burn, and, blending their song with the rising fumes, they marched around until all was consumed. The white dog, the emblem of innocence; the red, of victory over the enemy; and the blue, heaven's color, the sign mark of the Divine Spirit, which guided them to the worship of the Great Spirit.

The story "The Sacrifice of the White Dog" was first published in *The Church's Mission to the Oneidas*, ed. Frank Wesley Merrill (Oneida Indian Reservation, Wisconsin; Fond du Lac, WI: P. B. Haber, 1902), 56.

A Tribute to the Future of My Race

(1903)

Not a song of golden "Greek,"
Wafted from Aegian shores,
Not from an Olympian height
Come my simple syllables:
But from the northern of Wisconsin,   5
From the land of the Oneidas,
From the chieftain clan Cornelius,
From the friendly Iroquois
Comes the greeting of the wampum
And a tribute, humble, simple,   10
From the pines' soft, lingering murmurs,
From the "pleasant water courses,"
From the morn-kissed, mighty highlands,
From the breezes and the flowers
Nodding secrets to each other,   15
From the din of metropolitans,
From the wisdom of their sages,

"A Tribute to the Future of My Race"—This poem is Laura Cornelius Kellogg's only known surviving poem, published first in the Carlisle newspaper *The Red Man and Helper* on March 20, 1903. It was prefaced by the following introduction: "The following was read at the Sherman Institute, Riverside, California, recently by the author, a talented Indian maiden, well known to many at Carlisle. The occasion was the graduating exercises of the Indian school, where Miss Cornelius is instructor" (1). The poem is also reprinted in full, with annotations, in *Changing Is Not Vanishing: A Collection of American Indian Poetry to 1930*, ed. Robert Dale Parker (Philadelphia: University of Pennsylvania Press, 2011), 253–57.

I have caught this sage's epic.
Ye who love the haunts of nature,
Love the sunshine of the meadow,   20
Love the shadow of the forest,
Love the wind among the branches
And the rushing of great rivers
Thro' their palisades of pine trees,
Ye whose hearts are kind and simple,   25
Who have faith in God and nature,
Who believe that in all ages
Every human heart is human,
That in even savage bosoms
There are longings, yearnings, strivings.   30
For the good they comprehend not.
That the feeble hands and helpless,
Groping blindly in that darkness
Touch God's right hand in that darkness
And are lifted up and strengthened.   35
Ye, who sometimes in your rambles
Thro' the green lanes of the country
Pause by some neglected graveyard
For a while to muse and ponder
On a half-effaced inscription,   40
Writ with little skill of song-craft,
Homely phrases, yet each letter,
Full of hope, and yet of heart-break,
Full of all the tender pathos
Of the here and the hereafter—   45
Stay ye, hear this rude-put story
Of the future of a nation.
Many moons have waxed and waned
Since their chieftain clans were numbered,
Since from seas of rising sun   50
To the far coast of her setting,
From the white bear's colder regions

To the high-noon of their borders
Roamed an infant, warrior people,
A whole continent their own!   55
Ah, who were they? All barbarians? Were they men?
Without legend or tradition,
Without heroes, gods, religion,
Without thought of the hereafter?
Did they enter nature's gardens—   60
In her temples of the forest
With their warriors' hearts unmelted?
Did they tread her wreathed pathways
Without learning tenderness?
Did they see the rose's dew-drop   65
And not wonder whence it came from?
And traced savage eyes the hemlock
Without learning majesty?
Is it nature's law to teach not?
Ah, too often do we think not   70
That the human race for ages
Suffer countless throes, upheavals,
Ere they blossom beauteous.
But today my epic telleth
Not the lore of idle camp-fire,   75
Not the past so buried deeply
'Neath the mound of gracious kindness,
But of beauteous enlightenment.
Who has made it? Who will make it?
That the golden sun of freedom   80
May shine brighter and still further
Till our glorious America
Be the world's salvation—haven.
Ah, I've seen her high-born heroes
Who've attained life's highest summits,   85
Stretch their hands to weary climbers
Without thought of race or color,

That a man may yet be saved!
And among the foot-sore climbers
I've beheld a stoic brother   90
Climbing silently and slowly,
All unnoticed, all alone,
Till perchance, he puts his step where
In a moment he has lost it.
Then the world's quick recognition!   95
"He has fallen! He has fallen!"
Hark! A voice from yonder summit—
He is up, and tries again.
And—I can't tell how I know it—
But two guardian angels' trumpets   100
Blow against the gate of heaven,
And their descending volumes turn
To earth's bright gladness and her flowers.
Then another rises onward
With chieftain fire in his eyes.   105
I see him mount unmindful
Of the rocks and sounds of way
Till at length I see him reach it,
And he, too, stand among
The heroes of that band!   110
So for him who mounts through
All the hardships of the mountainside,
I pray, to him give patience,
For, what the future holds
In the imperial sway of Time   115
No man can tell. No sentence
Without first indubious conviction
And, ere conviction, just chances, give.
And, oh, ye sons of Tonner Hall
And all ye daughters, true,   120
Ye have it in your power to say
Of what, and when a race shall be;

Ye spring from noble warrior blood,
As brave as Saxon, Roman, Greek,
And the age that waits upon you all   125
Has begot a race of kingly men.
May your careers be as complete
As the arches of your mater halls,
And when the noon of mankind comes
May it find you all more nearly   130
With the noblest offspring
Of our dear, great land,
Such as Smiley, Pratt and Garrett,
Such as—oh, a thousand more
Along your young paths daily known!   135
Ah, they've taught us, we'll remember
Beauteous enlightenment,
Then to each with one accord
We will extend the wampum strand
Made of friendships, purest pearl,   140
Made of gratitude, deep-rooted,
Made to last eternal summers.
Yea, the hearts' right hand we give them,
Blue-eyed Royalty American,
Theirs, our native land forever,   145
Ours, their presence and their teachings.
Ours, the noblest and the best.

Overalls and Tenderfoot

(1907)

I t was five o'clock on the morning of a summer day, when the train from San Francisco emptied a motley crowd of mankind on the long platform of the Raymond stations. This was the last railway point into the Yosemite Valley. The crowd looked about stupidly to find the town. Grim desert sands and the scrubby sage brush were everywhere—but the town!—the tourists looked at each other, and finding a sympathetic ignorance there, looked abroad again for Raymond. Suddenly the sound of a bell came from somewhere, and with it the smell of bacon and eggs and coffee, which had a strong effect upon their curiosity.

They saw a girl in a khaki suit, some distance ahead, walking quickly in the direction of the breakfast, and they all exclaimed, "Why, how stupid! There is the hotel, of course!" and toward a long rambling building they disappeared, clearing the platform like so many subway ants. San Francisco was this time ahead of London and New York, Montreal, Spokane, Washington, Philadelphia, and Mexico. The girl in the khaki was already seated at a table in the dining room and being served when the rest came. At a table some distance from hers two men sat down. One was an Easterner, a tall, square-shouldered young man, with keen blue eyes. After surveying the room, he said, "I presume that," lifting his eyes in her direction, "is a Western girl. She

"Overalls and Tenderfoot" is a story Laura Cornelius wrote while she was an undergraduate student at Barnard College. The story was published in the student newspaper, *The Barnard Bear*, in 1907. We reproduce the story with the permission of the Barnard College Archives and Special Collections.

seems to be traveling unescorted! That may be the Western way of it, but I am glad she is not my sister or my sweetheart," and his lips came together decidedly as he looked into the other man's face.

"Bacon and eggs, beefsteak and fish," the waitress called at his elbow.

The other man, meantime, turned to look at the girl before replying—"Yes, she is evidently alone. However, she looks as if she could take care of herself. We are accustomed here to think that of her anyway before she proves something else."

"Do you mean to tell me that girls go alone on trips of this sort without making fools of themselves or being made fools of?" said the young man with astonished emphasis.

"I mean to say that such a thing is perfectly possible, has happened, may happen again, though such a trip as the Yosemite is rather unusual."

"Well, I'll be hanged!" the young man ejaculated as he turned his attention to the fish.

"Don't hang yourself too soon, this is only the beginning of the journey, you must remember," the other man admonished.

People were still busy eating and asking questions of each other or the waitress about the Yosemite, when the girl in the tan khaki rose and walked to the desk to pay for her breakfast. Every head in the dining room was turned toward her. A jaunty panama sat snugly on her yellow head. She was tall and slender, with square shoulders and a gait that said, "petticoats don't hinder me," yet who could say she was masculine?

As she turned from the desk, she faced all her curious travelers with a frank, open gaze. There was a suggestion of wonder and friendliness in her brown eyes, they thought, as she passed out.

"Isn't she the incarnation of health?" said a woman from Philadelphia to her companion. "What a graceful thing is an unaffected mind-your-own-business air, in a pretty girl!"

"Yes, it's health and youth and independence blended together, you see."

"Strange she should be alone!" the companion spoke again.

"Is it?" the other replied. "Why should we ask the whole world to be alike?"

At that moment a stage rattled up to the veranda of the inn, "Hullo, Manzinita!" shouted the driver of the four-in-hand.

"Hullo, Spikes," warmly returned the girl, and then stepping quickly to the edge of the platform she said in a low voice," "Now Spikes, I want to tell you something; you mustn't call me by my first name."

"No?" he said, inquiringly. "Is it a honeymoon up betwixt us?"

"No!" she laughed, "nor must you call me by my last. I'll tell you why when we get to the end of the Valley, or as soon as I get the chance. Now you can call me anything else—you trust me, Spikes."

Just as you say, Manzi—oh 'scuse me, well—Jehoshaphat! What in thunder shall I call you then?"

"Oh, anything will do; 'Ginger,' 'the Burrow,' 'Frisco,' anything."

"You ain't short on swell tailors in 'Frisco that can turn out a girl so sweet in overalls—Ha, ha, I'll call you Overalls!"

"Bully!" she answered. The tourists, more aggressive after break-fast, had hastened out, and had begun scrambling for seats on the stage.

"What's your name, sir?" the girl asked of the driver in a tone meant to be overheard.

"Spikes, madam—what's yours?"

"Overalls," she answered with a straight face.

"I guess you belong on the front seat," he said, by way of an invitation to the best seat on the stage. The Easterner seated himself one row behind.

"No stop till the relay—thirty miles from here—all up-grade, and one span short," replied Spikes to the volume of questions from the rear of the stage, while with one hand he cracked the whip and the big stage rattled its lumbering wheels to wonderful Valley.

◆

It was five o'clock in the afternoon when Spikes pulled before the second hotel. Its green lawn and busy fountain were a cooling contrast to the yellow sand, the dusty sagebrush and the dry rocks of the forty-five-mile journey. Everyone seemed overjoyed to get out, at least everyone slapped his ill-fitting duster good-naturedly while he blinked vigorously to free his sight from the sand on his lids.

Manzinita, without waiting for her companions, or shaking off the dust, ran into the office.

"Why, Manzinita, how glad we are to see you!" exclaimed Dunne, the proprietor.

"Please hush up," she said, and then taking the grey-haired man aside hurriedly explained. He laughed heartily, and answered, "Very well, I'll tell Mrs. Dunne she doesn't know you—or—you do. I'll tell her you are here, she'll be right up to see you."

"Ha, ha, I knew I'd come upon a new stunt. I felt it in my bones weeks ago," she was talking to herself while she unpacked the extra suit case. An hour later she came down in an embroidered white suit, her face aglow with new interests. Her cheeks had been slightly browned, and her eyes seemed larger and darker, while not a trace of dust could the sun find in her fluffy hair as she stepped out upon the veranda. No one was there since the sun had come around that late afternoon—except the Tenderfoot and Mr. Dunne.

"Pardon me," she said, addressing the proprietor, "but I see only three people out there on the tennis court, with odds much against the lonely one. Do they prefer to play that way?"

"No, indeed, they don't, they have been hunting all afternoon for a fourth. Do you play tennis?"

"A little."

"Fine!—a racquet, Kern," he called to the secretary. "I'll go introduce you to people," turning to her.

The Tenderfoot was frowning inwardly. "Thank you for the racquet," she replied, "but I will not interrupt your conversation longer; let me just tell them you let me come." She was off before he could leave the Tenderfoot, who was getting cloudy between another shock to his sense of property and the desire to go out there himself.

The three stopped playing as she approached the court, and the only young lady came forward cordially. "My name is Miss Brown," began Manzinita, "and I am sent out here by the proprietor."

"So pleased to have you, Miss Brown. I am Miss Campbell—allow me to introduce Mr. Slater and Lieutenant Phillips."

"You are very kind to come. At that distance, did you see how I was getting the worst of it?" asked Lieutenant Phillips.

"Not at all. I came from purely selfish motives," she answered, while with a pretty backhand stroke she returned a ball into the most unexpected quarter. "Whew! A pretty one," exclaimed Mr. Slater.

"I see our finish," returned Miss Campbell.

"Let's begin a new set," begged the Lieutenant.

Before they finished the game, the veranda was full of spectators again. Right and left men were commenting on the remarkably good plays the newcomer exhibited.

The sun had gone down when the players stopped with a score of 2–0 on games. The lieutenant was jubilant. "May I walk to the house with you?" he asked Manzinita, "You have saved my reputation! What can I do for you?"

"Shall we see you at the dance tonight?" asked Miss Campbell, much impressed with a girl who could take away the laurels she had enjoyed all summer.

"I am afraid not," Manzinita answered. "Why, don't you dance?" the Lieutenant asked in surprise. "Yes, I love it," she answered. "Then, why not?" he asked again. "Well—I—I—I am traveling alone."

They had reached the veranda. He stood perplexed and somewhat embarrassed for a moment, then looking at the girl again, he grew braver and said, "Then let me do the honors." The Tenderfoot was standing near and pretending to smoke, but, in fact, he was holding his breath for fear she would say "yes," and the match went out. She hesitated, then she saw the man she had been shocking all day.

"You are very kind. I shall be pleased to let you," she answered. As she went into the reception room the Philadelphians met her.

"We have been watching you play," spoke the elder woman, "and wishing we were girls again. You are just going in to dinner? Then come with us, we are on our way there, too."

As they entered the large dining room, Manzinita saw a large woman who, during the journey, had seemed to her like an Irish washerwoman in a gunnysack. She was now seated at the central table in the dining room. Her hands were glittering with innumerable diamonds, and her gown was of a giddy pink satin.

"Perhaps she did come with those ladies, but I doubt it. I think it is perfectly atrocious the way the Western girl is brought up. Do you think she is pretty, dear?" she addressed her husband.

"No one can hold a tallow candle to you, my dear Samantha," answered the new husband in an undertone. "Not even her."

"You think she is pretty then," Samantha spoke with some disappointment. "Oh—well—no—not exactly. She would never charm me, you know." "I don't think she is a very nice girl myself," finished Samantha.

◆

DeKoven paced up and down in the chill moonlight. "This climate ought not to be wasted in sleep," he consoled himself, as he discovered he had been holding a cold cigar stump between his fingers for some time. He threw it away with some impatience and looked at his watch. "By gad!" he exclaimed, "three o'clock—the stage starts for the Valley in three hours!" He retired. As he closed his eyes, the vision floated back again—a tall girl in white with faultless features, and a crown of golden hair on her well-carried head. He recalled how white her teeth were and what a soft brown her eyes. "And the voice!" he added aloud, "I should know it among a million!—but liking it all! I came to see the Yosemite, not a pretty female with such outrageous breeding as to pick up a confounded uniform she doesn't know—hang it all! I say," and with that he turned over and went to sleep.

◆

"I guess that there Kid Overalls don't want the front seat or she'd be around this morning," said Spikes as he brought up the stage to the steps of the "Wawona."

"At any rate, she can't have it now," DeKoven said as he sprang into the front seat beside Spikes. That moment a girl shot out of the hotel stables ahead of them on a wild bronco. The beast flew into the air, then came down abruptly on his fores.

"Who gave the girl that horse?" shouted the proprietor, rushing out. "She'll be killed."

"The idiot!"

"Jump off!" shouted the women, as they all stood up in the stage. "Sure enough, it's the Buster!" Spikes spoke with evident annoyance.

"By gad!" ejaculated DeKoven, as he sprang over the high wheel of the stage. The beast had reared, lain down, then had jumped up again. The women thought he was going to repeat his antics in the air—they covered their faces; some of them screamed, the men were running toward the scene. But too late, with one more mad plunge the bronco started down the road at full speed. Dunne and the rest of them stood hopelessly looking after horse and rider. As he met the stage at the gate, he said, "Well, if Buster couldn't throw her off, he'll get her to the Valley all right." It was still thirty miles but there were no relays this time; Spikes assured the tourists they would reach the heart of the Valley by noon.

"Where is she going with a beast like that?" De Koven asked of Spikes.

"Where she wants to, I guess," the latter answered. "A girl that can sit a hyena ain't much for wheels, and hosses, I don't guess."

The woman with the diamonds who, on the previous day, had entertained the stage-load with tales of her wealth and interests, her pedigree and the number of artists and writers she had met, began this morning with:

"That girl gets on my nerves! How does she dare to travel in decent company without a chaperon? Who can she be? I'd like to hear what my mother would say when she heard I was travelling with an adventuress. Imagine her letting me go like that!"

"You are well bred, Samantha, that is the difference; you could not possibly take such a step," the new husband answered. What else could a new husband do when Samantha was putting up the wherewithal of the long-deferred honeymoon, and this was his first trip to Yosemite.

◆

It was high noon. Instead of sand and rock, the Buster felt the soft loam under her feet. They had come to the lowest part of the Valley, and things green were thriving there. Trees grew up and even became gigantic. There was grass on the sides of the road and the Mariposa River sped along on its even course from the snows beyond the walls of rock. As Manzinita looked back, she felt the awful majesty of the surrounding mountains—and how small a thing in this Valley was a prank. The dignified calm that the most frivolous nature dare not break, stole upon her for the moment. When she dismounted in front of the hotel she was satisfied that she was an hour earlier than the stage. To her great relief, her aunt was not seeing people. She was confined, in fact, to her hammock on the back piazza, a portion of which she had screened for her special comfort while she wrote her novel. "Joy—now I will not have to explain at all," Manzinita whispered under her breath as she flew up the old-fashioned flight of steps to see her.

"This place, my dear niece, does not agree with me. There are too many tourists—too many curious people about; and then I always work better in a higher altitude. So I've planned this. Tomorrow you go up to Glacier Point and arrange for nice rooms for us there. My book needs a month of quiet in that pure air of the pines."

"Anything that suits you, auntie, suits me," replied the girl.

It nettled DeKoven to hear Spikes' opinion of Tenderfeet. He had actually said that no one could ride the Buster the way that girl had done—no, indeed, a Tenderfoot would not even have the courage to try. He, too, welcomed the green sport in the Valley, not so much as a stopping point as it was a release from that driver, Spikes.

That afternoon Manzinita walked down the Valley to see the founder of the Yosemite; he had become accustomed to look for her annually. This reckless girl always reminded him of his young days, when on a bold adventure he tried the unknown mountains, and after many days of hunger and exhaustion, he had come upon one of the most wonderful scenes the earth had to offer. However, on this afternoon, he did not know his young friend was coming, and Manzinita knocked at his small cabin door to no purpose. "I wonder if the poor old soul has died in his hermitage, and no one knows it!" She said to herself as she walked to the curtainless window and peeped in. "He is still alive," she said aloud as she saw a cat dozing on his huge chair, and a tin pail full of water in the corner of the room.

"Is the wizard out or dead?" called a deep voice at her elbow. She started, and turned upon DeKoven. "Oh, you startled me!" she said flushing.

"I beg your pardon," he apologized. "The butler is out, too," she said, recovering her usual composure, "but there are other windows in the house that are not busy if you would like to announce yourself." For the first time they had faced each other squarely, and they both laughed.

"Isn't one window able to stand two lookers?" he asked.

"That would be very improper," she answered with emphasis. "It would contaminate an Easterner. His mother wouldn't know him when he came home!"

He let out another laugh. "That wouldn't matter," he said.

"Wouldn't it?" she said, in surprise, and then quickly added, "Well, I must be going."

"Truly, I ought to, too, but I do not know which way to go if I started. I am lost. Isn't the hotel this way?" pointing in the opposite direction.

"Yes," she answered, "the hotel you left this morning is that way, but the hotel you want is not. That is, unless you want to walk thirty miles for your dinner."

"Have pity," he said, "won't you? May I walk home with you?" he asked in a different tone.

After a little hesitation she replied, "You may," with a note of coldness in her voice.

They talked of the Yosemite all the way home. She told him the wild-cat stories she had heard from the old man, and the different legends of the falls. The crisp touches of humor which she brought in, they laughed over together. DeKoven was really sorry that they returned to the hotel as early as four o'clock.

"Do you return on the third day, too?" he asked, with interest, as they were about to part. "Oh, no!" she answered to his dissatisfaction. "I am going to Glacier Point tomorrow."

She came down to dinner in a blue organdy with a slight train. DeKoven was looking for the same white he had seen the evening before, and when he heard her voice, as she joined the Philadelphians, he was surprised to see this tall, lithe figure in blue. The man from Spokane said to him as she and the elderly women entered, "That's the prettiest young woman in the dining room. I like the air about her. I wish she were my daughter."

"What about the trip to Glacier Point?" the young man went on, indifferent to the other's remark. "My opinion is that we better go there tomorrow instead of the next day. Perhaps we would find that so superb that we would want to spend all of the three days there instead of being here."

"It makes no difference to me," the elder man answered. "A trip like this ought never to be done in six days!" DeKoven spoke.

"No. I wish business allowed me to remain longer," said the elder man. "I should certainly stay."

◆

At nine o'clock, on the day following, everyone was getting into his or her riding habit at the little starting hub near the Happy Isles. The guide was a handsome cowboy. He picked out the nicest burrow for Manzinita, and said to her, "You've ridden beasts before. I'll give you the jolliest fellow in the lot."

"How do you know but what I am cringing, half-frightened mouse?" she asked him smiling.

"The brand ain't that kind," he answered, surveying her.

"The horse you've given that man has a wicked eye," she pointed with her crop toward DeKoven. "Don't you know he is a Tenderfoot?"

"Ha, ha," the guide laughed. "I told him on the square, that horse had guts, but he's too durn cocksure he can work him. It's the only pony on detail, and he gets to balking when we get up a ways."

"Give me a place where I can see the fun," she said.

When the long line of riders started off, DeKoven delayed until the guide said to Manzinita, "That horse you've got is used to bringing up the rear."

She pulled up her horse to let him pass. "I presume we have to obey orders here," she said, in half apology.

DeKoven only grew red and would not go on. His burrow chewed his bit and switched his tail. The guide looked back and saw the two delaying behind. He gave a peculiar call, and the pony started off without further ado ahead of the burrow before DeKoven could check him. He sat on his horse with the air of one who had always ridden and had nothing to fear either in himself or his beast. Manzinita thought to herself, "I wonder if he will keep up with that swell posture the whole of the thirty-mile trail." The little beaten path up the mountains became narrower and higher at each turn. Samantha, looking down at the precipitous sides along whose edge the line was passing, gave a wild scream, and when the guide asked her what was the matter, she answered, "I was only thinking of what Mama would say if she saw me go over the edge."

DeKoven's conversation with Manzinita was tinged with venom all the way.

"Spikes says that's a bad sign," she said to herself, and patted her horse in glee.

They were nearing Vernal Falls. The ascent was becoming harder and harder, and the path narrower and more winding. Suddenly the pony came to a dead stop. DeKoven entreated him in a gentle voice, but of no avail. He jumped off then and patted him but the ears were lying back and the tail was busy. The rest went without noticing the rear of their line. Manzinita said nothing, and her burrow seemed perfectly willing to bide the pleasure of his predecessor. At length, after his gentle measures were exhausted in vain, DeKoven's lips came together tight, then he mounted again, took from his saddle-bag some bright things and attached them to his heels. That was unexpected, for the pony and he did move, in leaps. In his ferocious retaliation, he ran up a short side trail that had long been abandoned because a huge boulder had blocked it. Manzinita held her breath. "Take care," she shouted, "these trails have many loose boulders and if a big one starts, it" . . . but, before she could finish, DeKoven had used his spurs again and the vicious pony had turned off the trail as he had come to the blockade. A boulder had started which in turn had sent others down the steep sides of the mountain.

As the horse branched off the trail, he met a heavy boulder in his fores, which brought him down ignominiously. In his fear of falling down the length of the precipice, he threw himself, with all his weight, and broke one of his master's legs. Manzinita had dismounted. She hastily put the two fingers in her mouth and gave a shrill call to the guide who, with the train of riders, had been sometime out of sight. Then she tied her burrow, and in another moment was bending over the heap of horse and human flesh. Both horse and rider feared to stir for fear of falling further down. The blood had left the young man's face; his strong, clear-cut features stood out more distinctly; his lips, which had been compressed, opened now to speak to her, but not a word would come, tho' the lips quivered.

"I have called for help," she said, "hang on—the guide will be here in a minute!" Then with her characteristic quickness, she recalled that the guide had allowed her to carry his lasso on the saddle. She rushed back and returned immediately with it. There were strong young trees standing up above them. Tying securely one end of the lasso to these, she brought the other end down, and lassoed in the horse. "Now you can stir, both of you," she said, and the pony breathed freedom in his captivity, and after some persuasion, he moved enough to free his rider.

DeKoven, now very white, refused the offer of her arm until he could not move his foot, when, without waiting for his pleasure, she fairly dragged him to a small level spot where he could lie at length without fear of continuing down the steep mountain side. Then, without saying anything more, she went back to the main trail and her saddle-bag and got her flask. "Thank you," he said to her as she poured some brandy down his throat. She saw a different man, in his eyes, from the one of a half-hour before.

Soon the guide came flying down the trail. "Over here, right off," she called to him as he dismounted near her burrow.

"Glacier Point is quite near now," the guide encouraged, as he put DeKoven into Manzinita's saddle, while the pony, having learned a lesson, was willing to take her on.

"Are the rest near?" asked DeKoven, breathing heavily with pain.

"About a mile ahead," the guide answered.

"There's a doctor from Spokane in the party," he said. "Perhaps he could help me."

"Don't ye fret," the guide answered. "We kin take care of yeah at the Point."

◆

A happy-faced girl was wheeling an invalid's chair through the soft lulling pines one afternoon at Glacier Point. The occupant of the chair looked like a perfectly healthy man. He was protesting vigorously to being wheeled by holding the wheels. The girl, however, teasingly continued, "If you do not stop," she said, "I will throw you out," at which he leaned back and looking up at the face above said,

"Well, may not a man defend himself?" But she paid no attention; she led the chair into the rich brakes which grew so tall and vigorously around them.

"Manzinita!" he said, and she started at the sound of her first name from the man's lips. "I've known you two weeks, but a man may meet his Waterloo in one day, may he not?"

"I must get some ferns for my aunt," she said, as she left him, and went gathering wild flowers and the brake, the smell of which he knew her aunt detested.

"Let me carry them," he offered as she returned. When she handed them to him, he whispered, "You witch, I love you and you've got to love me!"

"Oh, you are getting stupid!" she said. "Don't you know that is showing very bad taste on your part. I wouldn't have such an ill-bred creature as one that talks the guff on two weeks' notice."

"I am going to stay till I've got you," he said, conclusively. "You'd better not," she answered. "I've got to spend the winter with my aunt, Mrs. Whiting, in Boston."

"Mrs. Whiting?" he asked excitedly. "Which one? The ex-Governor's wife?"

"Yes," she answered.

"By gad!" he exclaimed. "She and my mother are great friends." "It's Fate," he said, "It's Fate."

"Fate!" she answered, calmly, "not a bit of it. It's you, you are getting locoed."

Essays

· · · · · ·

Building the Indian Home
(1901)

To attempt the solution of the Indian question is the duty of
every educated American Indian. Only when the Indians themselves demonstrate each step of the problem can the final answer be
reached. Years ago the mistakes in bringing up the American Natives
were made, not malignantly but unintentionally, and it must take time
before they can be remedied. Tangle up a skein of yarn in the effort
to make it into a ball, and what a vexatious piece of work comes of
it: knots are to be untied, and even to be cut sometimes. So it is with
our seemingly everlasting Indian question. But we will solve it yet. We
have lost much in experimenting upon it, but we have also gained, and
we must view this subject not too nearsightedly, not too far off, but
reasonably. There are several ways of reaching the correct answer of
such a problem, some pleasanter than others, and one of these is to be
found in the building up of the home.

The two civilizing influences that have operated upon Indians are
from the Government and the Missionary. If our great Government
is full of benevolence, the most of our missionaries devoted, and our
Indians capable, whence is the lack of better results? Wise methods
have suffered through poor machinery, and unwise ones have been
too potent. Through such a mill it is no wonder if we find the present
Indian as chaff. But it is from the lack of self-help that the Indian character, originally noble, has deteriorated. Ration-giving and tribalism

"Building the Indian Home" was first published in *The Indian's Friend* 13 (9),
May 1901, 2.

are the two evils which have fettered the development of the Red People. The Government has allowed both, and so indeed has the Missionary, and, while we cannot disregard bodily wants, the pauperizing of Indians in those qualities which made them proud, independent, and noble, was unnecessary. With the money the Government has expended in rations a system of loan funds might have been made to operate in the same way banks do among white citizens. Many Indians, while possessing acres, are land-poor in poor land. There is no money with which to start improvements, and they have no access to citizens' banks to relieve them temporarily from dire needs. Added to their poor knowledge of the ordinary pursuits of civilized life there is little or no compensation for their labor, their condition becomes disheartening, and rations and beggary furnish the only way out of these difficulties.

The present government of Indians is principally administered by white agents, whose offices, away out in wilderness of ignorant masses, can easily become monarchies, as indeed have some mission fields on Indian reservations. Such monarchies are dangerous things, especially when the interests of the monarchs are the chief object and conscientious workers are rare. The care of his own interests has curiously been denied the Indian. There is practically no government for him, since the surrounding towns will not and cannot admit him, nor is he ready for them. The absence of local government on reservations has almost completely paralyzed the useful faculties of Indian men, and, though government schools may continue to teach their children the rudiments of civilized living for an indefinite time, they will go back to reservations and have no use for these as long as reservations exist as they now are. Those "returned students" who have held their own at home are echoes of the past good hopes of their race, for it takes no ordinary character to live a civilized life on a reservation. On the tribal confines, as a rule, are avaricious whites whose habits of life have made them shrewd for their own interests. Their influence is certainly not elevating, and their attitude toward the Indian is not friendly unless he has something which they want.

Two influences on the reservation are of moment. These are the Police and the Missionary. The Police is the tool of the agent, and is as corrupt in most cases as some such in white municipalities. The Missionary varies in good works at different missions. Ecclesiastical equipment is not sufficient. The position being a public example carries a heavy responsibility and demands wisdom, for the ignorant masses will follow their white leader. Most important it is then that weak characters and even those of ordinary power be eliminated from both the civil service and the missions. Thus far reservation life summed up gives little incentive to living, for self-administration lies at the bottom of all race prosperity.

One cannot give a man the taste of anything through another man's throat, and the freedom to exercise one's own faculties is the only sure way to enlightenment. Self-help is a law of civilization, for it means work, and work means brain. I know it does. In reservation life the vital center, as elsewhere, is the home, and this has been the most neglected factor in civilizing the Native American. By some non-reservation believers, its ties have been scorned. Theirs is the belief that to wean the Indian child as soon as possible from the home is the way to civilize the race. It is an excellent way of hastening civilization, and, were the Indian not human, it would do very well. But the Indian is a lover of home. I have heard the most civilized Indian remark on reaching home, after an absence of many years, "After all, there is no place on earth like home." And this can be said of all Indian youth. They will sacrifice the comforts of civilization, the delightful companionship of enlightenment, and their hearts will turn toward the one spot whither home ties ever recall them.

This being true, it is sad to find a gulf separating Indian parents and children in interests. Why should this be so? Simply because Indian parents have been neglected, shut out from the enlightenment which they too might just as well have had through interpreters. Why should not a system of lectures be given them on different subjects in the same way that Christian teaching is reaching them? In fact, an elementary public school-like education could be given them thus. It is such knowledge that Indians like the Oneidas of Wisconsin have been craving. If you could converse with them in their own tongue, you would meet with such questions as these: "Tell me, you've been to school, how many rods to take off across the end of my forty acres to make so many acres?" Or this: "What degree of fertility in a foot of ground is necessary to replace the loss caused by the absorption of the atmosphere on it?" Their questions are sometimes not very clearly put, but their honesty soon tells whether or not your explanation meets their wants.

The Indians are silent students of Nature and they are diffident; but do not mistake their silence or seeming stolidity for lack of mentality. A strong characteristic of theirs is the love of the beautiful. In the most unattractive individual of them can be found an ideal that properly developed would be correct. There is every encouragement to think that they could make a race of artists. It is known among teachers of art that, out of every ten Indian pupils, eight will do justice to the instruction, and without much effort. Then why not cultivate this talent, and apply it to the home?

There are two theories at work on the race, neither of which is wholly right. The work of those who do not recognize human ties between parents and children is nothing less than the wreck of the home, whatever other good it may do. All Indians are not alike. Some will cling to the reservation in perfect happiness; others, with more ambition, cannot rest in its narrow confines. That the reservation ought not to be a receptacle of ignorance and degradation we well know; but since the home of the Indian is there, and his property is in the land, we cannot separate him entirely from it. That he should have a love for home is a sign that there is manhood in him, and the home is the center of earthly interests. The man without a home is a pitiable creature. In the history of the world the most far-reaching influences have come from the home, and from the humblest of these have been brought germs that have made nations. By the fireside the destinies of empires have been shaped, and in the home the most potent factors are the parents. Their guardianship over the welfare of youth is naturally the strongest as the most sincere. Love rules there of that same nature which brought redemption to the world.

Yes, to civilize the Indian we must educate Indian parents; and not only those of the future, growing up in the schools, but those already settled on the reservations. The mothers should be taught not only the art of needlework, but domestic science in its entirety. Someone says, "We already have field matrons to do that work." So we have; but one for each tribe is not enough. Specialists in each branch of the science are needed, and above all good cooking should be emphasized. After ages science has at last found out that one of the strongest roots of intemperance is poor cookery. Let more competition be encouraged by giving rewards for merit, and the Indians will be found not indolent but eager workers.

The care of local government is the need and the business of the men, and will hasten them into citizenship where they will have to earn their own homes, and living; and citizenship is the salvation of all peoples.

By education of both parents and children, the gulf which now separates their interests will be done away. The value and honor of labor and right living can best be learned, not in the institution, but in the quiet little world of home, which in the history of civilized peoples has never failed to be the best teacher of any race in any land. Nor should any despair if immediate results in such instruction as this are not seen.

The deteriorated Indian character was originally noble, and its degeneracy is due to conditions. This is its transition age and the race now shows itself at its worst. The momentum of forces existing before this age has been intercepted; the germs of hope have been nearly annihilated by years of oppression. But there is a blue vein in the American Indian that has not yet expressed itself, and from the resurrection of the present Indian may yet come forth a superior humanity. The efforts of his friends are worth that end.

She Likes Indian Public Opinion
(1902)

The last few issues of Carlisle's publications have so aroused my interest that I cannot refrain from humbly participating in an "Indian Council." Not that the pages of the little paper have been filled, lately, with literature superior than formerly, but the part in it I like better is INDIANS' public opinion.

I feel like living when I hear educated Indians advancing well-balanced ideas. It looks as if we are about to redeem our racial mental debility when we have opinions worth expressing, and express them.

For what, after all, is Public Opinion but literature? And literature in time makes and establishes the mental development of a people.

I like much perusing the artistic views of our own Native genius, Zitkala Ša, on The Indian Dance, and I had to listen to that exponent of Carlisle, Dr. Montezuma, for the practical side bearing upon the subject.

To this extent I agree with the former, that that element of our race which has no future is truly pitiable, that element whose present is a life of constraint and starvation of development, is a heartbreaking thing to look upon, but the latter points out that the present pleasure of the Indian Dance is a corruption of sacred rite, and since it is an irreverent imitation, its tendencies cannot be wholesome.

Naturally, the beat of the drum wakes up the human desire for recreation long pent up by the dead environment of reserve existence, and thither will go a weak youth, who once in the whirl of such doings

"She Likes Indian Public Opinion," *The Red Man and Helper*, October 10, 1902, 1.

forgets the moral and social codes that have replaced those of barbarism, only to wake up on the morrow, a shamefaced idiot, with the manhood gone, that perchance has been Carlisle's hard won years.

So debased pleasure can undo honorable labor, so is ultimate transition retarded.

And can we afford as a race, and individually, to lose thus not only time, which is gold, but honor, the greatest and our all?

Laura Minnie Cornelius
Seymour, Wis., October 1902

Industrial Organization for the Indian
(1911)

[THE CHAIRMAN: The next paper is by Laura M. Cornelius, on "Industrial Organization for the Indian." Miss Cornelius is a Wisconsin Oneida.]

Whether he is a citizen or not, or whether he has lands or not, whether his trust funds continue or not, whether he is educated or ignorant, one thing remains unchanged with the Indian: he has to have bread and butter, he has to have a covering on his back, he has to live.

Of all the phases of our national problem, none other seems so immediately important to me as our industrial status. It at once decides whether we shall become degraded toward pauperism or whether we may secure to ourselves permanent independence. Whatever our political or social status may be, we are and always will be tried and judged on our ability, individually, to maintain ourselves, indeed our very integrity depends upon it. I repeat what I have said elsewhere, that this country does not set aside the Indian because he is brown or because he wears beads around his neck. It is more often a question of soap and water, a lack of fitness to turn a good furrow in a field, or to labor by the sweat of his brow for what he eats. Now I am not saying that he shall be as clean as the man with a porcelain bathtub in his house, when the Indian has to haul water in a cup or an olla from a

Kellogg delivered this talk at the first meeting of the Society of American Indians at Ohio State University in Columbus, Ohio, October 1911; it was published the following year in the *Report of the Executive Council on the Proceedings of the First Annual Conference of the Society of American Indians*, 43–55.

mile away. No! What I do say is: the bathtub and the pipes must move to the Indian, and that he must make them move to him in a system. Not only this, but he must produce adequate supplies out of his own environment. He must labor—and he must labor to the best advantage for himself and not to the exploiter.

It is upon this conviction that I shall proceed in this paper. The good things of life must move to the Indian by a system. Instead of wasting what he already has, and looking for himself in the outside world, he must make his own world *at home*. This point of view is the result of some years of close economic study of the industrial conditions not only in this country but those of Europe, and a study, too, of the Indian himself.

Realizing that he was turning his face toward Caucasian institutions as his ultimate goal, I have looked into them critically, with his advantage uppermost in my mind, and I have become convinced that he cannot copy *everything* the white man does with advantage. Certainly, it is a mistake in some important phases of his industrial life to follow him exactly as he is today.

This imitation on the part of the Indian is an indication of our own weakness and inability to present a better program than his own. I do believe much of this is born of our growing disbelief in ourselves due to our having been misrepresented so long, and in deferring everything to the white man's opinions of us.

Under the heading "Industrial Organization for the Indian," then, I wish at once to suggest that the way out for the Indian, of his present situation, is along the lines of organization for himself and by himself—organization of those things which shall control his livelihood and which shall be based on a special consideration for his needs. In the present space allotted to me for this subject I can but briefly pass over a great many phases I should like to dwell upon at length, leaving out much of the detail.

Before I proceed further, I wish to be understood as to my attitude toward the "Pratt Ideal." I am wholly in accord with its idea of equal opportunity for the Indian, its belief in the ability of the Indian and the need of a proper environment for demonstration. And I am just as strong against Paternalism and Wardship and Reservations as a regime as any self-respecting Indian or educator can be. But I do not agree with certain failures on its part to calculate upon the possibilities of the Indian on the reservation, neither do I believe we can overlook the influence of human ties. A good majority of the Carlisle students, who have been taught to leave the reservation to establish themselves outside, come back to it even after they have learned trades. From unbiased observation this seems to point to the fact that the Indian's ties are very strong. He is naturally clannish, he does not seek to mix with the paleface either in interests or blood, down deep in his heart he feels superior to the ordinary white man—and the real Indian is. A proof of that is that after he has been surrounded by whites on every reservation for several hundred years, he has not amalgamated enough to have changed the face of his racial problems. What I do not see is the necessity of crowding him to become a white man, when opportunity is all he needs. I do not wish to be understood to mean, when I speak of the Carlisle student going back to the reservation that he is a failure. Far from it. I have been careful to observe certain localities upon this point, and I have found that Carlisle has no more failures than high schools in the outside communities, and in some instances less, in proportion to the population, than the outside.

A second factor, aside from the ties of home, is his interests in the way of allotments and inheritances on the reservation. The Indian naturally comes back to these if it is no more than to look at them.

This being the case, there seems the need of a complement to the Pratt Ideal.[1] It is this I propose to meet. Instead of forsaking what we already have in holdings, to go away to the white world of industry to be there too often wage-earners for life (I am taking into account the majority rule), instead of being fixtures in an industrial world, which is itself still largely problematic for the white man, I maintain that the line of least resistance to the greatest possible good under our present circumstances is to citizenize the possibilities and to reorganize the opportunities of the Indian *at home*; to organize the Indians' holdings into a system of economic advantages; to convert his large wastes into industrial centers which he can take care of to modernize his affairs and to assure him at least a comfortable maintenance if he will work. I believe in struggle and in competition in whatsoever vocation he shall prefer. I believe in struggle and in competition with the outside world. I am one who knows at firsthand what the knocks in it are. I am a product of almost every institution of the outside except the insane asylum and Tammany Hall.[2] Struggle is the making of men, but I do not believe in thrusting the weak, without due preparation, into the intense and unfavorable industrial strife of a foreign world. A while ago I said that I did not believe in copying everything the white man did, if we could improve upon it. I want to explain what I mean by that.

Some of the gravest problems in this country today are to be found in the industrial world of the white man. With all his acumen, with all his advantages, with all his training, the great masses of labor (who make the things he wears and the things he eats, and who serve the money despots) are by no means rewarded for their toil or taken care of when they need care, much less have they the leisure or the means or the energy for higher education. Why?

The social conscience in this country is not generally enlightened, and it is far from being ethical. Those that are enlightened are in a very small minority, and they have their difficulties in effectively bringing about legislation to the protection and betterment of labor, because public sentiment has to be educated first before it will move to anything, and it isn't so easy to educate it in a land where politics would control. There is something in the social order that is responsible for this. The development of intense individualism and the age of unprecedented prosperity no doubt are largely responsible for the selfishness of American people.

Look about you into the working world outside and see that first of all there is no uniform and happy adjustment between labor and capital in this country. For while the conditions of labor differ between the country and the city, between different localities, between cities themselves, they all come under one grand general wage system and modern capitalism. The wage system is a product of the nineteenth century and has not yet triumphed altogether above slavery and serfdom (the two conditions it aims to escape) for the reason that it is dependent upon capital, and capital in this land is suffering from acute despotism.

In order to save the cost of production, and to supply the growing demand of civilization (and in this it is evolutionary), capital has taken the work originally done on a small scale and put it into big machines; hence the factory system. The factory system is then at once responsible for some of the biggest problems for the Caucasian mind. Here are some of the evils to which it has given birth: child labor, employed in place of adult employment, with light-running machinery because it is cheaper; industrial accidents, due to large machines without protective appliances, because protection is an item of expense to the employer and the laborer himself is still too ignorant to demand protection before he takes the work that at any moment may take his limb and life; factory regulation and unemployment; unsanitary conditions and long hours—though the last two have been improved by legislation in the past few years, they are by no means above reproach today. Unemployment is the result of the invention of labor-saving machines and the unsettled condition created by differences between labor and capital.

The fact that capital is such a terrific power in the hands of the civilized but unenlightened is producing a class struggle in this democratic country of ours where they shout, "equal opportunity for all men," and then thieve it. The wage earner today is a wage earner always. Once he gets into it, he cannot get out of it. Let me quote one of the biggest economic authorities in this country, who says: "The great majority of men do not possess the abilities or the opportunities to secure the large capital necessary for the successful conduct of a modern business. For the masses, indeed, it is true and increasingly true that once a wage earner, always a wage earner."

Take particularly the wage earner in the city where the most of the population of the country is congested. Even a casual look at the labor market there is enough to show that the conditions of the white man's toil are far from being happy or equitable, indeed, they are tragic; look at the wan faces of the ill-nourished multitude closely packed like a lot of cattle, in a foul car hurrying to their work in the city. Follow a hollow-chested bent old man at forty-five years into the close shop where the wind never made a clean sweep, where the sun never had a chance to creep in through the high walls of the neighboring buildings; listen to the story of the boy [who had] to earn and save enough to buy his mother a home—he never did. Watch him go out of the dingy shop at six o'clock, a bent and sick old man, he would like one day off tomorrow, but he would lose his place and his means of support. He is still dependent upon tomorrow's toil for tomorrow's bread. Follow him into the old and dismal quarter of the city where rent is cheap and where the noises never cease. Follow him up the rickety old steps into the rented rooms, damp, sickly smelling dark rooms, whose windows closely face another wall, stay and hear him ask for a good sirloin, and see him get a red sausage and a dill pickle; hear him cough and remember that he helps to make the clothes you buy in the shops. No, I cannot see that everything the white man does is to be copied. The tragedy of young hopes and healths crushed out by the heavy heel of money despotism in the industrial world is not an unusual thing in this country. The average man in the white labor markets lives a miserable existence today that he may live another miserable day tomorrow, and so on till disease or accident take pity upon him.

I do not look with optimism upon these conditions, nor for any race of people under the sun. You may argue that the sweatshop is not the only industry into which the Indian can turn, and that there is legislation now against this evil. It is true, there is legislation and there is factory inspection, but here is what a thorough investigator of the particular problem says: "The effects of this legislation have been beneficial where they have been enforced, but with a shifting irresponsible population and a lack of public sentiment in favor of the law in the very quarters where it is most needed, it takes an almost superhuman vigilance to secure its enforcement, of the large cities where sweating has gained a foothold. Boston is the only one which may be said to have the system under control, and as a consequence of this control, a great part of Boston's clothing business is said to have been transferred to New York. The exact extent of the evil is not fully determined. The statistics are compiled from returns made by the manufacturers themselves, and many small establishments escape census enumeration, but at that there are 5,308,400 employees in the sweatshops in the United States."

I have given the sweatshop as only one of the evils of the white industrial world. Skilled labor has better conditions, of course, but outside of the agricultural pursuits, skilled labor, too, is confined to indoor life.

The Indian does not realize that under proper sanitation he is a superior man to any other class in this country, physically. The fact that he is an outdoor man is perhaps the chief reason why he has sustained himself and survived conditions of housing which is killing the white man, only he doesn't acknowledge it. His tendency to the great white plague is not so inherent as it is a matter of environment. With proper conditions thrown about him, which means returning to the observance of his original laws of health, the Indian would eradicate this tendency toward tuberculosis. The great white plague thrives in the indoor shop. Several years ago I had the pleasure of breaking the record on the investigation of the causes of tuberculosis in the city of Milwaukee. In this particular investigation we found that the average working family numbered five members, and the heads of families were earning nine dollars a week. When the rent and the fuel were taken out it left ninety-four cents for each one to live on per week. As a consequence the laboring population was dying from tuberculosis. These people represented not only the sweatshop but the general conditions of city employment. The white man laborer cannot earn enough to feed him properly, and, as for the sanitation of his house, the Indian teepee isn't a circumstance to the cheap tenement house. I have never forgotten the smells of the closed parlors with their heavy draperies and the dismalness of drawn shades. The tenement house of the city has since become a dread to me, and I fear some Indians who have an undue worship of Paleface ways will likewise follow closed windows and drawn shades. I may be departing a little when I dwell upon this beyond a passing mention, but when I have looked over the white man's conditions of living with the idea of putting the Indian into it, I have seen things that we too often pass over without due consideration.

Wherever there is intelligence in the land, there is a return to the Indian's habit of living out of doors. And when you stop to think that out of twenty-four hours each one of us is taking 25,000 breaths, it is easy to see that one of the reasons why we have been particularly free from the white man's foul diseases before he contaminated us is because we drew in health 25,000 times instead of poisons. An indoor race cannot have the reddest of blood.

It is a matter of statistics that as soon as a people have had long experience with tenement life and city employment they return to the country. Now then my plea is that we avoid the things that are killing off the majority of the laboring population in the country among the whites.

It has been agreed by all thinkers that the ideal life is the small community life, which combines the advantages of concentration with the health of the uncongested freedom. Before I go into the details of the organization I here propose, let me sum up the reasons why the Indian should seek to organize something different and better for himself than already exists.

1. He has lands, a valuable asset in the business world. He does not need to buy sites for the construction of industrial centers.

2. He has funds which could be called out for organization expense—enough of it to cover the whole Indian population with organization.

3. [He has] certain ideas of his own way of living, namely, the devotion to simplicity and outdoor life, and he ought to insist upon their being reinstated.

4. The conditions of labor in the outside world are inferior to the conditions which he can establish for himself.

The organization which I believe to be most effective for our uses is called the Garden City.[3] In this country, it has triumphed in the experiment on Long Island. In Europe, it has been tried extensively—the most modern examples being found in England and Germany and France. The kind I propose for the Indian I prefer to call the Industrial

Village, for the simple reason that it has been suggested to me that the name Garden City sounds too much like a utopian idea, or a soft notion of philanthropy. This thing I propose is a hard-headed, practical scheme which is not dependent upon charity to carry it out.

In distinction from the experiment in New York, the industrial village is not a relief from the congestion of population, but it is a planned concentration of population. The tendency in the cities to move back to the small community life is a sign of progress, and quite logical. Here are some of the chief reasons for it:

1. The social nature of man is more satisfied in a village than on isolated farms and the isolation of city life where families side by side do not need to know each other.

2. The advantages of systematized life can be readily and more economically secured. Sewage, lighting, and water-works can be had by a group of people of moderate means when the same people individually cannot have them at all.

3. The enforcements of regulations for the public good can be more effectively carried out. This includes not only the purely ethical institutions, but sanitation and education and amusements.

4. Facilities of transportation can be more easily secured.

5. The successful carrying out of commerce in modern times requires concentration of population. There is greater economy of manufacture and running businesses in the organized community. In this it is a practical school for wholesome citizenship and it develops municipal efficiency.

With the installment of the industrial village, there must be instituted at the same time the industry which shall be the source of revenue for the villagers. This industry among our Indians need not be the same for the different localities. We have among ourselves the consideration of the different stages of anthropologic culture to consider. There are four stages in the development to conventional civilization of any primitive people: first, the hunting and fishing stage; second, the pastoral or the keeping and tending of flocks; third, the agricultural; and fourth, the horticultural stage. All these stages the Indians of the United States had at the time of the advent of the Caucasian.

Some of them fished and hunted only, some of them herded the buffalo, some of them planted maize enough to trade or make it a tribute to their conquerors among themselves. The Cherokee actually knew and practiced the art of raising orchards and even of grafting. There is nothing more densely ignorant than the white man on these various stages of the American Indian's development, as is evident in the Indian policy. The Navajo is in the height of the second stage. The Nez Perce and the Oneida are in the height of the third stage. I might enumerate at length. It would be nothing short of folly to impose upon the Navajo a change of industry. The thing to do for him is to place his industry on a modern business scale and to go one step beyond: eliminate the middle man's interference with him. Instead of the white trader getting the 60 per cent of the profits as he does in the white man's world of commerce, let the Navajo so organize that he can sell his wares to the consumer direct and get 90 per cent of the profits.

In Oneida, Wisconsin, where soon every individual Indian will become a full-fledged citizen, the organization of the village we hope to make along lines which combine the foreign Garden City with the Mormon idea of communistic cooperation.[4]

The point of improvement on the foreign Garden City plan is a triumph over the white man's institutions of today the world over. The foreign and the American city both are corporate institutions, capitalized by money. Every member of the corporation holds so many shares of stock, which represent tangible assets. The man then who enters into the corporation must be represented by some form of money. If he does not have this, he either cannot become a member of the organization or else he must go in debt for it. Now there is nothing under the sun that is more unproductive than gold itself. Money is merely a medium of exchange for the products of the earth. That saying that "it takes an ounce of gold to get an ounce of gold out of the mine" illustrates my meaning. Money represents an exchange of values, and when you trace these values to their sources, they are soil and labor. In other words, the wealth of a country is in her soil and her men. Gold lies dormant in the earth till man comes along and hands it, and the only thing that never fails to produce is the soil. Herein is the failure of the modern systems of business to become at once equitable, in the fact that money represents the worth of a man. Now what did the Mormon do? How did he go into the desert with his destitute colony and establish economic freedom to every individual man the way it has never been done in the history of the white man in Western civilization? How did he keep from starving in the desert where there was no water, markets, or money? Someone among that colony had the right inspiration about organization. Someone reckoned out this defect in relying upon capital for everything. He had men and he had the soil. What did he do?

He saw that he needed water on the sand to make things grow. The Colorado River must be tapped. How was it possible to do it? Labor must do it, and it did. The Mormon practiced irrigation twenty years before the rest of the country did. He did it without money because he capitalized labor. Men were worth just exactly what they will always be worth when the estimate is right: men were worth just what they could do for the community. They brought that water from the Colorado [River] by the labor of their own hands, whether they were educated or ignorant. How were they paid? Each man was paid in shares of stock in the cooperative store and he received the best the community had for a living.

As soon as they established the water system, they put the seed in the ground, and they divided their labor so that no one man had more than twenty acres to look after. They placed every man at the oversight of a competent man who knew land value and the secrets of cultivation. They took no risks. Wherever their colonies went, they sent with them the expert who oversaw to the quality of industry, and to the economy of energy and space. Their traveling missionaries were men more bent upon learning the local conditions, the proper methods the secret of successes, the market requirements, the development and advancement of every locality, than upon converts. They took no risks.

And note how they understood the meaning of economy. They had to build a reservoir, for example. They did it with their own hands and thus avoided the rake-off to the contractor, the banker, the bonding company, and the promoter. They had 90 per cent of their value at home, and when they established their cooperative stores, this is the way they did it: they sent their wool, their hides, their grain, their mutton and their beef to the market and traded them in goods. They paid for the hauling of these in shares of Community stock. Now being one community, everyone was in the family. If a hard, lean year came along, he had credit given on his shares of stock, this being appropriable for payment.

At Woodruff, Arizona, 150 people used less than 600 acres making a distribution of 20 acres for adult labor per capita. The reduction of space to intensive use of the soil did away with too broad a distribution of one man's energy. This resulted in a greater success from twenty acres than outside individual farmers made on three and four hundred acres. At St. Joe, Arizona, there are two farms not larger than 20 acres that have amassed a fortune of $50,000 each for their owners, showing that men in the Mormon Commune may prosper individually according to their ability, which is the great note in the New Socialism.[5] When men are equal in their opportunities, they receive the maximum of economic advantage.

Where Socialism fails to triumph in this country is because under the present form of corporate rights, the individual has as many votes as he has shares of stock. A man, therefore, who has 51 per cent of all the stock decides and rules. And he may outdistance the small shareholder who may be a superior man to the organization.

There are two remedies I would suggest for this:

1. Apply the Rochdale system of "one man, one vote," regardless of the number of shares of stock, or,

2. Provide against 51 per cent control in the hands of any one individual.

The foreign American and European idea of the division of dividends to the shareholder is a communistic idea of capital and not of men. The Mormon idea is a communistic idea of men. In this institution, every man draws his proportion performed. Each man in it shall own lands, but the work and the advantages are communistic. The

Mormons today are the richest people per capita in the world. There is one precaution they took among other things. And that is they fortified themselves against the lazy man. If he could not perform a fixed minimum of labor he had to get out of the community. The community might take his property at its own price.

The principle of intensive cultivation as carried out by the Mormons has been carried out in other countries to a remarkable extent. Denmark, for example, is one-fourth the size of the State of Wisconsin, yet [it] supplies all Europe with butter and eggs.

The American scientific agriculturist is realizing that space is not necessary with soil for returns. The great note in Western civilization today is toward practical science.

A while back I said that we had four stages of anthropologic culture to consider in our organization. Let me reiterate in conclusion that no one industry can be uniformly installed on the reservations if we would intelligently handle every locality and group. Expert service must be secured to look over Indian territory,[6] to judge for what the locality is best adapted, and to find the market. The town-site for the Industrial Village should be chosen after determining these. In short, I believe that were the Industrial Village organized with the Mormon ideas of capitalization, combined with the European and American idea of the market, that we would secure the maximum advantage. That we must calculate to meet and to use modern business methods goes without saying, but the great distinction I wish to impress upon your minds is that to reach a state of economic equity we must follow the Mormon idea of making men the capital of the community.

In these pages I have not berated white institutions because they are white, but because all economists have agreed already that they are neither as economic nor as equitable as they hope to be. Let us take the natural advantages the race already has in its possessions and make for ourselves Gardens and teach the white man that we believe the greatest economy in the world is to be just to all men. It is my belief that the old saying, "Be good and you will be happy," is fast coming to mean, "Be happy and you will be good." Man is only a creature of circumstance after all. (Applause).

[THE CHAIRMAN: There will be no time for discussion. The next paper is "The Indian as a Skilled Mechanic," by Charles M. Doxon, an Onondaga and a graduate of Hampton, a man who is peculiarly fitted to speak on that subject, as he is himself a skilled mechanic, drawing the best wages of such. His paper possesses the golden quality of brevity. I take pleasure of introducing Mr. Doxon.]

Some Facts and Figures
on Indian Education
(1912)

The word education has several meanings to our race, and at the start I wish to clear up in our minds a common misunderstanding of the term. To some of our Indians at home, going away to a government school means an education from which we may expect anything and everything. To some others, anything the Caucasian does is "*educated*" and anything "Indian" is not. To those who have gone the whole way of enlightenment, education has another meaning. With them, there is a proper appreciation of the real values of truth wherever they may be found, whether in an Indian or Paleface.

These varying states of mind among us, with regard to the oncoming change in our racial life, have a very decided effect upon our attainment of education. One's attitude toward a thing is governed by the degree of light he has upon the subject, and, one's attainment of education is but the reflection of his understanding of what really constitutes it, and, since our ideals spring from these, it seems to me the duty of this Congress of the race to put out the watchwords and to define our ideals and standards.

I have never forgotten the figure for education an Old Nez Perce Chief gave at one Carlisle Commencement. He said, "When I was a boy the old chiefs used to say, as soon as you can climb a high

Kellogg delivered this talk at the second meeting of the Society of American Indians at Ohio State University in Columbus, Ohio, October 1912; it was published the following year in *The Quarterly Journal of the Society of American Indians* 1 (April 1913), 36–46.

mountain, the highest you can find, do not stop halfway and look back. Climb till you reach the top. There you can breathe deep and look into all the valleys. Then you can say, '*I have seen.*'"

There are old Indians who have never seen the inside of a class-room whom I consider far more educated than the young Indian with his knowledge of Latin and Algebra. There is something behind the superb dignity and composure of the old bringing up; there is some-thing in the discipline of the Red Man which has given him a place in the literature and art of this country, there to remain separate and distinct in his proud active bearing against all time, all change.

When Tecumseh was called to Vincennes, and intrigue and defeat were staring him in the face, in the open council, an aide to Gen-eral Harrison called him to the General's side by saying, "Your *white father* wishes you to sit beside him." Tecumseh answered, "My father? The sun is my father, the earth is my mother, upon her bosom I will recline," and seated himself with the ease of one who dares to be him-self. How different in tone is the expression we too often hear from the government school Indian as an excuse for anything he has done poorly: "Well, I am only an Indian!" I have no patience with this last expression. It isn't characteristic of our ancient pride, it isn't ours. It is born in the Indian service [and] it smatters of the Indian Bureau and mediocre custodian care. How different is the spirit of the Indian boy in public school who was asked by his fellows how he happened to beat Sammy Jones to the conduct prize, and he replied, "Well, I am half Indian; that much I got ahead of Sammy."

Under the philosophy of pantheism which the American native lived, there was a great regard for natural law. I for one am not certain that the discipline under it is not to be respected just as much as that under the artificial.

It has not been appreciated that the leisure in which the American Indian lived was conducive to much thought, and that the agitations and the dangers of the wilderness gave him a life rich in emotions. These, combined with his unobscured first principles and the stringent discipline to a high standard of character, really gave him an aesthetic education. His choice, when it is native, and not borrowed, is fine;

always the artistic thing in preference to the unattractive practical. He loved the beautiful because he had an educated sense of things.

Culture is but the fine flowering of real education, and it is the training of the feeling, the tastes and the manners that make it so. When we stop to think a little, old Indian training is not to be despised. The general tendency in the average Indian schools is to take away the child's set of Indian notions altogether, and to supplant them with the paleface's. There is no discrimination in that. Why should he not justly know his race's own heroes rather than through false teaching think them wrong? Have they not as much claim to valor as Hercules or Achilles? Now I do not say here that everything he has natively is right or better than the Caucasian's. Not at all, but I do say that there are noble qualities and traits and a set of literary traditions he had which are just as fine and finer, and when he has these, [f]or the sake of keeping a fine spirit of self-respect and pride in himself, let us preserve them.

One of the greatest thinkers in this country, Patten[7] of the University of Pennsylvania, says of race heredity, in connection with labor and poverty: "Children robbed of the treasures of their race-heredity by child labor, or by the poverty of their parents, show qualities in adult life which are only the defaced remains of what generous human nature implanted within them and would have developed under favorable circumstances."[8] I want to add to labor and poverty this other determination of the Indian service to kill the Indian into an ordinary paleface.

We want education, yes, we want to know all the educated Caucasian knows but we want our self-respect while we are getting his knowledge. In short, let us discriminate between the goods and the bads of civilization and the goods and bads of his own heritage; weed out as many of the bads as we can and send him along the way a finer type of citizen than if we turned him into a very average "white man" just to have him "white" in culture. This is what I mean by recognizing the real values of truth whether they are to be found in paleface or the Indian.

We live in a country that is young and gloriously admirable in many ways. But the growing heterogeneity of population makes polite culture less appreciated by the masses than it was even in revolutionary days. And where wealth is the ruling power and intellectual attainments secondary, we must watch out as a people that we do not act altogether upon the dictates of a people who have not given sufficient time and thought to our own peculiar problems, and we must cease to be dependent on their estimates of our position.

We meet with a characteristic attitude of the Indian service people in the person of the ex-supervisor of Indian schools. You will recall that several years ago the Press gave out as her view that the education of the Indian should be limited to the industries as contained in her own prescribed course of study.

Even an ex-commissioner's daughter exclaimed, on finding ourselves together in the New York School of Philanthropy, "Why should you be way out here studying the white man's problems? The thing for you to do is to go and get a job in the Indian service, while my father is commissioner."

These hopeless errors in the average mind are not inconsequential to us as a race though they can only be that to us as individuals. The hot-beds of these ideas are in the Indian schools and on the reservations. We have allowed the country to discriminate against us in the segregation of the Indian from the rest of the population. We have allowed ourselves to be cooped up for thirty-five years away from the same advantages the rest of the country is getting, and if we will sit down and take anything from the superintendent of a frontier Indian school, who was promoted by political pull from the calling of shoeing horses, we may as well make up our minds we deserve it.

Until we ourselves, in just such conferences as this, put our ideal upon the summit of the mountain, and let it shine out to us as the beacon by which we shall be guided, until we settle it that the only resting point in our search for the truth is the unit, or universal truth, however obtained, until we confirm by repeated examples the verdict of those who have tried to do us justice, we cannot emancipate ourselves from our own ignorance and the false notions of the paleface concerning us.

I want to quote a Frenchman who made an unbiased study of American life in 1831. The Gallic mind is always refreshing in its openness. He said: "The Indian in the little they have done have unquestionably displayed as much natural genius as the people of Europe in their most important designs, but nations as well as men require time to learn, whatever may be their intelligence and zeal."

Dr. Franz Boas of Columbia University, the greatest anthropologist in America, claims that so far as his investigations have gone, there is no difference between the brain of a Caucasian and that of an Indian, in actual weight and gray matter.

Besides the research of science, however, we have evidence of the power of abstraction in the Indian mind. History in its true representation gives us credit for generals and statesmen and sages and scholars in such personages as Sitting Bull, Geronimo, Tecumseh, Brant, Sequoia, Logan, and that Indian and statesman once mentioned as a nominee for President of the United States,[9] and so many others we have not space for them. The Caucasian discovered these men and since their time, since we have been subjected, there have been others like them, who for want of opportunity have died obscure.

Old Indian oratory is noted for profound thought, literary merit, and logic. I cannot help quoting here another Nez Perce, who was approached by an inspector with the proverbial proposal for removal. After listening patiently for some time he replied. He took a stick and described two circles on the ground of equal size. Pointing to one he said, "Through this the white man sees the world. Through this other, the Indian says goodbye." It made me start[le] when a Columbia professor used the same illustration in warning us as anthropologists in the field against inserting our own point of view into our investigations.

No, the Indian mind was not stolid and senseless, without penetration, just as it was not without humor. When Carl Schurz was Commissioner, a band of Crows came down to see him in Washington, one autumn. On meeting them he exclaimed, "I suppose that the Crows had to move South, now that winter is coming on." "Yes, they have come South," said their leader, "to get their shirts on."

But now what has our Red brother actually accomplished with a systematic educational system twenty-five years old? Dismissing the question of his capabilities, what has he actually done, and what has been done for him? What have been his opportunities?

There are altogether 357 government schools; 70 of these reservation boarding schools, 35 non-reservation boarding schools, and 223 day schools. The enrollment in these schools totals 24,500 children. Besides these there are 4,300 children in the mission schools and 11,000 in the public. Of the 11,000, the Five Civilized Tribes of Oklahoma have 6,900. The number of children of the race in school in the country then is 39,800. The last report shows an increase of nearly 2,000 [in] attendance over the year before. Yet, there are still 9,000 children without school facilities!

The statistics compiled by Carlisle of what her graduates have done with themselves are the best reports of the actual accomplishment of Indian education. I should like to hear more extensively from some of the graduates in this audience what those accomplishments are.

According to the usual method of averages used elsewhere, we should have about 54,000 Indian families. Allowing an average of three children to the family, we would have 162,000 of the young. Discounting the ineligibles, we should have at least 54,000 children of school age. The number accounted for in school and out of school is only 48,000, however, so that we have lost at the lowest estimate 5,200 children somewhere.

In 1906 I learned, through the President of the Indian Rights Association, that in Northern California there were 20,000 Indians in that state without any homes. Those, of course, would have children who were not in school or on any records, save their own foot prints on the mountain sands of the land which they once owned alone. They camp about the mountains till the season of fruit picking returns. I made a special effort to get these into Sherman Institute some years ago. They were speaking fluent English, Spanish and Indian, and were shrewder than other Indians who had not had contact with other people. But no people have very many children where the living conditions are hard and the staple food in the winter months is Mexican beans.

I am inclined to think that there are more children on some reservations who are not accounted for through some deficit in statistics. I noticed this in the thirty-eight reports from the various Agents and Superintendents on reservations that they seemed to tell haphazardly whatever came into their minds, some telling more than others, and some not giving much of anything beyond the attendance and the outlook. In 1906 I heard that there were three college-bred men who were Superintendents in the over 100 boarding schools, but I know that it has been the special effort of our Commissioner to improve the personnel of Indian schools. In many instances, however, such a thing is beyond any hope. This is characteristic of institutionalism. Wherever there are boarding schools, and the inmates lead restricted lives and are pinned too closely to the monotony of daily routine, besides being underpaid, we cannot expect to find the most progressive there, as a general rule. I have noticed that, in some schools, Indian employees are made most unhappy through the petty jealousies of some of the inferior white employees. Again, there are times when children are made to suffer for the animosities between Indian school employees. I mention this here not because it affects you and me so much as that if we are to be a protecting organization, this is one of the things that should command our attention.

The salaries of people employed in the service are entirely too small to [e]nsure us efficiency throughout the system. I do not mean to pass over the superiority of some of those who are employed in the Indian Service. One cannot help appreciating the noble service of some few earnest souls who are there through their sincere heart interest in the race who *are efficient enough to be acceptable anywhere else*. We all know them and appreciate them, but they are sadly in the minority.

There are phases in the Indian Schools which have their merits. For instance, one idea which has been installed in some larger school like that at Tulalip [Washington], recently, which can be full of fruit, is the organization of what is called "school cities." The students are organized into a miniature commonwealth and they themselves discharge the duties and activities of it. This is [based] on the idea of the George Junior Republic for the city boys, which is proving to be the making of some of the most efficient and high-minded citizens. Wherever the government turns over a boarding school to the state, as it has done in Utah and Colorado, these school cities ought to accompany the building.

Another phase of the non-reserve boarding school which is highly commendable is, of course, the outing system. But, when you stop to think of it, isn't it its contact with the outside world which makes it so useful?

The effective work the large institutions, like Carlisle and Haskell, have done is so marked that the evils of the System are almost lost in them. It lies in the fact that their heads have been personalities which are out of the general category of Indian schools. This just happens, though, because these men carry the system, rather than having the system carry them.

As for industrial training, this is splendid, of course, but the public schools are adding manual training and rudimentary agriculture now. The Commissioner, in his report, throws out a suggestion that more could be accomplished with a larger appropriation. We are much indebted to the Indian Rights people for their efforts to influence legislation in this matter in the past. This also suggests where one of the greatest services of this organization can be.

In the thirty-five years of Indian Education, the growth of appropriations has been as follows: 1877, $20,000; 1887, $1,211,415; 1897, $2,517,265; 1912, $3,757,496. But the year 1908 was the highest when the appropriation ran over the $4,000,000 mark. It has cost the government and the Indian to maintain these schools for the thirty-five years, just $74,723,375. This looks enormous. I can hear the paleface say, "And what has the Indian done with it?"

I want to ask that question of the government. What has it done with that $74,000,000?

I am going to take [the government's] own records. I take the state of Montana because it has a good number of schools and because its boarding schools are not exceptional in size or equipment. The actual cost of its five boarding schools, in site and buildings, sewage, light, heat in one school, and a water system in another, is $200,000. The furnishing, improvements and equipment to the point of running order is $300,000 additional, making an exact half million. For the twelve day schools, the same item of expense is about $60,000, making its expenditure thus far for both classes of schools, $560,000. The number of children of school age in the state is 13,759. The per capita expense up to opening school is $148. Remember that the teachers and the farmer, the cook, the disciplinarian, the laundries, the engineer, the clerks, the Superintendent and his wife, the matrons of dormitories, the nurse and the doctor and their various assistants have not been paid yet. When these are paid, the expense per capita will mount the $300 mark.

Their courses of instruction do not go beyond the grammar grades. In other words, they finish a public school course when they graduate.

In Oklahoma, the cost of educating a child in the public schools is twelve and one-half cents for each day of actual attendance. There are, as day schools go, about forty weeks of school in the year, making thus 200 school days yearly. This makes the tuition of each child $25 for the year. It should take the average child eight years to get through the public schools so that the cost of a public school career is just $200.

It is, of course, obvious that, were Indian children put into the public schools, most of them would require more expenditure than that; for carriage fare to and from home, which would have to be provided for in some systematic way because of distance and bad weather. There are those whose clothes would have to be looked after, but for the majority, $300 per year would be more than ample to place them in the best schools in the country. Now, as the Indian education stands, the difference between it and the public school is the difference between $25 per year for the white child and $300 a year for the Indian.

And what are we getting for it? In the boarding school every child is detailed to work half a day, so that the Indian child is getting a half year where the white child is getting a full year.

This phase of the Indian school has not received enough attention from this viewpoint, because the idea has been that the work done by these children is an industrial education. The difficulty lies here. Some of this is true, but the work in an institution of several hundred degrades into onerous tasks rather than the more practical lessons. The number of children who are working, who are incipient cases of consumption is large, because these are hard to detect until they come down in the last stage.

Another objectionable feature of the boarding school is this matter of health. Where there are several hundred together and a large percentage of them are afflicted with trachoma and tuberculosis and the means for their segregation is not sufficient, the well children are open to these dangers. Think of the danger of trachoma. Why, no immigrant can land in New York who has trachoma, but here we are exposing the youth of the race to an incurable disease. If this were done by one individual to another, it would be a penitentiary offense. I hear someone defending the Bureau. Go to the Indian schools and say to the nurses and the doctors that they shall not lose their positions if they will tell you the truth about the health conditions of the schools and we would soon enough find that the hospital equipment in the Indian service is nowhere near adequate to the demand. No one is working at greater disadvantage than this class in the service.

The white child comes from a well-established economic environment. That is, he has a home where the one idea in the community is to overcome deficits of material well-being. This child is continually asking of his parents to find a better means of support and accumulation. It calls for a *continual effort toward improvement*. The community life is organized; it produces and has markets, and money is in circulation in it as a natural result. Its social life is limited, by necessity, to recreation. It has personal liberties so long as it stays within a prescribed course of public law.

The Indian child's environment is the reservation, a world of deficits. The group has really custodian care. *There is no real personal liberty in wardship; there is no incentive in the community for any special effort; there is no reward for doing the right thing; the social life is not organized.* A group of Indians may dance a whole week without impairing their personal estates. There are no markets of their own making and their own responsibility. There is no money continually in circulation. As Marvin Jack, in his paper last year said, when money enters the reservation, it loses its elasticity. When rations and annuities come, they come like spasms. There is nothing being learned by the adult population from necessity. What they do, they do through their own sense of natural acumen or decency. The great wonder is not that they accomplish so little, but that they are not all outlaws.

The educative influences are centered in the agency or the schools, and what is the personnel of these institutions? They should be filled with well-paid, efficient social service workers. Instead, they too often need social service themselves. Originally the positions were filled by people who had political pull, just as there is still a lot of graft in spite of the Civil Service Reform, and in spite of a most efficient and sincere Commissioner and Supervisor of Indian Education, for both these men have large training and experience behind them. But here is a system: what are a few people to do with a large system, with a Bureau which is the most corrupt branch of the whole United States government?

What can we expect when we have such instances as this: a woman entered the service when she was fourteen and is now principal in one of the government schools. I should like to see a principal in the state public schools with no more preparation than that. Can the blind lead the blind? It isn't logical.

Is this $300 per capita for Indian education actually worth that to the race, the government or the child? If a child can go to the public schools in one of the most progressive states in the Union for $25 a year, the Indian child as he stands not getting the same education half a year, must have at the most $10 worth of education.

I should like you to be optimistic for the system, but this looks ridiculous to me: so apparent is the graft in Indian education that the one watchword I should like to emphasize on you all, more than any other, is that this body should not go out of here without some organization for independent research. We cannot ask for and push legislation without the figures in our hands as to our real status.

It would be far better if the children of the race were sent to surrounding public schools for a whole day. Suppose they had to have a delivery wagon to gather them up and take them home at night just the way that rural mail is delivered. Let these little fellows learn to fight their way side by side with the rest of the citizens of the country when they are young and daring. Let there be a lunch arranged for them for the noonday meal, and if their parents do not furnish them the clothes, they will demand it of them when they see other children's good clothes, and in reality they will by such indirect influences as this teach the community to move along with them.

Discrimination against the race in educational advantages because it is a convenient graft seems to be a general system in Indian education. The money spent in it is not going directly to the child's benefit, but it feeds a big machine which is not as efficient as the same grade of education in the country, at a fraction of the cost. For, at the rate of $300 a head for 6 years, there is an expenditure of $1,800, against $150.

The situation is simply this: we have both wealth and ignorance in abundance and we are the "easiest marks" for exploitation as a class that this country knows and, just as long as we ourselves can't help this, we need not expect any change. There are too many people interested in the perpetuation of the Bureau to insure us a change until we demand it, and the program I wish to suggest for this Society is:

1. A thorough investigation be made and our own statistics put on public record, together with a comparison of the conditions of general education in this country.

2. That we demand a special appropriation be set aside for higher education in colleges and universities and that, with this money, scholarships be given as rewards of merit to deserving students. These scholarships [will] cover tuition, board and clothing and necessary expenses to secure the student against embarrassment and the feeling of insecurity.

3. That we present a program to the Bureau, changing Indian schools into public schools wherever feasible.

4. That a campaign fund be provided to carry out this program by appropriation or by subscription from individual tribes.

In conclusion, I wish to be understood that this paper is only an aggravation to me. The amount of investigation I have done merely suggests what a field of surprises lies waiting for the Committee on Education, and for this Society.

Moreover, I have not space here to mention many other details which are of great moment for the future of the race. I appreciate the people in this system, who in all sincerity, are struggling against its odds, and I appreciate the laborious and scientific work Commissioner Valentine has done to improve these conditions. In short, I wish it to be understood that I am wholly impersonal in my critique of the system.

Our future is in the hands of the educational system of today. Those of us who have come thus far know how our youth have longed to reach the summit of the mountain. Let us not forget our own yearnings and the prayers of our ambitious young for opportunity. Let us climb the highest mountain, without looking back till we have reached the top.

Presentation at the Dedication of
Lorado Taft's Indian Statue *Black Hawk*
(1911)

An Account of the Unveiling Ceremonies at Eagles' Nest Bluff, Oregon, Illinois, July the First, Nineteen Hundred and Eleven, Frank O. Lowden, Presiding

RESPONSE [to Edgar A. Bancroft's address]—WYNNOGENE

MR. LOWDEN: *I now have the very great pleasure of introducing Wynnogene of the Oneida-Iroquois* (Miss Laura M. Cornelius), *who will make a further response to Mr. Bancroft's address.*

WYNNOGENE: Like the faint whispers of the last leaf upon the oak, when the northwest winds have done with summer, is the Indian's message to you. The ancient oracles are still. For him, even the golden glory of October's sun is set. No eagle plumes wave before my eyes as I look among you. The race is not here today. The race is not here, to rejoice with me for this great moment. And perhaps I may be pardoned that my vision grows dim as I look upon this mute magnificence before us, dim because:

> Tears from the depth of some divine despair
> Rise in the heart and gather to the eyes,
> In . . . thinking of the days that are no more.[1]

Charles Eastman and Laura Cornelius Kellogg offered individual "responses" to Edgar A. Bancroft's address, "The Indian," at the unveiling of Lorado Taft's "Black Hawk" statue at Eagles' Nest Bluff, Oregon, on July 1, 1911. The following year, Laura Cornelius Kellogg's response appeared in print between Charles Eastman's response and Hamlin Garland's poem, "The Trail Makers." *Lorado Taft's Indian Statue "Black Hawk"*, 71–82.

And dim, too, because this beautiful tribute, so long delayed to a deserving people, comes at last so freely given, so nobly conceived, so grandly memorial.

While it is with deep thanksgiving that I am thus privileged to represent the American Indian on this occasion, I have accepted this lofty honor with a profound regret that a Red Jacket, a Dehoadilun, or an Oskanundunah[2] is not here to immortalize in fitting speech an event which is the first of its kind in America, an event to which the American Anglo, no less than the Indian, must point with pride and gratitude in his heart as time mellows the pages of our history.

For my part, I cannot think of anything more long-enduring, grander in its significance, or more sublime in spirit than that which has the power to warm the hearts of two races in a common inspiration. The American Revolution was such an influence, and the hazardous frontier. Indeed, it is not so long ago since the oppressed of other lands stood side by side upon our shores tingling to their temples in the glow of a common purpose. It is not so long ago since the dangers of the wilderness beyond the Alleghenies gave birth to the real American Nation, no longer dependent upon the frontier of Europe for their initiative. But today it is not war, not the unbroken path in the wilderness, not the thirst in the desert, not the loneliness of the open plain, nor the treacherous pass of the mountain that bind us together. Wars and frontier are gone. The sentiments are growing out of other things: out of interests that, maybe, are more universal in their appeal, sentiments that go beyond the immediate self and are made of the larger sympathies for all men. Let me quote one of your literary artists, who says:

"The modern sympathy includes not only the power to pity the sufferings of others, but also that of understanding their very souls."[3] This is the sympathy which has brought us so pleasantly together here. This is the sympathy which alone can make the past redeemable. This is the sympathy that mothers the Arts. And lo, in its wake the earth grows more beautiful to the eye. How your poet has here caught an insight into the very soul of the Indian! How, with that kind of feeling which comes as the flowering of a people's culture, he has made of this place in the wood a Mecca to the lover of art! Today I have come to feel in a degree I have never before felt, that the American people may enter a large claim for worldly recognition in that art which is the hardest of the Fine Arts to attain, Sculpture.

You may recall how, some years ago, a British statesman and scholar asked, "Where are your American poets?"[4] I cannot question the definition of poetry in the Briton's mind when he asked that question. Nor can I here discuss with you the relative merits of our own sweet singers. Sufficient to say that, while one must admit the wild imagination of Poe and the rugged profundity of Whitman, he cannot compare them, or the gentle race of the New England *fireside* poets with the laurelled bards of the Aegean or British Isles. And, however much of the beautiful song has been produced in this country, the fact remains that, before Homer and Milton, we must admit that, in the whole history of the American nation there has yet been no conception that, in sublimity of theme, in dignity of treatment, in fidelity to atmosphere, can be called the American Epic.

But now what is this carving in stone, whose every line is full of the stately measure of the epic? What is this story, whose silent eloquence melts the heart as you look upon it?

"Thou foster-child of Silence and slow Time,
    Sylvan historian who canst thus express
A flowery tale more sweetly than our rhyme:
    What leaf-fringed legend haunts about thy shape
Of deities or mortals, or of both?"[5]

Done in a medium which has the first place in the esthetic hierarchy. Done to endure, as no other of the Fine Arts, the ravages of Time. Oh, I care not what the canons may be that divide one Fine Art from another. The Indian honored the prophet when he came. So let him always [be honored], whether that prophet carry in his hand the brush, the quill, or the chisel.

To me this Statue has gone beyond the limitations of speech. It has long passed the bounds of verbal expression. Were its essence to take other forms, I am certain we should hear in it the strains of beautiful music. Within its idealism is locked a great oratorio. Naught but the solemn harmony of some deep-toned sacred music could carry its meaning.

And perhaps, too, were we to look closer, we should find its noble lines returning to the boundaries of inland seas and crescent moon, or back to the stateliness of cathedral elm, find its hopes sailing the cloud-flecked blue overhead, its heroism leaping precipice and break with the daredom of the awful Tawasentha Niagara.[6] Aye, the spirit that has been caught in the marble mold is as large as nature itself. If this is not the American epic, I ask, what can be?

Rightly is its subject the American Indian. He who knows the throes of a Gethsemane; he who knows the blood-sweat of anguish; he who has sounded the very depths of a national tragedy, and done it after the teachings of his fathers, without a murmur; he who, too spiritual to survive the ravages of a material age, has been misunderstood and has passed under the ignominy of false charges; he who, like the Greek, belonged to a hero age they could not comprehend. Yet, when all is done, calmly he draws his simple robe about him and stands there mute and upright, looking boldly back upon it all, even as the eagle faces the glaring sun. Looking back to the East. Aye, even back to the welcome lodges of this father, surveying the past, as one who has finished the journey of life. How recently he himself stood there, with these words upon his lips:

"Beautiful is the sun, O, strangers,
When you come so far to see us.
All our town in peace awaits you,
All our doors stand open for you:
You shall enter all our wigwams,
For the heart's right hand we give you.
Never bloomed the earth so gaily,
Never shone the sun so brightly,
As today they shine and blossom,
When you come so far to see us.
Never was our lake so tranquil,

Nor so free from rock and sand-bar,
For your birch-canoe in passing
Has removed both rock and sand-bar.
Never before had our tobacco
Such a sweet and pleasant flavor,
Never the broad leaves of our corn-fields
Were so beautiful to look on,
As they seem to us this morning,
When you come so far to see us."[7]

How recent! I can seem to scent the aroma of the tobacco, as it smoked in rising circles from the peace-pipe. I can almost whiff of the savory sweetness of the new corn steaming in the old brown bowl, the chief's brown bowl, waiting for the hungry white guest. Could I but leave him there? Could I but leave them there, around the warming fires of the wigwam, giving and partaking each of the other's graces? Could I have been able today to say to all the American people, as I am able to say to this group, there is no debt but the debt of gratitude between us, how different had been the course of American history?

But perhaps it has always been so that the makers of a nation's glories have been individuals; some in statecraft, some in other mediums have come to herald new events, establish new regimes for the multitudes. It is an appreciable fact that today it is to the free mind of the artist we must turn for justice to the American Indian. To him we owe the debt of gratitude for establishing those subtle and most enduring impressions of an age and a people, which the American people, as a people, can only comprehend with time. But I am not here to unearth the long story of infamies, the great tragedy upon which this Moch-Pe-O-Zon-Za[8] gazes. Rather, I have come to thank you for the Indian where great thanks are due.

Who can misunderstand him who stands there against the sky, carved in stone, in the mighty truth of him? What dilettante can rob him of his dignity? What ignorance can abuse him? Aye, what baseness can touch him? Calmly he draws his simple robe about him and stands there, mute for that which has no defense, looking upon the nations of men, as they come challenging all to all that is lofty in spirit. Perhaps it is worth a national tragedy to go down to posterity an inspiration to all men. As I look upon him for the last [time], my heart within me says: Amen! There, let him stand, defying the very elements, defying injustice, defying defeat, so upright, so self-contained, so self-sufficient.

"O, every wind that nobs the mountain pine;
O, aching Time; O, moments big as years—
Each, as ye pass, swell out the monstrous truth!"[9]

Testimony during Hearings on H.R. 1917

Statement of Laura C. Kellogg (1913)

[In her testimony Kellogg criticizes the Indian Bureau and the general incompetence and graft of its employees, calling their work the "reign of paternalism." She also advocates for funding for the Lolomi industrial village plan, which will lead to economic development based on communally held lands and resources, as well as increased funding for day schools and funds for Native people to attend colleges. Kellogg argues forcefully for a protected autonomy and continued relationship with the federal government.]

Testimony before the Senate on the Indian Appropriation Bill

MRS. KELLOGG: Mr. Chairman and gentlemen, this matter of the investigation of Indian conditions is one of the most neglected in the whole Indian service, and when the Senator from Oklahoma said that it should be left to inspectors who are already an institution in this Bureau, I want to say from the Indian standpoint that it has been left to the inspectors for over 30 years with the result that there is actually no accomplishment in the way of getting at an intelligent understanding of the social conditions in the Indian situation, and that the social service side which is rendered by this Board of Indian Commissioners (in which service is associated Mr. Moorehead,[10] of Andover-William University, and men of that kind) is one of the greatest needs of the day, if you are ever going to settle the Indian problem.

Indian Appropriation Bill [H.R. 1917]; Hearings Before the United States Senate Committee on Indian Affairs, 63d Cong., 1st sess., pp. 94–95, 507–21 (May 8, 9, 12, 1913).

I know what the inspectors in the Indian service do. They go to these Indian schools, and they are entertained, and when they leave that place, they do not know anything more about what is going on than they did when they came. You will find in every Indian reservation—and disinterested people in every reservation will agree with me—that their service is wholly inadequate to meet the demand.

Now, as to the matter of the Indian Commission, I agree with the Senator from Oklahoma[11] that this idea of giving out a little dribble here and there to carry out a department service which should be one of the biggest, if you are ever going to proceed on an intelligent line with regard to Indian affairs, that this matter of giving a little here and there only kills any effective work that may be done by a central organization, and I suggest that the commission should not have $4,000 or $10,000 appropriated for, but that it should be given sufficient appropriation to cover the ground thoroughly and that if those men who have shown their attitude in the way of social service can serve without money, why should they not be asked to come into this service and help with the Indian Bureau to adjust this matter once and for all? Until it is done, there is no hope of getting at anything definitely.

I myself have been in the field and I know that when I compare the facts that I find at first hand with the commissioner's report—I know that Commissioner Valentine made a special effort to have statistical work done. I know that there are many things that are waylaid through the avenues that come to the Indian Office, and unless you clean up the personnel of that investigation, and trust it to such men as are on that commission, I do not see what effective work can ever be done by the Government. It seems to me they are of the utmost importance, and instead of being wiped out should be encouraged and should be invited to cooperate with the Bureau of Indian Affairs.

THE CHAIRMAN[12]: I would like to ask the commissioner how these men are appointed. Who appoints them?

Commissioner ABBOTT[13]: The President.

THE CHAIRMAN: Are they officials of the Government?

Commissioner ABBOTT: In a sense—in the sense that they are appointed by the President and subject to the call of the President or the Secretary of the Interior, and in like manner, I suppose Congress, for report of the results of their investigations. [. . .] (p. 95).[14]

◆

Senator TOWNSEND:[15] Mr. Chairman, I understand that two or three persons have come here this morning with the understanding that they would be heard, and then the committee would be through with the hearings. Mrs. Kellogg and others are here by appointment. I move that Mrs. Kellogg and any other persons present who desire to be heard on any matter pertinent to the bill be heard.

The CHAIRMAN: I had supposed all the hearings had been closed with the criticisms and attacks that have been made. It seems to me we have had sufficient hearings to enable us to take this bill up and dispose of it.

Mrs. KELLOGG: Mr. Chairman, I ask for the passing of two items in the early part—

Senator ASHURST:[16] If you will pardon me, I will say that Mrs. Kellogg, on the day that all parties were notified to file statements with the committee, rose and said that she wished to be heard for a few minutes.

The CHAIRMAN: I want to call the attention of the committee to the fact that on the 30th of this month the fiscal year ends, and the tariff bill will be reported within the next two weeks to the Senate, and we will have to confront the proposition now of getting this bill through the Senate. I would like very much to have it passed before the end of the fiscal year.

Senator TOWNSEND: I am just as much in favor of closing the hearings as anybody, but I think where persons have information that would be useful to the committee, they ought to be heard.

The CHAIRMAN: By unanimous consent, unless there is objection, the hearings will proceed ad infinitum.

Senator OWEN:[17] I desire to enter an objection to that proposition.

ADDITIONAL STATEMENT OF MRS. LAURA KELLOGG:
Encouragement of Industry among the Indians

Mrs. KELLOGG: Mr. Chairman and gentlemen. I wish to be heard on (1) the item on page 9, line 6, of the bill which reads "For the purpose of encouraging industry among the Indians and to aid them in the culture of fruits, grains, and other crops, $100,000, or so much thereof as may be necessary, to be immediately available, which sum may be used for the purchase of animals, machinery, tools, implements, and other equipment necessary to enable Indians to become self-supporting." (2) Item on page 15, lines 6–19, relating to the provision of school facilities for the Navajo children in Arizona and New Mexico, for which the appropriation is $100,000. (3) On reimbursable funds generally. (4) The Lolomi Industrial Village as the only comprehensive solution to the Indian problem.

Items 1 and 2 attracted my attention as being parts of the argument of No. 4. Back of the whole Indian problem is obviously and primarily the question of self-support and effective education. And the blame falls to the Indian, who is charged as being backward and indifferent and not responsive to the efforts of the Government and philanthropy to put him against his feet.

Granting that some effort has been made both by the Government and philanthropy in his behalf, and that the Indian population today is helpless and that an off-hand proof of these things is that this appropriation is still an absolute necessity, I shall proceed to dissect the Indian situation from the Indian's standpoint and to prove how the measure I propose meets it.

The present plight of the American Indian in this country has reached a point where he is face to face with the problem of race deterioration and extinction. And by extinction I do not mean the assimilation of one race by another, the contemplated end of this Government's policy in Indian relations; I mean that wholesale demoralization to which death is the redeeming end.

The census report gives the Indian population to be a little over 265,000. The report of the Indian Bureau gives it a little over 322,000 as an argument that the birth rate is on the increase over the death rate. It is a well-known fact to all who know Indian reservations that the intrusion of palefaces and negroes into the allotment rolls in recent years has a great deal to do with the sudden increase of the Indian population.[18] A great number of the negroes who have been thrust upon the Five Civilized Tribes of Oklahoma, for example, tell vivid stories of how they came from Louisiana and Texas, Georgia, and Alabama in colonies, solicited by paleface investors prior to the allotments among these Indians, and that they were paid so much money to claim connection with these people, whom they had never known before. In the last report of the Commissioner of Indian Affairs, the estimated death rate and birth rate of the Navajos are even. Occasionally I see editorials in the local press denying the facts represented by various agencies on the matter of prosperity among the Indians. It has been my interest to meet men outside of the various Indian reservations and to get their point of view of them. All these facts have made me very skeptical as to the estimates which proceed from the Indian Bureau.

All indications point to a deplorable state of affairs in the race under which birth cannot be prolific. Where disease and poverty flourish, infant mortality may be suspected. And as far as the old Indian is concerned, he is dying from a certain form of nostalgia—the broken heart.

The health question of the race alone is a large index of the social and economic conditions around it. The report of the Marine Hospital Service,[19] which has made such a thorough and commendable investigation, particularly on the subject of trachoma, gives as its estimate 22.7 per cent of the race afflicted with trachoma, and about 25.5 per cent with tuberculosis, this latter being a conservative estimate. Practically half of the Indian population is therefore sick with two hundred diseases against which there are prohibitory statutes in the national laws. This investigation, moreover, states that the largest number of those afflicted with trachoma is those in the Indian boarding schools.

Already, then, the young generation to whom we look for the future is largely blind and hollow-chested, dividing its meager energies between languor and pain and having one foot in the grave. [. . .]

To this I would add that the hospital facilities in Indian schools are usually wholly inadequate to accomplish anything like proper segregation of the sick. Moreover, the maintenance of large boarding institutions requires a great deal of labor to keep them in any kind of order, and there are children performing drudgery work, who ought to be in sanitaria. The part of the appropriations used for actual nourishment is not always sufficient to keep a child in battle trim against tuberculosis.

There have been doctors in the Indian Service who have been of the caliber of the instance I am going to give. A physician examined for trachoma several hundred pupils in one boarding school one day. He went from the infected to the clean children without once disinfecting his instruments.

What response shall we expect from the youth whose energies are eaten out with disease and misery? What spirit, what initiative so necessary for the trials of civilization, are we making for the foundation of independence and civic pride under these conditions?

In conclusion, if I were a physician, and by malpractice maimed your children for life, or if I knowingly came from a case of smallpox and without disinfection entered your homes and brought death to you, would I not be charged with criminality and punished accordingly? That is what Federal supervision has accomplished for the race.

When such barbaric conditions as the scientific investigation of the Indians' health has disclosed emanate from the institutions for the so-called "civilization of the Indian," I am alarmed at the mention of any new ground to be broken. And unless a totally different course in education is to be pursued in the introduction of school facilities for Navajos, there is the danger of contaminating and demoralizing one of the last few groups who have maintained their superiority because they have resisted the paleface's civilization so far. The Navajos are full-bloods. Out of a population of 10,000 they have only 75 disabled people: 11 per cent have tuberculosis, 15 per cent trachoma, being smaller percentages than other Indian populations of this size. They are in the height of native development of the pastoral stage of ethnic culture. They are morally superior and clean, shrewd and thrifty, as the following figures will show. They have 162,000 horses and mules, valued at $1,660,000. They have 10,000 head of cattle, valued at $200,000; 700,000 goats and sheep, valued at $1,380,000. Their annual income is $311,552.

There is a partial explanation why they have maintained their native integrity and health in the following. Several years ago the geological surveyors tried to enter the Navajo country and to pitch their tents there. The Navajo chief, who, by the way, has never been to school, answered them: "No, you shall not pitch your tents among my people. We are healthy. We are clean. You come and you will bring your whisky, your painted women, and your dirty diseases, and the same will happen to us as has happened to all out Indian brothers."

The Navajos hold their property in common, and they appear to be better off than any other Indians in the country. I predict that interests in the country who covet what they have will be forthcoming to persuade Congress that the allotment act should be enforced as a step toward the "civilization" of these Indians.

There is no stronger proof of the failure of this Nation to civilize the Indian than the contrast between the groups over whom Federal supervision has held a "reign of terror" and these Navajos who have been freest from the hand of paternalism . . . [.]

But, to return to that item, "For the purpose of encouraging industry among the Indians, $100,000," etc.

I have not the time to criticize in detail the actual processes of encouraging the Indian in industry beyond some few facts which disclose whole situations. I appreciate, however, this provision of $100,000 for the encouragement of industry among the nearly 300,000 Indians. But I want to ask, is this enormous sum to be spent by the expert farmer of the Indian service?

Last year one of these "experts," I am told, had the Indians in one of the Dakota Indian schools cut up turnips for seed after the manner of preparing potatoes for seed. He had the untutored mind sowing onion sets and corn broadcast and harrowing them in. His crop came up to the hilarious derision of the whole Indian population in the vicinity.

Among the Chippewas in Minnesota they tell a story how their "expert" did not know the difference between onion seed and radish seed, so to get over the difficulty he mixed them, so he wasn't short of a crop, anyway.

Recently I heard of the promotion to the supervisorship of agriculture of an agent whose agency farm of 30 acres was so renowned for cuckle burs that, when I visited the reservation, an Indian escorted me there to show me one of the sights of the locality.

In another agency the "expert" did not know how to water a cow upon the assumption of his duties, so he finally concluded that drinking cups were made for mouths and went about with a bucket of water and a drinking cup. I would suggest that Congress inquire whether or not this item is not to be consumed in drinking cups.

In one school where Indian girls were supposed to learn needlework, the girls, who already knew these stitches when they came, poured over some Mexican drawn work and embroidery till their eyes gave out, and when their wonderful exhibit was over, the superintendent's wife took it away for her trousseau, as a token of the Indians' esteem for her.

The economic environment of the Indian today is worse than it was in the time of his own primitive institutions; the lack of social organization on Indian reservations is appalling. This is an environment of deficits: there is no industrial system, no money in circulation, and what money does enter the reservation loses its elasticity at once; there grows up a discrimination against the Indian in business; he must pay higher interest and give more security in the local banks; these things all combine to make him a pauper.

I spoke a while ago of "the reign of terror" of paternalism. I want also to try to read a little philosophy into the policy. Like the rest of the Government, but more accentuated in form, paternalism has been a policy of extreme centralization. Under the cloak of civilizing the red man by supervision, and as a check to the Indian wars in the early days, grew up the reservation and ration system. It, in effect, grew to be a design for the purpose of depleting the Indian tribes.

The nature of bureaucracy is to perpetuate an anomalous growth, and the Federal policy in Indian relations has no equal in the achievement of such an end. Various ways have been devised within the Indian Bureau from time to time whereby more Federal patronage might be paid. There are any number of Indians competent to fill the positions of these people, but they do not get them. If the American Nation would only come out and acknowledge that under the name of civilizing the Indian it has in truth been undoing him, there would still be a degree of justice in it. But when it charges to the Indian all the demoralization it has brought upon him as his inheritance, it has heaped upon him not only plunder and outrage but the stigma of inferiority.

Charged indeed to his response are all the unpleasant aspects of a false position; all the deficit of managerial incompetency, all the defeat of a false system.

It has not even stopped to analyze him ethnically. As a matter of fact, at the time he came in contact with the European the four stages necessary to the attainment of a conventional civilization had been accomplished by him. Few Indians comparatively were in the nomadic stage in the West. The plains Indians were in the second stage, namely the pastoral. They herded the buffalo and made things from his hide. In the East the Iroquois were in the third and fourth stages. Their political organization was complete. They had even entered upon offensive warfare, which is the forerunner of expansion and nationalization. Their colonies paid tribute to them and were under control. The Cherokees [. . .] even knew the art of grafting trees. So that in the fourth stage of horticulture the Indian was represented. As for the Aztec, who was a North American Indian, he was a civilized nation.

The policy of Indian relations as late as after Monroe's administration assumed that we were all of the first stage and, instead of seeing that we were none of us stationary even in that, dealt with us below our natural state of development, and since we have, in reality, retrograded.

The percentage of Indians who, from the most deplorable environment, have forced their way to the front and have beaten the paleface man at his own game in the outside world is larger than the Indian is given credit for. I have rarely entered a city or town of any size where I have not been able to find this type of Indian. When the Indian crosses the reservation line and his abilities and attainments become the equal of the best around him, he is lost to the Indian population. There is nothing sinister in this. It merely goes to establish the fact that there is no such a thing as social discrimination against the Indian—that in this country where we perpetuate prejudices is in the economic environment.

The most cultured people of the city of Muskogee and other towns in Oklahoma, for example, are to be found among those Indians who, under the regime of the Indian Territory, maintained their own educational systems far ahead of the public and private school systems there today. Impartial people of the outside tell that these people had a curriculum in their seminaries which does not exist in any educational institutions in the state of Oklahoma. The response of the Indian, in lieu of the absence of actual statistics, must, however, for this time, be made on the side of his resistance. Someone has said, "The wonder is not that the Indian has done no more, but that he exists."

It is a remarkable fact that after four centuries of wars, harassment, eviction, disease, whisky, outrage, the Indian has not given way before. With his leadership consumed by massacres, with a beggarly educational system a little over 30 years old, and his own institutions removed without adequate substitution, he has emerged to the point of being ably represented in every profession.

This did not come through the Government Indian School. This system hurts. It does not aim to get down to the bedrock of finding his needs and fostering his own set of perceptions through which he might evolve to other steps. No. The Government has instead tried to tell the Indian child [that] everything Indian was to be despised. In the place of his own tales of heroism, he is told about Uncle Remus.[20] When I went to a little country paleface school as a child, the rude inquisitiveness of the paleface children was a constant annoyance to me, and one day I told my mother about it. She replied: "You must pardon these schoolmates of yours when they talk like that. You see, they do not have chiefs in their families."

Right there is a suitable critical point in our transition. The Indian child in the Government school is taught he must forget everything Indian instead of being told to respect the things that are respectable in his own culture. In the words of G. Stanley Hall,[21] of Clark University, one of the biggest educators in the world, "[t]his educational system is making a pinch-back white man instead of a good Indian." All the races of the earth who come into the melting pot of the United States have had their period of early race development.

The Roman Catholics declare that if they can get hold of a child in the first seven years of his life, he will be a Catholic always. Race development and individual development are not so far apart. The most impressionable stage of primitive life should be handled with the study of the care by a government that educational institutions take with children. I cannot, in this time and space, dwell at greater length, upon the educational system. From the Indian's standpoint, however, I may say, in conclusion, that the education and civilization of the Indian so far as the Federal system goes, is a rank failure. Here was the type of primitive man with which it started. Scientists and romantic observers alike agree that the highest type of primitive man in human history was the American Indian. In physical excellence he was Greek. Disease, insanity, anything abnormal was a burning shame, to be avoided before the man was born. In his code of ethics he maintained the same standard. He did not lie; he did not steal. The lawbreakers came to his own execution. He did not need jails and penitentiaries. Cowardice and treachery were punishable by death. Today they are encouraged and made by the Indian Bureau. In his institutions he was close to first principles. He lived the laws of nature. Sociologists claim he worked out cooperation in a way no race has ever done. He had no paupers, no insane asylums, no hospitals, no churches. He left no brick and mortar monuments, but he put his monument in the man. A cockeyed, superficial, vulgar, gluttonous civilization, burdened with fallacies, met him, and has been four centuries in accomplishing his demoralization. His resistance and ethnic tenacity are no less remarkable than the barbarities of a Christian era. Even today we need but to compare the old unamalgamated Indian, superb in his own sober dignity and poise, with the average sick miserable weakling of the Government school.

And now, I have come to the most critical point of the change I propose. When the maladministration of a people's affairs resolves itself into a problem of race deterioration, one of two things is inevitable—either a complete change of policy and management with regard to them or the extinction of the race. We need no further demonstration to show that the Indian Bureau is a vulture. It feeds on carrion. It will perpetuate itself by killing the manhood of a race till they become so helpless they will forever need its custodian care. This Nation has spent eighty million for the civilization of the Indian in the last 30 years. While it has spent more for the insane population of the country, nevertheless, it has a right to demand some showing for this money. And if the charge is going to fall upon the Indian's response, then is the final settlement between the American Indian and this Nation at hand. I have come here this morning to say that the only thing to do with the Indian Bureau is to do away with it.

That the end of the American Indian is citizenship goes without saying. Whatever his own likes and dislikes may be with regards to this, it is inevitable that his relation to the State in which he lives must be the same as that of any other people who come under the flag. But it is also true that paternalism has not prepared him for his step and that he is not ready for it without preparation.

For many years I have looked into Caucasian institutions with a critical eye, and the only conclusion at which I can arrive in the face of conditions is that the day of economic equity for the paleface man has not yet arrived in this country. The struggle between deficit and surplus, between labor and capital, between fallacies and truths for him is not settled. The realization of his highest hopes is not yet. With all his education and property, I fail to find the sense of social justice in him that the Indian originally possessed. What is the defense of a democracy which claims to lead the world, when one of your greatest economic authorities can say, "The great majority of men do not possess the abilities or the opportunities to secure the large capital necessary for the successful conduct of a modern business. For the masses it is true and increasingly truer that once a wage earner, always a wage earner."[22]

I cannot see any superior advantage in putting a girl at 14 behind the counter for $8 a week, where she is obliged to lunch on 15 cents till she goes to swell the number of white slaves. I cannot see the advantage or the justice in the great army of the industrial world having to spend the most of a lifetime in small, dark rented rooms or factories on a salary or a wage which is only a license to continue the same miserable existence indefinitely. The world of civilized labor is overworked and underpaid and cramped in its childhood, and when its impulses are distorted in manhood it is thrown into a dark cell, and when it falls to illness it becomes a public charge with a stigma dogging its steps to the end of life. This is the way civilized people take care of their social and economic income—the man. The white slave and the white plague are nothing more or less than glaring indications of the true conditions of your economic life. The inconsistency of a civilization which will consume billions building hospitals and asylums, and at the same time be producing inmates for them is a shock to my sense of proportion. With all his experience, with all his acumen, with all his advantages, with all his progress, with all his capital, the paleface has not settled his own problems. I cannot see the economy in introducing the deteriorated Indian into the ranks of the civilized oppressed.

I have often been asked: if the Indian is deteriorated, what is the use of trying to save him? I have not lost all hope in the possibilities of the race. His quick response to an environment that is halfway advantageous has been provided to my knowledge too many times. His pride can still be revived; his spirit can be lifted. With all he possesses in material wealth he should be given the utmost advantages of an economic environment. I have had in mind the things which are needed and which are still in his command toward this end. He has ample property, ample capital, and ample natural resources to start with.

The Lolomai Industrial Village[23]

I have searched the world of organization for the one institution which must touch the Indian at every side, which shall involve him in personal and social responsibility, which must have the power to push and to punish him justly, which must lift up his spirit and give him back his pride, which must engage him in actual employment that will teach him at every turn, which will satisfy his gregarious wants, which will give him not only legitimate amusements but also a means of livelihood, an incentive, and reward for labor. A permanent home in surroundings he may love and value, and in which he may be secure, a home in an environment which will insure to him health by a proper system of sanitation and hygiene; in short, where economic and social advantages will insure to him peace, health, education and competition for efficiency.

The Lolomi industrial village is the result of this search. The word "Lolomi" is a Hopi term which means not only "good" but [also] "beautiful."

The consensus of opinion among sociologists and economic thinkers is that as the ultimate solution to the problems of modern civilization, there is bound to be a return to the soil and the small community life against the evils of rapid urbanization, and that the way to avoid the haphazard and ugly growth of towns and cities is to plan the concentration of population beforehand and thus prevent them from growing up on false values by speculation, which is such a large feature in the growth of modern towns.

The garden cities[24] of Europe are examples of the successful and happy carrying out of these theories. Bournemouth at Birmingham, Letchworth, and Hampstead Heath are some of these in England, while Frankfurt in Germany and [blank in the original] in France are splendid examples of those on the Continent, while Garden City on Long Island, N.Y., is a fine example in this country.

While these towns were mainly built for the relief of congestion in large cities, there is nothing to prevent towns being built for the promotion of industry.

The Mormons in this country have proved beyond any doubt the feasibility of legitimately concentrating population around industries. No community knows the higher meaning of incorporation better than the Mormons. Today they are the richest people in the world.

Not so many years ago they were an oppressed and destitute people. They went to the deserts of the West and without money, demonstrated that labor rather than money is the stable capitalization of organization. Each man among them labored regardless of whether or not he was a professional man or a laborer. A combination of the various principles which have been well tried should be the bases of the Lolomi industrial village.

In England, the garden city is incorporated by special act of Parliament.

The Indian needs a protected autonomous government. To this end, he should be incorporated into these communities by a special act of Congress. And as far as the outside world is concerned, the village and industrial sites should be condemned. Till there is such a provision against graft, the Indian cannot hope to hold what he possesses in the way of town sites.

The various states of ethnic culture in the race should be one of the considerations in the system. The full-blooded Indian believes in communism. He does not understand and cannot handle other forms of property. Let us protect him in it by law, rather than by allotment and the removal of restrictions make him a target for exploitation.

For the Indian who has had his allotment, the danger of the local interests getting a hold of his shares of stock under a State charter is a very serious one. Originally it was my idea that the Indian would do better under State control than under Federal, but just such things as were contained in "the Mott report"[25] have shown me that to change from the Indian Bureau to local interests in most states is only a change in the set of grafters.

I would suggest that a minimum of 20 acres should be required to be pooled by every individual Indian of the allotted class. So that the Indian with the fee-simple title may not be interfered with in his right to sell or to leave the reservation if he wishes, but the improvidence of those who have been allotted has been so largely demonstrated that, unless some provision is made to still protect the Indian community where they are incompetent citizens, we stand a chance of having paupers on the hands of the State and county.

Were a Federal incorporation of Indian communities demonstrated to mean economic advantages and protection, it would encourage them to hold their allotments and would be the making of the great majority of the Indian population who still have their trust patents.

As to the form of capitalization, in Indian communities this should be half labor and half money; that is to say, in the charter is set the minimum number of hours out of each day each able-bodied man shall perform. With the Mormons, each community started out with communistic principles in the use of public utilities. There was the cooperative store as one of the first institutions. Upon the books of the community each man was given credit for the number of hours he labored, the same as a wage earner would be paid, only he was not paid in cash. He had credit at the store and whatever above this was left after his living came out of it was credited to him in the sinking fund. The part the capitalization of the money half would play would be the paying for the medium of the industry or industries to be established, the home, and the installation of public utilities; that is, water, sewage, light, and heat systems should be out in by the corporation.

Contracts for the building of comfortable and artistic homes should be left to architects after an open competition, and that the city Lolomi would be complete before it is entered by its inhabitants. The site for the residences should be picked, where there are trees and water and natural attractiveness, and at least 1 or 2 acre spaces between each home reserved. An out-of-door sanitarium or a hospital should be built where a community is diseased.

In another part of the village should be the markets, the cooperative store, a savings bank, the theater, the cooperative kitchen, and such other institutions as may be necessary. In a zone outside the village should be the work gardens. If the community is agricultural, the plowing and the cultivating should be done by steam plows and adequate implements to carry off the work with dispatch. A scientific agriculturist should ride a horse up and down and supervise each man's labor.

If it is a pastoral community, an expert stockman should supervise who understands market conditions as well as other things. The Indian has money to pay for brains and efficiency. Men of large organizations are worth their large salaries, and it is time we turned to them.

As to the form of representation, the large capitalist has usurped power in corporations because he has as many votes as he has shared. If the Rochdale system[26] of one-man, one vote were established, this evil would be done away with, while the progressive man who acquires more stock than the backward one can have his income according to his deserts.

It would take seventy-five million to install such a system as this throughout every Indian reservation in the country, but when once such industries were started on this scale, they would be self-sustaining, and the only changes of failure would be in bad management. A vigilant board of directors, composed of men of incorruptible character, could handle this end, and if such a system deteriorated into another source of low-browed plunder, it would be conclusive proof that the character of the American Nation is incorrigible, and it would be time for the American Indian to take his last stand regardless of consequences. Till a red-blooded economic system enters the desert of the reservation, where hope is dead because oppression, sickness, and poverty in all their unloveliness rule, all the money appropriated for the civilization of the Indian under paternalism is so much thrown away.

Till the Indian home has running water and proper ventilation, till the Indian mother knows the lessons of hygiene and sanitation, till the father is encouraged and rewarded for right effort, and secured in his possessions and his home against the harassment of exploitation by the local grafter and paternalism, till children can stay at home during their tender years and have educational attention without being taught to lose their race respect, till the Indian family has plenty to eat and plenty to wear and right influences around it, till we meet depletion with nutrition, helplessness with self-support, till we meet destruction with construction, till we teach the young generation back their race respect, and teach them to discriminate between the good and bad things of this civilization, we shall not only continue to need appropriations, but there is fast approaching the time when the unsuspecting citizen of the country will have to pay for the barbarities, the ruination, the pauperization of the grandest type of primitive man.

Senator GRONNA:[27] Mrs. Kellogg, did I understand you to say that you advocate among the Indians the economical and ethical system employed by the Mormons, or did I misunderstand you?

Mrs. KELLOGG: The Industrial system only. I am not versed in the ethical questions of the Mormon institution. I do not advocate Mormonism, but I certainly do the industrial system of the Mormons.

Senator GRONNA: You referred to the industrial system?

Mrs. KELLOGG: Yes, sir.

Senator ROBINSON:[28] Would you withdraw all Government supervision of every kind?

Mrs. KELLOGG: I most certainly would not. I would withdraw the supervision of an inferior Bureau, with its personnel of people who do not understand the large questions involved in race deterioration.

Senator ROBINSON: What kind of supervision would you substitute?

Mrs. KELLOGG: I have suggested here that Congress should pass a special act incorporating these Indians.

Senator ROBINSON: I understood that.

Mrs. KELLOGG: Now, the thing that I suggest would be a civic federation board.

Senator ROBINSON: Would they be Federal officers or merely citizens?

Mrs. KELLOGG: Both.

Senator ROBINSON: Why both?

Mrs. KELLOGG: Because the legislative side would intelligently come to such people as are on the outside, and who do not understand always the complexities of the system to be undone.

Senator ROBINSON: Is that not practically the system, the fundamental system that exists now? We have the Board of Indian Commissioners, you know, and we have the Bureau of Indian Affairs.

Mrs. KELLOGG: I certainly would not recommend that the Board of Indian Commissioners should be taken as an effective achievement of the other side.

Senator ROBINSON: I do not mean to criticize, or to approve, either. I simply call your attention to the fact that now we have a dual system of control. We have a board of commissioners who are prominent citizens of such high character that they are calculated to inspire respect and confidence, men who have given their lives, or the greater part of it, to the sociological and economic questions, and in addition to that now we have the Bureau service, which you have condemned. Now, suppose that this system, which you suggest is established, and that in one given locality does not prove an economic success, what would be your suggestion then? What assurance have you, in other words, that it would be successful?

Mrs. KELLOGG: I have the idea that it would not fail as a system. Wherever the Indians have brought themselves together naturally in villages, you never find want and pauperism there.

Senator ROBINSON: You are proceeding to recognize, then, what we understand to be the natural method of life of the Indian?

Mrs. KELLOGG: Exactly.

Senator ROBINSON: It is true, however, that there is a wide divergence in character between the different tribes of Indians, is there not?

Mrs. KELLOGG: Yes, sir; there is. I have spoken of the four stages of development and—

Senator ROBINSON: Take the Indians as they actually exist; some of them are far shrewder, perhaps, than others?

Mrs. KELLOGG: Yes, Senator.

Senator ROBINSON: And some of them have a very much higher standard of personal character than others?

Mrs. KELLOGG: That is true.

Senator ROBINSON: Now, then, the economic system or plan which you have might work with a certain class and might probably fail with the inferior class. What would be your plan?

Mrs. KELLOGG: My plan is to make this system so elastic that it would cover every condition, and that it should be established only after a thorough investigation, such as this committee proposes, of every locality where the social conditions are taken note of, and the grade of intelligence and ability and the tendencies toward certain industries taken into account. There is not a group in the United States that I have ever seen that will not respond to some effort for their benefit. They are tired of the roving, wandering life and persecution, and when you introduce a system where you build them up on a foundation which, if they would perpetuate, it would give them the comforts and the necessaries of life, it would to my mind be successful.

Senator ROBINSON: Have any experiments been made along the line of the plans you have suggested with the Indians?

Mrs. KELLOGG: There is a very splendid example. I discovered it just recently in Shiprock, New Mexico, where the Indian agent who went there happened to be a [R]ed-blooded man and he took those Indians who were going the way of the other Indians and he bought cattle for them, bought thoroughbred stock and took off his high collar and went out and actually labored with those Indians side by side in the field, with the result that they are coming up in a most remarkable way. The response is tremendous.

Senator LANE:[29] Up on the coast of Alaska there is a village colony that is a self-sustaining colony, is there not, Mr. Commissioner?

Commissioner ABBOTT: I do not know about that. That is not in our jurisdiction.

Mrs. KELLOGG: As I was saying, in giving them a limited area, I would never, for instance, give the Indian in the nomadic stage more than 5 acres of land to take care of, but truck farming in any part of the country is successful around these Indian localities. Take farming in the way it is carried out by scientific agriculture today, it would give them all the living that they require and more, and just the moment you build them up to that stage they would begin to develop and clamor for more. It has been proved by statistics in agriculture that 3 acres is sufficient to maintain a family of five in truck products.

Senator ROBINSON: You would not advocate the striking out of this provision until some better system is devised; you would not advocate abolishing the Bureau now.

Mrs. KELLOGG: No. I want to be understood, with regard to the measures that I propose, that we most certainly would not cut this off without substitution. That change must only be gradual, and I think this committee is on the high way to the accomplishment of the biggest thing that has ever been done in Indian history in this country when it proposes a thorough investigation based on scientific facts so that we know what we proceed from and what to avoid, and to see what institutions were to be taken hold of. I welcome that investigation most warmly as the first step. It is one of those reforms that I have suggested before. I have a list of four of those that I will mention briefly. The first would be the investigation; second, the creation of a social-service department in the present bureau.

Senator ROBINSON: What does "social service" mean?

Mrs. KELLOGG: It means such a department as university settlement work. That is the thing I had in mind, putting university settlement work in the Indian Bureau. That is to say, take people who have been trained to looking into social conditions among people who are not upon their feet, people who have already studied these questions—let them come in and look upon the Indian from that standpoint and get statistics, not only on his status as a ward, but as to his local needs, and his standards of living.

Senator ROBINSON: After all, the uplift of any race, like the uplift of any individual, must come rather from within than from without.

Mrs. KELLOGG: Exactly.

Senator ROBINSON: You can spend a million dollars and have your high-strung theories, and create your boards and abolish them, but until you inspire credit and hope and confidence in the heart of the Indian, he will continue to deteriorate.

Mrs. KELLOGG: Just so.

Senator ROBINSON: It then simply becomes a question as to what is the best process, and what are the best means of accomplishing that end.

Mrs. KELLOGG: Exactly.

Senator ROBINSON: I presume the theories that you advance here you are not wedded to further than to believe that they would constitute an advance over the present system.

Mrs. KELLOGG: I have lived all my life on a reservation; that is, except what periods I have been away at school and abroad and traveling, and my experience has been that the self-help of the Indian has got to emanate from within. We have got to get hold of his psychology. As an example of this, the best people in the land do not understand the Indian. He himself—this present generation of Government school Indians—do not understand themselves, but you take the old Indian and he will tell you out of his own philosophy the things that are the matter with the race, what is best for the Indian. He has his own idea as to what he would do if he could.

For example: here is an instance that [I] came across in Colorado. A man, who was very well disposed toward Indians, came to their assistance; and he brought them to me. He said, "Something must be done for these Indians; they are starving on the Great Divide." In the course of the conversation, I proposed this very measure—the building of little industrial communities among them. He said, "You cannot do that. The Indian does not get over this fact that he will be forever hampered by certain superstitions which he himself has." He said, "Wherever an Indian dies in this community, they burn up his house. If you had a $1500 cottage there, how many of those could you be building with a habit like that?" I called those people aside, and I asked them their own point of view about it. I said, "You do not defend yourselves against these charges when they are made. Now, is that true?" The chief answered, "Over there on the Great Divide we have no brick, no mortar, no lumber; our houses are put together with anything we can lay our hands on, and the ax and mud, and the result is they are ugly structures, full of dust and dirt and holes, and when an Indian dies, we are afraid if somebody else will go and live in his house he will die of the same disease."

Senator ROBINSON: You were interrupted a while ago when you were announcing your third suggestion. You said you had four on your notes?

Mrs. KELLOGG: Yes, Senator. Third, I want to have an appropriation of $100,000 or $150,000 for college education for Indians. That is one of the great lacks in the race. I know hundreds of Indian students who are clamoring and anxious to get a college education who have positively no way of getting it, no money to pay even their transportation to the universities.

Senator ROBINSON: That is also true of thousands of white people—

Mrs. KELLOGG: But you have your colleges—I did not mean to interrupt you.

Senator ROBINSON: I was just going to say that to me that is not the larger side of the question—the higher education of the Indian— because my observation has been that, when one advanced far enough and has the advantages of education, he has the usual advantages to obtain it in some way.

Mrs. KELLOGG: Some of them will go to the Indian service, and it takes forever to lay enough by for this purpose. The years of youth have passed away before enough can be accumulated with which to get university training, and particularly for the Indian, he should be put upon a ground of advantage in that for the reason that the whole world outside is obsessed with the idea that he cannot do things. If he were to go to the university and wash dishes on the side for his living, his energies would be deflected and not focused upon the things he is trying to accomplish when he already is under disadvantage.

Senator TOWNSEND: What is the object of having these spe-cially-educated Indians? What would you expect of them, especially?

Mrs. KELLOGG: I know this much, that the moment you edu-cate an Indian individual as far as going through the university, that we are done with the Indian problem as far as that individual is concerned.

Senator ROBINSON: What advantage is it to the Indian race?

Mrs. KELLOGG: If we educated every one of them, we would not have any Indian problem. You have to develop leadership—

Senator ROBINSON: But you cannot do that with any particular number of them under the present state of affairs.

Mrs. KELLOGG: The principle is this—

Senator ROBINSON: Have you observed that the college-bred Indian is a benefactor to his race? I mean peculiarly helpful to his race, or does he follow the bent of the higher white civilization and leave his race rather than tend to help them?

Mrs. KELLOGG: They usually come home and try to do something for the race, and then they fall flat. They fail because they are working against a system that is perfectly hopeless, and one man cannot do it without assistance from either legislation or a large fund to work with. The environment of deficits must be changed to meet the average college training. The fourth suggestion is with regard to the health department—the transfer of the health department into the public-health service. That was a suggestion made by Mr. Sloan.[30]

Senator ROBINSON: You have discussed that?

Mrs. KELLOGG: Yes, sir.

Senator GRONNA: You believe in the reservation schools—these boarding schools that you refer to, do you?

Mrs. KELLOGG: Yes, decidedly. I think they are way ahead of the boarding schools. The child coming home at night to the father and mother brings with him something for them to think about. I think the day school—the country day school—as an institution of the land is a very splendid one.

Before closing I want to say that this system I propose, of course, would be subject to an investigation and to an adjustment of itself to the conditions of the locality that it involved but the fundamental principles of it, I believe, would apply to all reservation Indians.

That is all I care to say.

Mrs. Kellogg was thereupon excused.

Statement, US Senate Committee on Indian Affairs (1916)

Statement of Mrs. Laura Cornelius Kellogg

[In her testimony, Kellogg calls for a congressional "scientific investigation" to uncover the demonstrated incompetence in the Indian Bureau. She also presents her proposal for industrial development and for instituting a policy of self-help, expressing the wish to "continue the common ownership of the tribe."]

Recall of Agents or Superintendents by Indian Tribes Hearings before the United States Senate Committee on Indian Affairs

Mrs. KELLOGG: Mr. Chairman, I have a bill that I think is apropos to this discussion here. I do not intend to introduce it for the next 30 days. I have been working on it for many years, and I want to say with regard to Senator Johnson's[31] bill and Senator Lane's[32] bill that my plan does not subscribe to theirs, while I think the spirit of their bill is very splendid and is something that is bound to come. But it seems to me rather piecemeal legislation. It does identically the thing that Senator Page[33] has mentioned—it proposes to try it out on a group of Indians who are very well prepared for this sort of thing. My bill goes back to the principle that was suggested by somebody else, that you cannot make any kind of gain with respect to the Indian situation without getting radically down to the root of the evils.

I want to say this in regard to the investigations that have taken place by congressional committees. There has never been anything

64th Congress, First CIS Hearings (64) S. 53, 1916, pp. 4–15. Kellogg's statement and discussion begin on page 9 and end on page 15.

like a scientific investigation. Men have gone out there and have had hearings. You may take volumes and volumes of that kind of testimony and you can go on with your investigation indefinitely, but when it comes to getting the consensus of opinion or the consensus of the facts of the situation, you cannot do it unless you make a house-to-house campaign and count the evils and count the number of times they appear and take into consideration the conditions with respect to them.

Now, that is what I have done, and I have learned to look at this matter rather coldly, for the reason that I have tried everything else and found nothing else to do. As far as the work of philanthropy is concerned, it has always failed for the simple reason, as Senator Walsh has just stated, that it does not give to those people the handling of their own business matters originally. Unless a bill is founded on an economic basis, I see no solution to anything, however high-minded or however ideal in spirit it may be.

As to [. . .] Senator Lane's bill, I have found a public sentiment that is as much on the side of the bill as it is against the parties we are hearing from in the press. The public sentiment in this country is ready to condemn the Indian situation in the hands of the Government, and what is more, we are not going to subscribe to it. We are not going to be indefinitely the puppets of another race, and that is exactly that we have to look forward to nothing but pauperism. This is a proposition that is based upon government, that is going to be a self-government, and not in opposition to the principles of democracy, and if it is done, I begin to see a little hope, and I think we will stand the searchlight of public sentiment.

I have this feeling about the Secretary of the Interior. I have great faith in his ability and in his spirit for right provided a program was presented to him to which he could subscribe. But nothing has ever been done like that. Nothing has ever been said to the people of the country on which they have been asked for more than their vote and their intelligence upon it. Philanthropists have gone out there and said they would give $5,000 for a lot of starving Indians. They have repeatedly told me what the $5,000 did: "I am merely subscribing to a condition that will come up again next year," and that is the difference between the scientific social service and philanthropy that is given at random.

In the investigations of the joint commission, I think Senator Lane was responsible for one of the biggest documents that was ever brought to the enlightenment of the public—that is the Document No. 65 which was printed by the Bureau of Municipal Research and Investigation of Business Methods of the Indian Bureau.[34] That document would convince anybody that the present order of things has got to go, and I say this, that whether this bill or mine passes or not, the time has come when the Indian will have to resort to the same measures that the labor movements have resorted to and that the Russians resorted to 10 years ago in Russia. We will not be under the yoke of a government that is unjust, that is as flimsy, that is as hopeless, and that is as ruinous as the present one, and I wish to be heard within the next 30 days, Mr. Chairman, upon that point.

I think if there is a spirit here to cooperate with a measure that would hold water, that that is the measure. I have spent a good many years of my time on it and I have gotten the opinions of many men who have engaged in large investigations like the Bureau of Municipal Research, and all of them have pronounced it very feasible and to be the economic solution to the problem.

Senator CURTIS:[35] I judge, Mr. Chairman, from what Senator Page said a moment ago, that he thought perhaps I was in favor of this measure. I want to state that I have not committed myself to this measure at all. I want to help the Indians, if I can do so, get in a position where they could file their complaints and be heard without danger. [. . .]

Mrs. KELLOGG: Senator Curtis, I want to ask what is the objection to keeping an Indian an Indian provided he is a better Indian than he is a white man?

Senator CURTIS: There is no objection to that, but what I meant was that they wanted to keep him under their control all the time. Of course, you cannot change an Indian if he is an Indian. But the Government wants to keep him under its fingers all the time. [. . .]

Mrs. KELLOGG: Senator Walsh,[36] you might mention another point there, that when you classify the Indians, you have Indians who believe in communities, Indians who want allotments, Indians who want their funds outright, and Indians who want citizenship right away, so you cannot always go on the basis of competency as other things come in.

Senator CURTIS: That was the point I made a moment ago.

Mrs. KELLOGG: There are a great many Indians who want to be withdrawn or who rather want the restrictions removed, who are really not competent to take care of themselves. Instances of that character occur on reservations everywhere. The landed interests, the merchants, come and work these Indians up and get a certain amount of money from them—what they have. So that is again a question that would enter very largely in the equation. I have provided in this bill that a system of "communizing," as I call it, shall be worked out, whereby we eliminate the man who has no sympathies with the man who wants to have communal holdings.

Senator CURTIS: But you continue the common ownership of the tribe?

Mrs. KELLOGG: Yes, sir; I continue the common ownership.

Senator CURTIS: Both money and property?

Mrs. KELLOGG: Both money and property; yes, sir.

Senator CURTIS: They get the common money and the common property of the tribe?

Mrs. KELLOGG: Yes, sir; and there is provision made to promote those things. Now, on the other hand, as to the colonizing of these other individuals, I would like to see that worked out to some such way as Untermeyer[37] and Jacob Schiff[38] have worked it out for the Jews in New York. They have gone to any young man who is worthy and said to him: "Here is $200. There is a very splendid colony in Illinois or Wisconsin. We must return to the soil. You go out there and look over this proposition. We will take for you a farm and stock it and put improvements on it, and it will be in running order when you step into it."

Senator CURTIS: Has that proven a success or not?

Mrs. KELLOGG: Yes; so I am told.

Senator CURTIS: The movement in Colorado was a failure, I was told.

Mrs. KELLOGG: Well, I was told by people who ought to know, that it worked out splendidly.

Senator CURTIS: In Wisconsin and other states?

Mrs. KELLOGG: Yes, sir; in the agricultural belt.

Senator CURTIS: I have no personal information about the Colorado scheme; I was told that it was very successful for a year but of late it had not been successful.

Senator WALSH: I agree that in any plan suggested here there should be a constant incentive to the incompetent to qualify himself to get into the competent class.

Senator CURTIS: That is what I had in view.

Mrs. KELLOGG: The organization as it goes on has a banking system attached to it out of the Indian moneys, and it carries with it also a life insurance, and in that way we are not speculating with the Indian's money. Also, with regard to the men who have perhaps $500 or $1,000 or $2,000, whatever it may be, we start them according to their own abilities but with that foundation, and we will be eventually able to take care of the Indian who has not anything but himself if he is a good man.

Senator JOHNSON: Well, Mr. Chairman, what is the disposition of the members of the committee with regard to this bill? Senator Clapp and Senator Curtis, as I take it, raised practically the same point, only expressing it in a little different way.

Senator CLAPP:[39] I do not think there is any contention. I think myself that the complaint might perhaps be better made by the majority of an assembly. I see some advantages in the other way, but there are some advantages in its being done in that way. There is no real contention upon the subject. I quite agree with Senator Curtis, I do not see why this should be done in any spirit of hostility to the department. [. . .]

Testimony before Senate Subcommittee on Senate Resolution 79

Survey of Conditions of the Indians in the United States (1929)

[Kellogg's testimony is part of a larger contingent of Haudenosaunee leaders from New York State testifying about the conditions they face, raising issues that will continue to be of importance throughout the twentieth century. Kellogg's husband, Orrin J. Kellogg, also testifies, providing historical, political, and financial contexts of their activism on behalf of Haudenosaunee people. Besides giving her own testimony, Kellogg translates for another Haudenosaunee leader, Chief Oak, who does not speak English. She responds sharply to the criticisms of the Bureau of Indian Affairs members about her work in Native communities, arguing that Native people are capable of making decisions about who can best help them. She turns allegations of fraud against her back at the Bureau employees, whom—in her direct and characteristic style—she calls "anaemic, slimy fingered, hothouse fellows." She also advocates for a continued "protected autonomy" status of Native tribes and a continued relationship with the federal government.]

Hearings before a Subcommittee of the Committee on Indian Affairs

[The subcommittee met, pursuant to the call of the chairman at 10 o'clock a.m., in the room of the committee in the Senate Office

US Senate, 71st Cong., 2d sess. (March 1, 1929), 4857–925.

Building, Senator Lynn J. Frazier[40] presiding. Present: senators Frazier (chairman), Pine,[41] Wheeler,[42] and Thomas[43] of Oklahoma.]

The CHAIRMAN: The hearing will come to order. This hearing was called especially to hear, or at least at the request of, Mr. and Mrs. Kellogg, from New York State. They have been down here for some time, and have insisted on a hearing, and we are glad to give them a hearing; but this is called at their request, and especially for the purpose of hearing them and some other witnesses that they have here. The first witness on this list I have is Mrs. Laura C. Kellogg.]

Testimony of Mrs. Laura Cornelius Kellogg

(The witness was sworn by the chairman.)

The CHAIRMAN: Kindly give your name and address to the reporter.

Mrs. KELLOGG: Laura Cornelius Kellogg, Seymour, Wis., and Syracuse, N.Y. I am of the Oneida Nation.

I come before you, gentlemen of the committee, with what I have to say condensed into three parts. I represent the Six Nations of New York. I am executive secretary of the Six Nations.[44]

The CHARIMAN: Very well, proceed.

Mrs. KELLOGG: The first part deals with the serious situation among the Six Nations of New York, created by the fact that the Six Nations have valuable properties which are being thrown into jeopardy because those who covet them are using powerful political means and propaganda to oust them from their rights, and because the Six Nations, while they offer a tenacious resistance, are not properly protected. They are a people who have wonderful traditions, who are organized, and who have a superior legal status peculiar to Indian relations; one which they have faithfully kept, and one which entitles them to the highest protection in the land, the protection of the United States Government.

I shall attempt to show how, historically, they became entitled to this protection; how the courts and the Six Nations interpret that protection and what has been their experience lately in seeking it. Secondly, I shall present an Indian reconstruction program which the Six

Nations have adopted for their own rebuilding and which I believe solves every other Indian problem in the land. Thirdly, I shall show in detail how the Six Nations contemplate carrying this out. Now, I am going to offer here, Senator Frazier, a history of the Six Nations, which is too long to read this morning.

The CHAIRMAN: Very well; it will be printed in the record. (The statement referred to will be found printed at the end of this day's proceedings.)

Mrs. KELLOGG: I am going to proceed into the heart of the reasons why we are here, introducing it only with such bits of history as are connected with the treaty relations between the Six Nations and the United States Government, upon which a lot of their troubles are hanging.

Here are a group of Indians, 16,000 in all, occupying some 78,000 acres in reservations in New York or colonized in small groups in Western States and in Canada. Their legal status is peculiar to Indian relations. They have a treaty with the United States Government which gives them the status of an independent protectorate of the United States under this treaty of 1784,[45] confirmed and added to in their treaty of 1789.[46] They are a protected autonomy, with the title of the original territory vested in them, and United States protection absolutely guaranteed to them. In specific language the United States ceded all right and title to them to territory they reserved to themselves out of their Iroquois domain, in return for their ceding all right and title in the Ohio Valley to the United States Government.

This peculiarity of status came from remarkable circumstances. In the first place, the Six Nations Iroquois had a superior social order, a civilization of their own when the white men came. According to our own history, corroborated by Spanish, French, English, and Dutch historians, their domain extended from Canada as far as Montreal and the Great Lakes to the Carolinas, Florida, and west to the Mississippi and Tennessee, with an irregular eastern boundary running into the southern part of the New England States. They had acquired this territory by conquest from other tribes, and they had many tribes under their protection from whom they collected tribute in kind.

Prior to the Revolution they met and treated with foreign nations as do other nations of the world. They sold the most of this territory to the Dutch and the English and Pennsylvania giving the warranty deed in each instance. They reserved for themselves and their posterity in their last transaction with the English in 1768, a tract containing some 18,000,000 acres in the States of New York and Pennsylvania plus the Ohio Valley, set aside by the English survey known as the Sir William Johnson line of property[47] in their last treaty with Great Britain prior to the Revolution. The Revolutionary War came on, and with the experience of the English people in the French and Indian War[—]where one of their historians truthfully said of the Six Nations' part in it, "Our victories are purchased at the expense of their blood"[—]both Great Britain and the United Colonies solicited for their assistance.

Both were able to get some, though the majority of the Six Nations remained neutral. Early in the war the English, who through the late Sir William Johnson had a great hold on Gen. Joseph Brant,[48] were able to get the alliance of those who would follow Brant.

Upon this break in their ranks, the Oneidas pleaded with the Six Nations that they could end the war by allying themselves with General Washington.

However, the Six Nations said, "This is a conflict between father and son. We have been friends to both; we will take part in the conflict between them on neither side."

However, as time went on, as the Revolutionary conflict became intense and it was fought over their territory, the Oneidas were nearly wiped out by General Butler[49] in one of their villages. They broke neutrality on this occasion immediately, and took with them all the fighting men they had and those of the Stockbridges and Brothertowns, their adopted people, and those of the Tuscarora Nation.[50] Your historians say that the Revolutionary War was won with the help from these people. The relations between the Six Nations and the people of the United States followed.

Some years after the treaty of 1784 was concluded, the State of New York, despite the constitutional provision against any State making separate treaties with other nations, made separate treaties with the individual nations of the Six Nations; fraudulently and criminally over the protest of General Washington to Governor Clinton these transactions went on. Rum was used to get the signatures of individual Indians, who in many instances were nearly white men and who had no authority or ability to sell. The United States Government, however, has never O.K.'d one of these transactions.[51]

Out of these 18,000,000 acres that the Six Nations had reserved for themselves out of their enormous domain, together with the Ohio Valley, there is left today only 78,000 acres in the State of New York in their small reservations; and now they are being threatened with eviction practically from their homes in these small reservations.

Mr. MERRITT:[52] May I ask by whom?

Mrs. KELLOGG: Yes, I am going to tell that. At this moment the citizens of Syracuse have introduced a bill in Albany—with the assistance of your Commissioner of Indian Affairs, so they claim—whereby these citizens are going to take these lands from the Onondaga Indians, which form a tract 4 miles square, near Syracuse through the State of New York.

The CHAIRMAN: Yes, with authority?

Mrs. KELLOGG: They are soliciting the government of the State to help them secure a dam site on the Onondaga Reservation, which would mean the flooding out of the Onondagas, because it is the most economical way that the city of Syracuse can protect itself from the flood waters of Onondaga Creek.

As a matter of fact, I think Mayor Hanna[53] has been down here to consult with Commissioner Burke[54] on this question, I am informed, and in that case the citizens have gone to the Onondagas and spoken to them and told them that they were going to get this over there for $15 an acre, because they had the Commissioner of Indian Affairs to assist them get it.

Now, we want to call the attention of this committee to the fact that the Commissioner of Indian Affairs has no just and proper relations with the Six Nations Indians. Under their treaty of 1784, there was never a hint of their being brought under any kind of control under a bureau. They had the right of self-determination that the bureau would necessarily cut off. They have never subsequently made any different arrangement with the United States Government themselves. So, the original agreement of 1784[55] stands as it was made, today.

We, of course, are very solicitous of this committee that some sort of protection be given us at this particular moment, because if we are not helped all these influences which have started since six years ago to oust us out of our rights will continue, depriving us of our right to self-determination with the connivance of the Bureau of Indian Affairs. The very moment that the Six Nations introduced a program of self-reconstruction there, an enormous propaganda was brought on, with paid agents, we do not know of whom, whether by the States or whether these individual politicians who are interested in the lands we wish to recover, or whether it is with the direct understanding between them and the bureau. We do know this: that every influence which can approach the Six Nations, and that has done so, has gone to the bureau and gotten the sanction of the bureau for assistance on their side. We do not know that the bureau reaches out clear to Canada in its sinister suggestions as to what shall be done to those of us who are trying to exercise our autonomy. I want to say, in connection with this experience, that I, personally, with other citizens of the Six Nations, was arrested like an ordinary thief and brought before a foreign court, in Canada, and the arrest was based upon the fact that the Six Nations people were located, a part of them, in Canada, before there was a white man on this continent, and that these same groups of the Mohawks were still on that side of the St. Lawrence, on that side of the survey that divided them into Canada, later, under the Jay treaty,[56] when they were United States subjects.

This state of affairs we do not recognize, because there is only one relation which we do recognize, and that is that relation between us and the Government of the United States of 1784. All others have been fraudulently gotten.

This status allows the Six Nations in their reconstruction program to go to any part where their citizens may have gone, whether it be over the Canadian border or in Oklahoma or Kansas or any other State where they may have been colonizing, and solicit through their council the assistance under this reconstruction program, about which I am going to speak later, because it has relation to the enormous litigation we started.

We were arrested in Canada on the ground that we were soliciting money under false pretenses, and that there was a conspiracy to defraud the Mohawk people who, through their councils, had accepted our proposal and had assented to the levies made for this particular purpose, which in each instance were not exorbitant. A propaganda was started on the ground that here were these thieves who were filling their pockets with money because we had instituted the policy of self-help, having discovered this protected autonomy through an action in the court. We decided we were sick of the conditions of Indian life, we were sick of poverty on every hand; we were sick of ignorance and of our inability; we were sick of the influence that opposed us at every turn. There is not a man with any degree of initiative in him that has any kind of credit among all Indian peoples, including the Six Nations, who does not feel this. We are sick, all the Indians of the United States, of our being forced into that status practically by the action of the bureau, of everlastingly being submerged like penitentiary wards of the United States Government. We are sick of being plagued with the white man's filthy diseases; we are sick of being held down until we are plucked of everything that we possessed; we called our original people together, the chiefs of the great confederacy, and we said, "We will take inventory. Let us see what we are able to do. Here is our legal status. From there on it is our fault if we do not make some legal progress, when we have everything that any group of Indians need in the United States to go on with a program of self-help."

We made a survey of our population on the reservations, of the assets, of our man power, of the particular kinds of minerals, and what properties there were, and we ended up by recognizing one other thing which is prevalent among all Indians of any part of the United States, and that is the development of sycophants among us, so that it makes us hopelessly unable to ever do anything with ourselves, without a few of these English-speaking pinch-back men[57] among us everlastingly in the pockets of the white men, who have the bureau standing right behind them in every instance. There is not a group of Indians in the United States which is not always having help given to, that is trying to do away with Indians. They are the fellows who always get the help from the bureau. They are the fellows that are everlastingly filling their pockets from outside for destroying the rest of us. They put on fine clothes because they have fine jobs; and, when tourists come along, what happens is that the bureau points to them as "progressive Indians."

Now, there is a system of espionage growing up in this country that is alarming in its extent. In this most subtle way the Commission of Indian Affairs suggested to the Commissioner of Indian Affairs, on the Canadian side, in this instance to see that we were put into trouble, and I told you what it all ended up in. We brought our case before one of the biggest courts in Montreal. We secured the biggest criminal attorney in Montreal. We had had no hearing in the United States in our case. All the propagandists joined hands to throttle the Six Nations because they had the protection of a court that went into the facts, and our case was tried, and the outcome of that trial was that we were never even called on the witness stand. The thing was so flimsy that the jury was for us, and they brought in a verdict of not guilty; and when the distinguished judge gave his instruction to the jury, he used these words:

"I am not surprised that the Six Nations should look for more and more independence. They say they have the right of self-government. There is no doubt of it. They have just as much right to govern themselves as the legislature of the Province of Quebec or as a municipality has to make its own laws."

The CHAIRMAN: How long ago was this case?

Mrs. KELLOGG: That was a year ago last October; and in a communication which we will present to the committee upon this investigation of these facts, we shall introduce before you letters from Commissioner Burke wherein he suggested that his inspection force should be used in seeing—

Mr. KELLOGG: If they could find anything.

Mrs. KELLOGG. They did not find anything. I want to say this. We charge the Indian Bureau with propaganda, pernicious propaganda, criminal propaganda. They acknowledged it themselves on the witness stand in Montreal. They sent one of their anaemic, slimy fingered, hothouse fellows over there, and when he got on the witness stand he was compelled to tell that the Bureau of Indian Affairs has instituted propaganda against the Six Nations, and when our attorney asked him how much money he had used in this propaganda, he stated that it was not much, but enough to employ one man and for the printing of that literature.

We want this commission to look into this fact. We suspect that this Indian Bureau's propaganda over the United States to deceive the public as to the wonderful things it does for the Indians has some fund behind it somewhere that we do not know about, and we want to know if our protector, the United States Government, is spending money to have somebody vilify us before the public, and to incriminate us in court and exterminate us in this country. (Addressing Mr. Merritt) I do not know how you dare go about unescorted, but—

Mr. KELLOGG: Do not.

Mrs. KELLOGG: I want to get some of the important things here. I understand our time is limited. I am not through with all these things, but I want to hasten on so that I may give some of the other delegates who are here some time to say something.

There is some fact connected with the fact [that] the Six Nations [have] brought forth a reconstruction program for themselves wherein they made up their minds to do this. They were going to incorporate, entirely outside of politics, a trust instituted to take care of all their assets, and this trust would become the banker not alone to the Six Nations but to all the Indians of the United States, through which they may pursue the securing of their liberties. This trust would have under it, separately incorporated, model villages which would take care of the social side of the problem, all of the health questions, and all of the social questions like education, morals, recreation—all those things were to be controlled by that. They have, right now, this idea of locating this model village community at the Onondaga reservation in Syracuse, which is a most beautiful spot for such a thing. This is also the capital of the Six Nations.

We went about, first of all, to clean house. We had corrupt chiefs in our councils that had been in there, instituted by outside influences, and with the help of the Indian Bureau with white agents who are always running around after something we have got, whether it be the elimination of somebody who might be a possible leader, whether it be properties, in one form or another, whether it be influence of some kind, whether it be the character of the people—

The CHAIRMAN: What do you mean by "white agents"?

Mrs. KELLOGG: I mean white agents; that they were introduced the moment we started litigation. There showed up a man who was trying to dictate to the Onondaga Council to hire a certain man who was an attorney, sure enough, in the State of New York, and that when the Six Nations caught onto the fact that this man was committed to a program of helping the State of New York and that he wanted to get the contract in order to submerge us—

The CHAIRMAN: You did not mean, then, that it was an agent from the Indian Department here, or anything of that kind?

Mrs. KELLOGG: No, but I want to say that they are always in touch with the Indian Bureau; they always get their inspiration, at least, out of the Indian Bureau. There has been money transferred in this propaganda; and we have known people who have passed checks— at least, some of our people have—and we had a detective who was present when it was done in one instance, with the white, paid agent, who, by the way, is out in the propaganda. He claims to be one of the best friends the Six Nations have.

Now I want to get back to this question of intervention.

Before I leave this, I want to charge here that we believe there is a coalition between the Bureau and those political interests in the State of New York against the Six Nations. We want it looked into. We started this litigation to recover 18,000,000 acres of land in the States of New York and Pennsylvania, out of which we have hoped to get a settlement from some court enough for our reconstruction program.

I want to stay off your legal ground, Mr. Kellogg, so that you will have that to present.

In going about to do that, the Six Nations started litigation for the recovery of these 18,000,000 acres of land. All trouble immediately started. They were entitled to United States intervention. Their attorneys came up here, and we have come up here to Capitol Hill, and they have gone to the departments, and when they went to look over the ground, they found that the Solicitor General of the Interior Department had taken the recent stand that the Six Nations had intervention coming from the United States. Our Wall Street attorneys had solicited this of the Department of Justice, and the assistants in the Department of Justice likewise all agreed that we have intervention coming from the United States.

Just the moment that a telegram was sent by the Assistant Attorney General of the United States to the United States attorney at Syracuse for the northern district of New York, to intervene on behalf of the Six Nations, the assistant attorney general of the State of New York came down here and stopped the Department of Justice from acknowledging that intervention was our due. In one of their letters, of which there are several, written by the Attorney General to attorneys and to friends of ours who had pressed him for his opinion on this matter, he expressed several different opinions. On one occasion it is laches.[58] Now, laches was definitely disposed of by the Boylan case[59] in the appellate court. It was decided the question of laches did not operate against the United States as the guardian of the Six Nations. The effect of this state of affairs whereby we have no machinery to come and speak to the United States Government about our trouble, is that we were denied a hearing before the Senate Indian Affairs Committee by Senator Harreld,[60] because we had no legislative bill before this committee. We went to different places, and finally we should have gone, I think to the Judiciary Committee, at last, had it not been for the institution of this committee.

The effect upon the social life, upon the everyday life, of these Indians in these reservations is something that we cannot endure and we will not endure. Right now, after we have exercised the first right of self-determination, white agents are busy at night handing out money to our eliminated chiefs, the chiefs that we have thrown out of our council because of this corruption. We decided upon one thing at the meeting on our program, that if the Indians of the United States were ever going to get anywhere, it could not come from the outside; it would have to be an internal organization of the tribe. At the present time nobody is able to get a consensus of opinion out of the Indians, because of the bureau's selected pets who constitute business committees, all of which are against the regular institution on the basis of councils, who have plenty to say, and who know what they want, but are never even permitted to come to Washington.

On the Onondaga, they drew us into a petty trial over the question of who was the authority on the Onondaga Reservation. There was no change in that personnel except for the elimination of seven or eight chiefs other than the head chief. Nevertheless, we have been in the courts, and the income from the Onondaga sand-bed leases has been held up in the courts in order to make the Six Nations paupers while they are having to fight the whole world.

The CHAIRMAN: Who brought those actions?

Mrs. KELLOGG: The local people. They can always operate through bad Indians. That is what happened in this case, and we want, at the termination of these hearings, to know if there is any place in the United States Government that we can go to for assistance, and where we can prove who is who among our own people, how we are constructing our government, how we are pushing our program, what our policies are, and who we are, so that hereafter this question which the Treaty of 1784 supposed would always be easily adjusted, can be definitely settled for all time. Right now, in the Mohawk Nation, there is all kinds of commotion over the fact that two Indian bureaus are always dealing with the affairs of the Mohawk Nation, and there is also a lot of persecution—

The CHAIRMAN: What do you mean by two Indian bureaus?

Mrs. KELLOGG: One is the bureau at Ottawa.

The CHAIRMAN: Oh, the Canadian bureau?

Mrs. KELLOGG: When the Jay Treaty was made, the Mohawk Council held it up for three years, telling these commissioners, whose names I do not now recall, that they should put their boundaries outside their reservation. They finally agreed that they would lift up the line into the sky. After they passed, the line fell down and what happened was that there is a division of the Mohawk territory, running through, which absolutely balls up the affairs of the Mohawks into such a state that the Mohawk chiefs cannot do anything with self-government without interference from Ottawa and without interference from the Bureau of Indian Affairs over here. I am going to allow them themselves to tell some of their own stories. Right now the Cayuga Nation in northern New York is threatened with the extinguishment of its nationhood by the fact that New York State offers to settle now, at this late day, for 160 square miles of territory that it has never fully paid for, and the Six Nations do not wish any of their people to accept this money because of the litigation that we have started as the Six Nations confederacy, in the court, to recover these through the court.

I do not see that I am going to have the time here—it is a quarter to 11 now—to go into the details of the reconstruction program.

Mr. KELLOGG: I would not, now, Mrs. Kellogg.

Mrs. KELLOGG: And I think if I might leave that for a probable future, I should like to have Mr. Kellogg, perhaps, supersede me to present the legal situation, as he deems best, on what I have left out; and then I should like the Mohawk chief[61] to be heard, and Chief Crouse[62] of the Onondagas, and Chief Eels[63] of the Cayugas.

The CHAIRMAN: Have you any questions, Mr. Merritt?

Mr. MERRITT: No, except I want to make this short statement, if she has concluded her statement.

Mrs. KELLOGG: I have not concluded it. I have rested it now. I am never through, so far as the Bureau is concerned. [. . .]

Testimony of O. J. Kellogg[64]

(The witness was sworn by the chairman.)

The CHAIRMAN: Will you please state your name to the stenographer, and your residence?

Mr. KELLOGG: O. J. Kellogg; Seymour, Wis.; office at Syracuse, N.Y.

Gentlemen, there is a lost man somewhere up in what is now the State of New York. That man became lost soon after the Treaty of 1796.[65] Up until that time he was located very prettily, a great deal better than any other Indians in this country.

He had a treaty with the United States Government, started in 1784 and finished in 1789, by which the United States Government guaranteed him protection in 18,000,000 acres of land in consideration of his ceding of this title to the Ohio lands—the lands in the Ohio Valley. The Federal Government ceded all right and title that it had to this 18,000,000 acres of land; and by the treaty of 1796, which is explanatory of the treaty of 1784, the Federal Government had put into the treaties a provision that not one foot of this land could be sold except if it was sold to the sovereign, the United States Government.

This was to these Indians on the ground of their help in the Revolutionary War, and in the trying times of 1776 to 1783.

Today what do we find? That little remnant of the people claim from the State of New York that 78,000 acres left.

When this Government started to protect the Six Nations, they had 18,000,000 acres of land. They protected them down to 78,000 acres, and now they are trying to protect them out of that.

Gentlemen, if your committee comes up to New York, I think we will be able to show you things that you have never seen in any other State. Land was taken away from the Mohawks, the Onondagas, and the Cayugas by so-called state treaties. Not one of those treaties was ever validated by the United States Government. Not one of those pieces of land was ever offered to the United States Government for it to purchase. Today these Indians are down to 78,000 acres of land. They had 18,000,000 acres of land which the United States guaranteed them they could keep. They have only 78,000 acres today. Whose fault is it? Partially [it is] that of the United States Government; partially it is the fault of the government of the State of New York.

The Federal Government was poor during those early years. New York was a whole lot more powerful. The Federal Government could not go in there and force the State of New York at that time to live up to the treaties. These treaties were confirmed by the United States Senate and promulgated to the world. The New York Senators fought them bitterly. Even Governor Clinton came down here and fought them bitterly; but they were passed in spite of that, and were the supreme law of the land.

Article 1, section 10, of the Constitution forbids any state entering into any treaty or alliance with any other nation. The very fact that this land, 18,000,000 acres less 78,000 acres, was taken by treaties made by the State of New York with individual members of the Six Nations, shows that the taking of it was not legal. Not one foot of it was ever surveyed. Gentlemen, it was just the same as Germany, or some other foreign nation, coming over here and buying property in the State of Wisconsin; or, Senator Frazier,[66] in your State of North Dakota. It cannot be done under the law and under treaties.

Senator WHEELER:[67] Let me interrupt you to ask you a question. You say it cannot be done under the laws and under the treaties.

Mr. KELLOGG: Yes.

Senator WHEELER: Why have you not gone into court on it?

Mr. KELLOGG: We are in court now; but we cannot get a foothold because the Federal Government will not intervene; and Charles E. Hughes,[68] our opposing attorney, has twice knocked us out of court because these Indians cannot sue for that purpose without the enjoinder of the United States.

Senator WHEELER: What is the idea of you coming before this committee with it? There is nothing we can do about it that I can see.

Mr. KELLOGG: Absolutely, there is something you can do. You can decide the status in the State of New York. You can help us to get Federal intervention, if you think the case is good.

Senator WHEELER: We have not any more right to decide the status of the State of New York than you have.

Mr. KELLOGG: No. The status of the Six Nations Indians in New York.

Senator WHEELER: Yes.

Mr. KELLOGG: I want to tell you this. On that 18,000,000 acres of land there is not a patented deed issued by the United States Government. It is all issued by the State of New York. Practically all of that land is held on leases, and not on patented deeds, or warranty deeds.

Senator WHEELER: Was all of the 18,000,000 acres of land in New York?

Mr. KELLOGG: No; part of it is in the State of Pennsylvania. It runs clear down to Pittsburgh.

Here is a statement showing the whole thing from beginning to end, with the decision of the court on the matter. New York appointed a commission of the legislature to make an investigation, and here is the report of that committee, and I would like to file it for the record.

Senator WHEELER: It is all right to file it, but I do not think it should be made a part of the record.

The CHAIRMAN: You think it would be better just to file it as an exhibit?

Senator WHEELER: Yes; as an exhibit. Why should we fill up the record with a complaint?

Mr. KELLOGG: It is a complaint of a lot of other treaties in the State of New York of things going on now that we want this committee to investigate and look into; for instance, the fact that they are taking away certain lands—trying to—by a bill in legislature.[69]

◆

Senator WHEELER: Are these Indian wards of the United States?

Mr. KELLOGG: They are certainly wards of the Government.

Senator WHEELER: Technically?

Mr. KELLOGG: Judge Ray's[70] decision in the Boylan case said they were wards of the United States Government. They are aliens and have never given up their rights of self-government, but they are wards of the United States Government.

Senator WHEELER: What judge said that?

Mr. KELLOGG: Judge Ray of the northern district of New York. Also, it was appealed to the appellate court and they sustained Judge Ray.

Senator WHEELER: They sustained him as to what?

Mr. KELLOGG: As to the fact that they were wards of the Government of the United States.

Senator WHEELER: How did that come up?

Mr. KELLOGG: In making a test case on 37 acres of land in that case. The land got into white hands.

Senator WHEELER: You are the attorney representing in that case?

Mr. KELLOGG: No, I am not the attorney. I am just the agent of the Six Nations, representing them in this hearing. The attorneys in that case are in New York.

Senator WHEELER: But you have your lawyers representing them?

Mr. KELLOGG: They made a little test case up in the northeastern part of the State, and the rest of it is not in court.

Senator WHEELER: Why is it not in court?

Mr. KELLOGG: Because they have had a test case going on for five years, and we have never been able to succeed because we never could get the Government to come in with us. They promised us they would, but they do not do it.

Senator THOMAS: Have you a contract with them?

Mr. KELLOGG: Yes.

Senator THOMAS: Have you a copy of that contract?

Mr. KELLOGG: I have, I think.

Senator THOMAS: Would you mind submitting that also to the committee?

Mr. KELLOGG: Absolutely (producing paper).

Senator THOMAS:[71] For the benefit of the committee, without reading the contract, just state the nature of the contract, and what it provides for.

Mr. KELLOGG: It provides for carrying on these investigations before the committee, furnishing the committee with evidence, and so forth; for organizing the Six Nations into a body that can be a nation; reorganization work that has been going on for the past five years.

Senator WHEELER: This contract was made on the 9th of February, 1929.

Mr. KELLOGG: Yes.

Senator WHEELER: This contract reads as follows. [Reads the agreement][72]

[. . .]

Senator THOMAS: Are you employed on a salary?

Mr. KELLOGG: No, sir.

Senator THOMAS: In connection with the work with the Indians?

Mr. KELLOGG: No, sir; I am not.

Senator THOMAS: Have you ever collected any money from the Indians to represent them?

Mr. KELLOGG: I have.

Senator THOMAS: Over a period of how many years?

Mr. KELLOGG: Four and a half years, I think.

Senator THOMAS: Tell the committee about how much you have collected.

Mr. KELLOGG. Well, now, Senator, I have collected money for the Six Nations as well as received money for the Kelloggs. There is a difference between the two.

Senator THOMAS: Tell the committee how much of each.

Mr. KELLOGG: I cannot tell you exactly. The treasurer of the Six Nations is here and can tell you how much has come in that has never gone through my hands.

Senator THOMAS: Can you give us some idea about it?

Mr. KELLOGG: The attorneys have gotten something like $27,000.

Senator WHEELER: What attorneys?

Mr. KELLOGG: Wise, Whitney & Parker.

Senator THOMAS: How much of that have you received?

Mr. KELLOGG: I have nothing to do with the contract in any way, shape, or form; do not come under their contract.

Senator WHEELER: How much money did you collect personally, yourself?

Mr. KELLOGG: For ourselves, do you mean?

Senator WHEELER: How much money did you personally collect, and how much did you get for the Indian tribes?

Mr. KELLOGG: I should judge somewhere around $50,000.

Senator WHEELER: You got that?

Mr. KELLOGG: I think so. Of course, we have not had that for ourselves. That has gone largely to the Six Nations.

Senator WHEELER: You said you collected that.

Mr. KELLOGG: No; the Stockbridge and Brothertown in Wisconsin. Why, Mrs. Kellogg, too. We were through. We helped them organize under the united tribal agreement, and then we quit and did not care to go ahead with it any further. They have their own organization in which they agreed that they should pay the Kelloggs $1 a month, per member of the Stockbridge and Brothertown Indians in the State of Wisconsin. That is what we have been drawing for expenses, and so forth, and a great deal of it has gone into the expenses of the Six Nations to keep up the organization.

Senator THOMAS: You stated a while ago that your claim is for the recovery of 18,000,000 acres of land in the States of New York and Pennsylvania?

Mr. KELLOGG: Or the equivalent.

Senator THOMAS: That is the point I want to get at. What do you claim would be an equivalent of that?

Mr. KELLOGG: Cash.

Senator THOMAS: How much cash?

Mr. KELLOGG: We do not know. It has got to be done by agreement with the United States Government as a party to it.

Senator THOMAS: You have a claim pending in court, or you sought to establish it?

Mr. KELLOGG: We have a claim pending in court for one mile square on which the Aluminum Co. property is located.

Senator THOMAS: Can you give us some idea how much?

Mr. KELLOGG: And they have tried twice to get together with us for a compromise, and have asked and agreed to compromise with us if we have got the United States Government to come in, and compromise with us.

Senator THOMAS: Whom do you mean by "they"?

Mr. KELLOGG: The St. Lawrence River Power Co.

Senator WHEELER: Who are they?

Mr. KELLOGG: It is a corporation owned by the Aluminum Co. of America, situated on this mile square in the State of New York.

Senator THOMAS: What I am trying to get is some idea of the property value of that claim.

Mr. KELLOGG: Our attorneys have told us that we should recover $500,000,000; but we will never get it—we never expect it.

Mrs. KELLOGG: At least $500,000,000.

Mr. KELLOGG: At least $500,000,000.

Senator THOMAS: Your contract calls for 2 per cent?

Mr. KELLOGG: Yes, it does.

The CHAIRMAN: Are you an attorney, Mr. Kellogg?

Mr. KELLOGG: Yes.

Senator THOMAS: That would be $10,000,000?

Mr. KELLOGG: If we would get anything like that; but you know well enough that we never will.

Senator THOMAS: You would not object, then, would you, to the Senate committee assisting you in helping establish this claim?

Mr. KELLOGG: That is not what we ask. We do not ask the Senate committee to help us establish that claim.

Senator THOMAS: What are you here for?

Mr. KELLOGG: We are here to get the Senate committee to look into the wrongs that have been done to the Six Nations of New York. We want them to make a survey of conditions up there and recommend to the United States Government, or to the Treasury Department of the United States Government, that they intervene and settle this question for all time to come.

Senator THOMAS: You regard this committee, then, as a sort of court of last resort in this matter?

Mr. KELLOGG: No, we do not. The biggest part of this territory has never been in court at all.

Senator THOMAS: Why do you not get in court on that?

Mr. KELLOGG: We cannot get in court on all of it, because we have been into it twice on this mile square, and the Federal Government would not come in and intervene in the case.

Senator THOMAS: If that be the case, do you not think any law that we might pass would be set aside by the same courts that have heretofore denied your case?

Mr. KELLOGG: No; I think a recommendation from this committee alone would force the Federal Government to act.

Senator THOMAS: I beg your pardon. I just want to get this idea, so far as I am concerned.

The CHAIRMAN: Proceed, and be as brief as possible.

Mr. KELLOGG. That is about all. We want you to come up and look over the situation in the Seneca country.[73] There we have a city of 20,000 to 25,000 people on leased land.

Senator WHEELER: Land of the Indians?

Mr. KELLOGG: Yes. Every building on that land is paying lease money.

Senator WHEELER: Paying to whom?

Mr. KELLOGG: To Mr. Harrison, collector of lease money.

Senator WHEELER: Mr. Harrison is a representative of the Bureau of Indian Affairs?

Mr. KELLOGG: A representative of the Bureau of Indian Affairs, agent for the Six Nations.

Senator WHEELER: I did not hear the first part of your statement, so that I may be asking some question that the committee has already heard answered; but you say Mr. Wise is one of the lawyers for the tribe?

Mr. KELLOGG: Yes.

Senator WHEELER: Where is Mr. Wise?

Mr. KELLOGG: He is in New York City.

Senator WHEELER: Why, if you wanted to discuss some legal principles here, did you not have Mr. Wise come here?

Mr. KELLOGG: Because Mr. Wise and the other attorneys asked that I should come. They are in court, and they did not care to come before the committee and take up those matters. The abuses of the Six Nations are a separate thing from anything that is put in court.

Senator WHEELER: Your contention is that the Indians are under the supervision of the Indian Bureau at the present?

Mr. KELLOGG: They certainly are at present. That is, they are not now under any bureau, but under the Government's supervision. The Indian Bureau claims they have no supervision over them to any extent; but the treaty and the law is laid down that they are under the Government, wards of the United States Government, and as such it is up to you people to protect them. With the State of New York there is a dual control there. They have appointed agents under the treaty, but the agents can do nothing but distribute annuities, and they have taken the whole thing into their hands, and have been doing it for 50 years.

Senator WHEELER: I cannot understand from your statement, at all, what authority this committee has in the matter. That is the reason I suggested this to you. Are you an attorney?

Mr. KELLOGG. Yes, sir.

Senator WHEELER: I wish you would tell us what authority we have got in the matter under our resolution to assist you in getting into court?

Mr. KELLOGG: You cannot assist us in getting into court at all. That is not what we want here.

Senator WHEELER: You were suggesting a moment ago that all this committee had to do was to pass upon it, and if we passed upon it, then we could have the Department of Justice act.

Mr. KELLOGG: I think you could have the Department of Justice state, or the general counsel, to the States of New York and Pennsylvania; not the court.

Senator WHEELER: But this committee has no authority to do anything.

Mr. KELLOGG: But you have authority to look into all things concerning Indian affairs, and this comes under the Indian affairs of this country.

Senator WHEELER: You say first that you are under the Indian Bureau and next that you are not under it.

Mr. KELLOGG: We are not under the Indian Bureau, but under the control of the United States Government.[74]

Senator WHEELER: How do you contend that you are?

Mr. KELLOGG: Made so by the treaties of 1784 and 1796.

Senator WHEELER: What provisions in the treaties? Have you the treaties?

Mr. KELLOGG: I have not got them with me.

Senator WHEELER: Why did you not bring the treaties here?

Mr. KELLOGG: The treaty of 1796 provides this. I can give it to you.

Senator WHEELER: I do not want just your bald statement about it. I would like to get at the facts, and not your conclusions.

Mrs. KELLOGG: May I just say that I presented to this commission—

Senator WHEELER: This is not a commission.

The CHAIRMAN: This is a committee of the Senate.

Mrs. KELLOGG: That I presented to this committee facts which I think entitle the Six Nations to an investigation. In the first place, there is no machinery in the United States Government to which the Six Nations can commit themselves. We are not under the Bureau of Indian Affairs. We have tried it all out. On Capitol Hill there is no one that we can go to, to be heard. The social order of the reservation is very largely affected, and the people are threatened out of their property by the state of things that is created by this.

Senator THOMAS: Would that same condition happen in regard to all Indian tribes if they were turned loose like your tribe has been turned loose?

Mrs. KELLOGG: It would, under the Bureau. They have interfered where they have no business to interfere; where they have no right to interfere. Right now they are before the Legislature of the State of New York trying to force the Onondagas out of the little they have.

Senator WHEELER: Who is before the Legislature of the States of New York? What evidence have you of that?

Mrs. KELLOGG: We have here statements in the public press by people of responsibility who have introduced the bill in the State legislature, who claim that they have the promise of Commissioner Burke that there will be no trouble in their securing this from the Onondagas.

Mr. MERRITT: That statement is without any basis of fact whatever.

Senator WHEELER: You mean the statement that the legislator made, if he made it; is that it?

Mr. MERRITT: Yes; that the Indian Bureau is interfering in any way in regard to that matter. Our jurisdiction is very limited so far as the New York Indians are concerned, as I stated to the committee before you came in, Senator Wheeler.

The CHARIMAN: Have you anything further, Mr. Kellogg?

Mr. KELLOGG: Not until I can find what I am looking for, for Senator Wheeler. Go ahead with one of the other witnesses.

The CHAIRMAN: I understand you have some of the Indians themselves here to be heard.

Mr. KELLOGG: Yes.

Testimony of Chief Louis P. Oak

(The witness was sworn by the chairman.)

The CHAIRMAN: Please state your name.

Mrs. KELLOGG: Do you want me to interpret for him, Senator?

Senator WHEELER: You speak English, do you not?

Chief OAK: No.

Senator WHEELER: Have you any education?

Chief OAK: No.

Senator WHEELER: You have been to school, have you not?

Chief OAK: No.

Mrs. KELLOGG: He says he has never been to school.

The CHAIRMAN: Proceed.

Senator WHEELER: Have you not some Indian who can speak English? We cannot take up the time of the committee with a witness testifying through an interpreter.

Mrs. KELLOGG: He has a very brief statement to make.

Senator THOMAS: Mrs. Kellogg, do you state to the committee that he cannot talk English and cannot make a brief statement to this committee in English?

Mrs. KELLOGG: I said he had a brief statement to make.

Senator THOMAS: You do not answer my question.

Mrs. KELLOGG: I did not say that.

Senator THOMAS: Do you tell the committee that it is necessary now for you to act as interpreter for the chief to make a brief statement, that he cannot make a brief statement in English so that we can understand it?

Mrs. KELLOGG: I do.

Senator THOMAS: Very well.

(The witness proceeded to testify through Mrs. Kellogg, acting as interpreter.)

Chief OAK: I represent the Mohawk Nation. They live on the boundary line between the United States and Canada. I come from that country which was reserved to the Mohawk Nation by the Six Nations at the time of the treaty of 1784, established between the Six Nations and the United States Government.

Prior to that time, each of our nations in the Indian Government sold territory according to a constitution which the ancient civilization possessed, and each gave a fee simple title to those nations like Great Britain, Holland, and a State.

At present time there is a state of affairs among my people which is very upset, due to the fact that the Six Nations now have found no place to go to be heard. There seems nothing arranged between the Mohawk Nation and the Six Nations and the United States Government, where we may take our troubles. We have left out of all the loot since 1784, a reservation 6 miles square, from which was sold fraudulently, without the consent of one official of the Mohawk Nation or the United States Government, a mile square of territory upon which the city of Massena and Ordmont is located. Upon that mile square is located the greatest water power in the United States.

Senator THOMAS: From your information, state the name of this water power, so that we can identify it.

Chief OAK: A part of the location is on the Grass River, which is near the St. Lawrence, or into the St. Lawrence.

Senator THOMAS: Has the power been developed?

Chief OAK: Yes; the power has been developed. We have no Indian name for it. It is the location which the St. Lawrence River Power Co. occupies. The development of the Aluminum Co.'s plant is upon this property.

Senator PINE: It is in Canada?

Chief OAK: No, it is in the United States.

The CHAIRMAN: Proceed.

Chief OAK: These people have no title to this territory. The Mohawk Nation never sold it. There were three people who had no authority, who were mixed bloods, and whom we suspect they got, who made the transaction. There are a lot of islands involved, in the St. Lawrence, in the same status as the 1 mile square of Massena.

Senator THOMAS: Let me ask you another question there: Has this Indian tribe ever tried to get a jurisdictional bill through Congress to give them a right to go into the Court of Claims to present any claim they ever have against the Government?

Mrs. KELLOGG: Are you asking me that?

Senator THOMAS: Yes.

Mrs. KELLOGG: No, they have not. They do not consider that the matters belong to the Court of Claims. They have not a claim against the United States Government; they have a claim against the State Government and individuals.

The CHAIRMAN: Would they not have a claim against the United States Government in regard to the violation of the treaty that was made that you have referred to?

Mrs. KELLOGG: After we have tried all over Capitol Hill and have found that no one wants to hear us on our troubles, and we have no place to go, we shall probably start that action. That is what we want to determine here.[75]

The CHAIRMAN: Let Chief Oak proceed, then.

Chief OAK: What I want to ask this commission to do is to look into the value of that water power, to subpoena the books of the Aluminum Co. that is located upon it; to investigate as to our status on the territory which was originally ours and which we believe we have by every right under the sun. We should like to know where we belong. Our people are getting crowded on the reservation that they now possess. We want those matters ascertained that they now possess. We want those matters ascertained somewhere.

Senator WHEELER: How long ago was it that they took over this power site? I want to know approximately; has it been 8 or 10 years, or 6 years or 2 years or 4 years? Approximately, how many years has it been? I do not want it exactly.

Chief OAK: I cannot say exactly the number of years, but it is longer ago than 10 years.

Mrs. KELLOGG: I can answer you on that, Senator. They acquired the property in 1825.

Senator WHEELER: In 1825?

Mrs. KELLOGG: Yes.

The CHAIRMAN: Have you any further statement?

Chief OAK: No.

Testimony of Livingston Crouse

(The witness was sworn by the chairman.)

Mr. CROUSE: I am of the Onondaga Nation. I live near Syracuse, N.Y. Gentlemen, I am here to represent all Onondagas. I am here to tell you some of our troubles on the Onondaga Reservation near Syracuse. We have had considerable trouble with the State, yearly, fighting the State from annihilating the Indians and making them citizens. That is practically what they really want to do, to wipe us out and get us off the reservation.

I am asking this commission to come out and investigate the sand pits that we have out there, and the lease to the stonecutters. We have a valuable stone on the reservation, leased to the Patten Jones Cut Stone, of Syracuse, who are required to lease from the Indians through the Indian State agent.

The CHAIRMAN: Do you mean the State agent or the agent of the Indian Bureau?

Mr. CROUSE: He assumes the right to lease.

Mr. MERRITT: It is the agent of the State of New York.

The CHAIRMAN: The State of New York or the department here at Washington?

Mr. MERRITT: It is the agent of the State of New York.

The CHAIRMAN: The State of New York?

Mr. MERRITT: Yes.

Mr. CROUSE: The agent assumes the right to lease these properties to the people of Syracuse.

Senator THOMAS: Let me ask you a question there. Perhaps it will help me. Have you any complaint against the Indian Bureau that you want to state here? Have they done anything that you do not approve of, or do you want them to do something that they are not doing?

Mr. CROUSE: We have come here to get some help.

Senator THOMAS: I am trying to find out what help you want. That is my purpose.

Mr. CROUSE: I am trying to tell you just what help.

Senator THOMAS: I have gotten the impression that your complaint is against the State of New York.

Mr. CROUSE: Yes.

Senator THOMAS: And you have no complaint against the Federal Government?

Mr. CROUSE: We have a complaint against the Federal Government because she has not done her duty in accordance with the United States treaty.

Senator THOMAS: Tell us in what particular.

Mr. CROUSE: The reason for that was that they have not protected us.

Senator THOMAS: In what particular?

Mr. CROUSE: Under the treaty provisions it is provided that we are to be protected in these 18,000,000 acres of land, and the United States has never done so. Instead of protecting the Indians, they have simply slept, lain dormant, and never protected the Indians.

We have considerable property. Statements were made here that we had 18,000,000 acres of land. Now, we have only 2 by 4 miles square in the Onondaga Reservation, and now the city of Syracuse is threatening to take over for a dam site, and that will flood the Indians entirely out of the reservation.

Senator THOMAS: They propose to pay you, do they not, for your land?

Mr. CROUSE: They propose to pay probably enough to last a week of rations.

Senator THOMAS: The laws of New York provide that no one can take your property without first condemning it. A commission will be appointed to appraise the property, if it is for a public purpose, the court must pass upon that first, and after the appraisal is made and the award fixed, if you are not satisfied, you have a right to appeal to the court and have the matter tried out before a jury of the citizens of the jurisdiction wherein the property lies. Are you afraid that the procedure will not protect you in the amount of actual value of your property?

Mr. CROUSE: I say, yes.

Senator THOMAS: Proceed. I will not bother you any further.

Mr. CROUSE: Yes. In the first place, the State of New York, I do not believe, has any right to condemn the property under the treaty. How could we have condemnation when we are supposed—

The CHAIRMAN: Are you referring to a treaty with the Government, or to a treaty with the State of New York?

Mr. CROUSE: I refer to the treaty of 1784 with the Government.

The CHAIRMAN: Did your Six Nations have treaties also with the State of New York, do you know?

Mr. CROUSE: What do you say?

The CHAIRMAN: Did your people have treaties with the States of New York as well as with the Government of the United States?

Mr. CROUSE: We had State treaties.

Mrs. KELLOGG: Pardon me; you said with the United States. May I answer this under your question, that there is no State treaty with the Six Nations. They are all with separate nations of the Six Nations.

The CHAIRMAN: The separate nations made treaties with the State of New York?

Mrs. KELLOGG: Yes.

Senator WHEELER: Is your contention that the separate nations had no right to make treaties?

Mrs. KELLOGG: Absolutely; under the constitutions of the Iroquois and under the Federal Government.

Senator WHEELER: But there is nothing in this treaty that I can see that would prevent the Indians from entering into a separate treaty with the Government.

Mrs. KELLOGG: We have the letters of George Washington and Governor Clinton, and other people who have made a study of those things, together with other historical documents, which are too bulky to state here.

Senator WHEELER: I do not see anything in the treaty. I have been trying to look over the treaty here.

Mrs. KELLOGG: You see, protection was guaranteed the nation. Will you look on page 23, Senator, where the treaty of 1789 specifically provides—

Mr. KELLOGG: The United States Government reaffirmed the treaty of 1784 and added to it that specific language that no interference would be made in the treaty rights of this tribe. I have a decision here to the effect that the fee of the lands of the Onondaga Indians is claimed by the State, right now, under this mixture of treaties.

The CHAIRMAN: Let the witness complete his statement.

Mr. CROUSE: We also have another development. We have salt pipe lines running through the reservation. They acquired a lease to some of the property from the chiefs, which, as I understand, was given for 25 years, and for which was paid $25, I believe, that the lease called for. There are 4 miles of that pipe line running through the reservation. The chiefs did not want to do that, because the leakage of that salt would destroy the property along the road. Now, we are having trouble with it. It has spoiled the springs along at the homes of the families, and it destroys the trees—the leakage; and practically there is nothing that can grow on the land where the pipe line runs through;

but when you go over the line into the city property, the salt company has to pay about $40 to $50 just right across a city lot. They have to pay $40 there; but on the reservation, 4 miles long, they never pay a cent. Now, the 25 years has been up for a good many years, and it has never been paid, and nothing has been renewed, and we have never received a thing out of it. We tried to take the matter up with Syracuse lawyers, and, I don't know, they do not seem to take interest; and how in the world we are going to do, I don't know; and the fact is, one lawyer, when I asked him what would be the first thing we are going to go against, said: "The first thing is, your property is not appraised. We could not place a valuation."

Now, we have treaties there, so that the Indians there in the reservation are simply nothing. The Indian agent—the State agent—leases; he makes leases for these individuals for agricultural purposes. They have taken practically all of the best land that we have out there, and the Indians have not much land there to work.

Senator THOMAS: Let me ask you a question about that pipe line. You say the pipe line carries salt water?

Mr. CROUSE: Yes.

Senator THOMAS: And the company that operates the pipe line has the line across your property?

Mr. CROUSE: Yes; they had a lease, which expired probably 12 or 15 years ago.

Senator THOMAS: Who looks after this reservation—that is, the tract of 4 miles?

Mr. CROUSE: The chiefs look after it.

Senator THOMAS: Have not the chiefs made any complaint about damage being done by this pipe line, to that company?

Mr. CROUSE: Yes, we have been to the company and told them, and finally they discovered a new spring on the reservation, and piped fresh water for us, because of the complaint to the Indians.

Senator THOMAS: The lease no doubt provides that the pipe line shall be maintained in a good condition, free from leakage, and if it does, and the pipe leaks and destroys your property, it would be a simple matter to require that company—

Mr. CROUSE: I do not believe it specified that. It is just simply a right of way. The State road runs through the reservation, and I believe there is some agreement made with the State along the road of that highway, right in the highway, and of course when the leakage of that salt occurs, it runs down, naturally, in the yards and around the trees, and some valuable fruit trees have been destroyed by it.

Senator THOMAS: Do you want this committee to come up there and look over the matter?

Mr. CROUSE: Absolutely.

Senator THOMAS: And see what damage is being done?

Mr. CROUSE: Yes.

Senator THOMAS: And then to try to protect you against his damage?

Mr. CROUSE: Yes; and I also want to have the commission to look into the quarry lease and sand leases. I want that, also. We are in court with that now.

Senator WHEELER: I do not think this committee has any right or any jurisdiction in that matter at all.

Mr. CROUSE: Well, may I ask who has the jurisdiction?

Senator WHEELER: If the facts are as you say they are, you have a right to sue these different companies for damages in the courts, just as you have a right to go in the State courts up there and sue them.

Mr. CROUSE: Years ago my sister was working in the city, and was on board a street car and the front trolley took the switch and turned the car right end for end into a ditch. That was right in Syracuse, right at the outskirts of the city. The result was that her death was caused by the accident. We immediately sued the street car company. The street car company said this, that since the State has no jurisdiction over the Indians, they have no right to bring actions in the State, and we were thrown out of the court.

Senator WHEELER: I cannot conceive of a court holding that.

Mr. CROUSE: It was thrown out of the court; and we again tried, and carried it up into the Supreme Court of the State. It seems that the Supreme Court said that the surrogate should appoint administrators over these, and I was appointed as one, to see that all the details and the mortgages, and so forth, were paid, and we finally got a settlement from the street-car company of $400, after paying the fee of the—

Senator WHEELER: That was not the fault of the Government.

Mr. CROUSE: I know.

Senator WHEELER: The Government has not got anything to do with that.

Mr. CROUSE: Then the Government looks upon that kind of a deal with the Indian, then—

Senator WHEELER: Not at all; but the Government has not any authority whatever. Why, if these Indians are not wards of anyone, are you seeking relief from the Government?

Mr. CROUSE: The Government has some authority over them.

Senator WHEELER: Not at all. I know in the case where the Northern Pacific Railroad runs through the Blackfoot Reservation, if an Indian riding on a Northern Pacific train is killed on that train, his heirs have a lawsuit against the Northern Pacific Railroad, and the United States Government does not enter into it at all. Those cases are perfectly plain.

Mr. CROUSE: Well, it is a question of jurisdiction. We cannot get anything from the State. Then, where does the Indian stand? Where does he get his protection? That is what we are here for. Am I an Indian or am I a white man? Tell me that.

Senator THOMAS: I would like to get your viewpoint. What aid do you think should have been given you in either of these cases, in your judgment, by the United States Government?

Mr. CROUSE: I think that the Senate should look and delve into this matter and clear it up, and have it brought before the Senate and Congress, and have a settlement made for the lands that were wrongfully taken from the Indians, and that the question of jurisdiction should be settled once for all on that matter.

Senator THOMAS: Do you think you have a claim against the United States Government for any purpose, or to cover any incident or any neglect of theirs?

Mr. CROUSE: Yes, I think that the United States Government owes us protection, because we gave up all the Ohio Valley for this protection. If that treaty of 1784 is neglected, then where does the United States get its right to the 18,000,000 acres of land?

Senator THOMAS: I am trying to get your case. I do not live in that section, and I am trying to get your idea of what your rights are and wherein they have been violated. I am trying to get all the information I can from your viewpoint.

Mr. CROUSE: Well, you were asking about the question of jurisdiction.

Senator WHEELER: The trouble is that most of these questions are legal questions, and I think it is unfortunate that you did not have your lawyers down here to present the jurisdictional question, so that the committee would get some idea as to whether or not we did have any jurisdiction. I am frank to say to you that on the face of it, under this treaty, unless there is something in regard to it that I do not know about, I do not see where we have any jurisdiction in the matter.

Senator THOMAS: Let me ask you another question. How many Indians do you represent?

Mr. CROUSE: About 500 Indians.

Senator THOMAS: Where do they reside around Syracuse?

Mr. CROUSE: Around Syracuse.

Senator THOMAS: Do they live on a consolidated reservation, or do they have allotments, or either, or neither?

Mr. CROUSE. No; they have a reservation; a public domain of the Onondagas.

Senator THOMAS. How large?

Mr. CROUSE: About 2 miles wide and about 4 miles long.

Senator THOMAS: Do all those Indians live on that reservation?

Mr. CROUSE: Yes.

Senator THOMAS: Do they have allotments, or have certain tracts of ground been set aside for the use of each family?

Mr. CROUSE: We buy from one another improved land; and we buy from one another only as improved lands. We hold property and houses, and some valuable houses on the premises.

Senator THOMAS: Is this land deeded, and have you patents to it or deeds to it?

Mr. CROUSE: No; we have no patents. We just occupy it. There is a big tract where any Indian can go and clear up and build, and it will be his.

Mrs. KELLOGG: May I elucidate as to that?

Senator THOMAS: Yes.

Mrs. KELLOGG: Under the constitution of the Iroquois there was an individual holding of property among themselves. After that was satisfied, the rest was claimed as a common domain.

Senator THOMAS: And the remnants of this tribe live on this common domain?

Mrs. KELLOGG: They do. Still, they all have their original assignments handed down to their heirs, and a part of it is incumbent to them.

Senator THOMAS: Do they have the right to sell or mortgage?

Mrs. KELLOGG: No right to sell or mortgage. It has not been alienated.

Senator THOMAS: Who has title to it?

Mrs. KELLOGG: The Six Nations; the Onondagas.

The CHAIRMAN: Our time is getting very short. Is there anything further?

Mr. CROUSE: The power company has also come on the reservation and set up a line through the reservation for the purpose of forcing the line through into the city, and they have built a building there and cut off through the Indians' woods for this line, I guess about 14 feet wide where they have cut that timber.

Senator THOMAS: Were the Indians paid for that privilege?

Mr. CROUSE. No; the Indians were not paid.

Now, the State agent under the lease wants to collect on the lease from the stone quarry and on the sand leases, and he wants to take the right away from the chiefs, rather than having the Onondaga treasury do the collecting, as we have always done before; but the State agent is assuming the right and tried to go to these companies, and he takes the money, and wants to take that and put it into the annuities.

The CHAIRMAN: In other words, the State agent of New York assumes the right to lease your property, and the State courts say you have no standing, that there is no jurisdiction, in the courts; is that it?

Mrs. KELLOGG: Absolutely.

Mr. CROUSE: Yes.

Senator THOMAS: Mr. Chairman, I would like to make a suggestion, and give it such publicity as it may deserve, as to all Indian tribes in the United States that have business organizations—and those that do not have business organizations should proceed to perfect one—that we extend to those tribes the invitation or reserve the privilege of having prepared and furnishing to this committee any suggestions, grievances, claims, or what not, that they would like to have this committee consider. If that could be done, we would have something concrete to act upon and not have to depend upon the statement of a man who does not probably understand what his rights really are.

The CHAIRMAN: I think that is a very good suggestion.

Testimony of Chief Elon Eels, of the Cayuga Nation

(The witness was sworn by the chairman)

Chief EELS: I come here, and I am very glad to be permitted to appear before the committee, and I want to tell you that I am now residing on the Seneca Reservation, because all my land is disposed of, I suppose; but in the late years I have been kind of investigating, after I became chief.

We had a claim against the State of New York. We got a claim for just the profit share, they call it, on the lands that were sold, and the profit of that. It was sold again, after the State got our lands, and in six months after that they sold it at auction sales at the capitol grounds at Albany, and that was sold for $4.50 an acre; and they only gave us 50 cents an acre. That was $4 profit on the acre, and so they allowed us 5 per cent, I think it was, of that profit, and they pay us in the annuity form, which amounted to $40 a year, and we were getting $7 a year then. I know you are in a hurry, and I am just going to give you the main points. I intend to file some statement hereafter, more definite in the details.

After the Senecas heard where we resided, they said, "We want to share." There was the chance for them to come in. The way the attorneys made the bill, it states that the Cayugas wanted to buy the land, or pay for their rights. I did not agree with my attorney. That is not my will, the way he put it, because after that investigation of mine I found out that there was some reservation there; that the Cayugas were just crowded out. We believe we have a tract of land there that never was sold, and that is why I am here. I want your help, if you have got a chance, which I believe you have, to locate that tract of land that was not sold; and so I refused to pay any amount of money to the Senecas by believing I want to go back to my own reservation where I live, where my forefathers lived; and so that is how I refused.

Now, the way I understand, the State officials have been trying, and they have hired some agents to go to work and destroy us. They want to make out a bill, and if we sign that bill, and we pay for the right of staying on their reservation, it would mean that we would have the same rights, the same privileges; and I believe when we come under that agreement it would destroy the Cayuga Nation. That is the way I believe. That is one reason I refused. I want to stay Cayuga, and I want that reservation of mine, where I say we were placed, I think, and I have found and I was told that there was a reservation there; that we were just crowded out from that. That is the part I would like to look into, and I am asking the help of this committee here. If you want to ask some questions, I will answer.

The CHAIRMAN: Are there any questions anyone wants to ask?

Chief EELS: As I say, I want to file a statement so that there will be more to it; it will be facts, that is.

The CHAIRMAN: You can send your statement to us and we will consider it.

Chief EELS: Yes.

The CHAIRMAN: Mr. Merritt, do you want to make a statement now?

Statement of Edgar B. Merritt,
Assistant Commissioner of Indian Affairs

Mr. MERRITT: Mr. Chairman and gentlemen of the committee, referring to the statements made to the committee as to the Cayuga

Indians, I would like to read the following paragraph from this House Document, No. 1590, Sixty-third Congress, third session. [Reading:]

"The Cayugas also sold their land to the State and gradually migrated westward, locating first in the Ohio Valley, but finally removing to the Indian Territory and becoming affiliated with other tribes there. A few Cayugas still remain in New York, residing principally with the Senecas and Tonawandas—the latter an offspring of the Seneca Tribe—being frequently designated "the Tonawanda Band of Seneca Indians." The State paid the Cayugas at the rate of 4 shillings per acre and thereafter sold the land for 16 shillings per acre. About 1853, representatives of the tribe began to petition the State for the difference in price between the one paid to them and that received by the State. Finally, in 1909, the legislative assembly authorized the land commissioner to adjust and settle the claim of the Cayuga Indians against the State for a sum not exceeding $297,131.20, with an additional allowance of $27,131.20 for legal expenses incurred."

That is just in response to the statement of the gentleman.

As to the Indian problem of the Six Nations in New York, I would like to say that we in the Indian Bureau appreciate the difficulties of this situation. Our jurisdiction is very limited. Under existing laws we do not attempt to exercise administrative functions over the Indians of the State of New York. Those Indians have been living there for hundreds of years. Their land is included within one of the original 13 States. They have treaties with the States as well as with the Federal Government.

Senator WHEELER: When did they enter into those treaties with the States?

Mr. MERRITT: When?

Senator WHEELER: Did they enter into a treaty with the State of New York before New York became one of the original States of the Union, or afterwards?

Mr. MERRITT: Afterwards.

Senator WHEELER: I notice that this treaty of 1794 apparently recognizes the treaties with the State of New York.

Mr. MERRITT: Yes.

Senator WHEELER: Is that your understanding of it? [Reading:]

"Art 2. The United States acknowledges the lands reserved to the Oneida, Onondaga, and Cayuga Nations, in their respective treaties with the State of New York."

Mr. MERRITT: The Federal Government recognizes those treaties. There has been introduced in Congress legislation on this New York situation. There was a bill introduced (H.R. 18735, back in 1914, in the House of Representatives, by Congressman Clancy, I believe, and that bill appears printed in House Document 1590, Sixty-third Congress, third session.[76]

Senator THOMAS: Was that introduced in the New York Legislature or in the United States Congress?

Mr. MERRITT: It was introduced in the United States Congress by the Congressman representing those Indians in the House of Representatives.

The Department of Justice made a report on that bill on September 28, 1914. This report was signed by Ernest Knaebel, Assistant Attorney General, and he discussed the situation in New York. There are also some resolutions by the Board of Indian Commissioners in regard to the New York situation, in this report. There is also a report by the Secretary of the Interior on this same bill under date of January 22, 1915, in which the Secretary of the Interior goes into the New York Indian situation somewhat. Back in 1914, I requested Mr. John Reeves, then a law clerk in the Indian Bureau, to go to New York and go into this New York situation and make a report to the Indian Office concerning all phases of it. This report is dated December 26, 1914, and it is printed in this same document referred to.

Mr. Reeves was also kind enough to prepare an appendix giving references to the treaties, and giving statute references, and also other specific references concerning court decisions and leases relating to the New York Indians. This is a very valuable document on this subject, and we would like to have this document go into the record, because I think there is no document in the possession of the Government that gives so much information on the New York situation as this document, No. 1590, Sixty-third Congress, third session; and if there is no objection we would like to have that printed in this record.

The CHAIRMAN: Without objection, it will be printed in the record.

Senator THOMAS: Your Bureau published another document that gives information about the total number of Indians in that State, and the numbers and names of the tribes and location of Indian agencies, and so forth?

Mr. MERRITT: Yes.

Senator THOMAS: I personally would like to have a copy of that document, and when I get it I would be very glad to insert that in this record.

Mr. MERRITT: Yes, sir; we will be glad to furnish it.

(The two documents above referred to will be found printed at the end of this day's proceedings.)

Senator THOMAS: How many tribes does your Bureau exercise jurisdiction over and is it in contact with?

Mr. MERRITT: There are about 200 tribes in the United States living on about 190 reservations. There are about 350,000 Indians in the United States and about 225,000 of those Indians are under the jurisdiction of the Federal Government.

Senator THOMAS: Do these several tribes of Indians have, as a rule, a business organization in each tribe representing the tribe?

Mr. MERRITT: Some of them do. It depends upon how advanced the Indians are. Most of the Indians have organizations of some kind, either a business committee or a tribal organization.

Senator THOMAS: What would be your reaction to the proposition I made a moment ago, to send out word to these various tribes and ask them to present in a written, concrete form any statement that they care to make, which they, of course, would hope or expect to be of benefit to them, in connection with future legislation?

Mr. MERRITT: We would be very glad to have such a statement from the Indian organizations on the various reservations.

Senator WHEELER: The trouble with these Indian organizations you mention on the reservations, is this, that the Indian agents on those reservations seek to control, and in many instances do control, the Indians by appointing as policeman and other things of that kind those who are subservient to the bureau. At least, that is the way it is reported to me.

Mr. MERRITT: That is the claim, but I do not think there is much to that.

Senator WHEELER: I have seen some evidences of it in Montana. I do not know how it is on other reservations, but I have seen some pretty practical evidences of it in Montana, the way they have operated there. I do not know what they do in other States.

Mrs. KELLOGG: They do that in New York State.

Senator THOMAS: That might govern as to some feature, but I do not think that would govern as to every claim that the Indians might have, away back. I do not think the Indian agent would deny them the right to present any claim away back. They will never be satisfied until they have these claims presented and have some adjudication on them, and I think the sooner we get into that the better it will be.

Mr. MERRITT: When I first went into the department I was a law clerk, and I drafted a general jurisdictional bill that would permit all Indian tribes to go to the Court of Claims. I believe that every tribe in the United States should have an opportunity of presenting their claims to the Court of Claims, and that the Indian should have his day in court.

Senator THOMAS: Are they not getting that now from Congress?

Mr. MERRITT: Since that time a great many jurisdictional bills have passed Congress, and there are only a few tribes now that have not had an opportunity to go to the Court of Claims, who have real claims against the Government; and personally, I am in favor of every Indian tribe in the United States having its day in court and having the opportunity to go to the Court of Claims.

Senator WHEELER: Coming back to this New York case, what is there in the treaties that gives the Bureau of Indian Affairs any jurisdiction over the New York Indians at all?

Mr. MERRITT: Our jurisdiction is very limited. Congress has not passed legislation giving us jurisdiction over the Indians of New York the same as other Indians in the United States. It is my belief that there is need for legislation affecting the New York Indians. They are now more or less under the jurisdiction of the State of New York; but there is a twilight zone there, and there is some doubt as to the jurisdiction in some cases and I think that Congress has authority to pass legislation affecting the Indians of New York State.

Senator THOMAS: Are these Indians affiliated up there? Do they work together in any particular? Are they associated and do they have meetings so that they can get together and form a joint request or memorial to Congress?

Mr. MERRITT: They have their local organizations.

Mr. KELLOGG: May I ask one question, believing that it may help out considerably?

The CHAIRMAN: Yes.

Mr. KELLOGG: Mr. Merritt, do you know whether your Bureau or Interior Department or the Federal Government ever went into an agreement with the State of New York whereby they ever assumed jurisdiction?

Mr. MERRITT: No, I know of no such agreement. I think, Mr. Chairman, that I ought not to let pass without a very vigorous denial the statement made by Mrs. Kellogg in regard to the Indian Office attempting to influence either the Canadian Government or the Legislature of New York or any of the officials of the State of New York.

The CHAIRMAN: As I understood Mrs. Kellogg, there was a representative of the Bureau here, present up there at the trial in Canada.

Mrs. KELLOGG: Yes, there was.

Mr. MERRITT: Yes. We were asked to have a representative here at that trial, to show the records of our office in regard to Mrs. Kellogg and her methods of collecting money from the Indians.

The CHAIRMAN: You were requested by whom?

Mr. MERRITT: By the authorities of Canada. I believe it was Mr. Kellogg himself who admitted here this morning that they had collected from the Indians approximately $50,000 in recent years.

Mr. KELLOGG: Yes.

Mr. MERRITT: Our records show that these Indians have been grossly abused in this collecting business. The assertion has been made that they were going to get a large judgment, amounting to many millions of dollars, and if the Indians do not pay the Kelloggs $1.25 for each member of the family every month, then they are going to be denied participation in this $500,000,000,000 or $500,000,000 that they will get after a while.

Senator THOMAS: What do you base that statement on?

Mr. MERRITT: I base it on complaints that have been received in the Indian Office and complaints that have been received by the Department of Justice, and just to show the method of defrauding these Indians by these alleged friends of the Indians, who are constantly abusing the authorities so that they can build up sentiment to collect money from these Indians, I would like to have inserted in the record a statement prepared by the Department of Justice on this subject.

Senator THOMAS: Do you have that statement?

Mr. MERRITT: We have the statement here.

Senator THOMAS: Is it long?

Mr. MERRITT: Not very long. We have information in our files which shows that they have gone so far as to require these poor, helpless Indians to sell their chickens in order to pay them $1.25 a month, and they have been told that they are going to get this judgment of $500,000,000, and if they do not pay this money to these people, they are going to lose their participation in this judgment.

Senator WHEELER: Mr. Merritt, the thing I am more interested in—of course, if that is going on it should be stopped, but what I am more interested in—is the question as to how we should go about it, if you feel that Congress can help them. I mean, what is the occasion of collecting this information? What was the occasion of the collecting of the information with reference to these people?

Mr. MERRITT: The Department of Justice collected the information. There was a complaint made against them by the United States attorney in Wisconsin, that they were defrauding Indians.

Senator WHEELER: Using the United States mails to defraud?

Mr. MERRITT: Using the mails to defraud, and also collecting money, personally. It shows that they have been collecting as high as $500 a month from these poor Indians.

Senator WHEELER: If they were doing what you say they were doing, using the mails to defraud, of course, the Department of Justice should prosecute them for doing it. Has the Department of Justice ever filed any prosecution against them?

Mr. MERRITT: They have investigated the cases and found out the methods of collecting the money.

Mr. KELLOGG: Mr. Chairman, may I say—

Senator WHEELER: You just sit down. You have had your say. Now, why was it that the Department of Justice did not prosecute them, if the facts are as you say they are?

Mr. MERRITT: They collect this money—

Senator WHEELER: My question is, why has not the Department of Justice prosecuted them, if they are doing as you say?

Mr. MERRITT: It is rather difficult to get enough evidence to convict in a matter of this kind, notwithstanding the fact that it is well known that they are actually collecting the money.

Senator WHEELER: But if what you say is true, there is a perfect case against them for using the mails to defraud. If they have been going out and talking to these Indians and telling these Indians that they were going to collect several million dollars, and they would not be able to participate in it in the event that they did not pay a dollar a head to these Kelloggs, and then, in carrying out this underhand scheme, they used the mails or wrote letters in connection with that, there is a perfect case under the Federal statutes of using the mails to defraud.

Mr. MERRITT: We have a great many complaints about it, but it is rather difficult to convict in a case of that kind.

Senator WHEELER: But, Mr. Merritt, I have prosecuted any number of cases of just that sort. Now, there should not be any difficulty in getting a conviction if the facts are as you say they are—not in the least.

Mr. MERRITT: As to the remedy for this situation, it is my view that there should be legislation by Congress so as to give a definite jurisdiction to the Federal Government, and so that the line of demarcation between the State government and the Federal Government will be absolutely clear. We are not seeking additional jurisdiction over any Indians. I would like to have these New York Indians be an example to the Indians in other States, and be absolutely free and independent of the Federal Government. These Indians have been living for hundreds of years in the State of New York. For the last hundred years they have been surrounded by a civilization and they are now surrounded by the highest civilization to be found in the America.

Senator WHEELER: I cannot agree with you on that. [Laughter.]

Mr. MERRITT: There is the greatest opportunity in the world for those Indians to stand on their own feet and to be absolutely independent of either the State or the Federal Government, because they have every opportunity to make good in their homes, on their lands. Also, there is every opportunity to find employment in the State of New York in the large enterprises surrounding these reservations. However, we recognize that those Indians do need assistance to be extricated from this jurisdictional situation in which we find them, and, after investigation, if the Congress wishes as a matter of policy to turn those Indians over the state government, it will be absolutely agreeable to the Indian Bureau.

On the other hand, if they find, after an investigation that their interests can be best protected by the Federal Government having jurisdiction in the matter, that will be entirely agreeable to the Indian Service; but we are not seeking further jurisdiction at this time.

Senator THOMAS: Why should not your Bureau give this matter some attention and make us some recommendation in the matter?

Senator WHEELER: Yes, I was just going to suggest that.

Mr. MERRITT: We have given it some attention; and at the suggestion of the committee we will be glad to give it further attention and to have legislation drafted for submission at the next regular session of Congress. I think it will take—

Senator THOMAS: We can never get any place unless there is a motion made. I move that the Indian Bureau be requested—

Senator WHEELER: Please let me make a remark before you make your motion.

Senator THOMAS: Very well.

Senator WHEELER: I was going to say, I think it would be well for either your legal department or the Department of Justice to analyze these treaties and the laws, and advise the committee with reference to the exact status of the situation, as to whether or not we can legislate with reference to this.

Senator THOMAS: I will make my motion to cover that.

Mrs. KELLOGG: May I say a word before your motion?

Senator THOMAS: I do not care.

Mrs. KELLOGG: I just want to ask the status of this commission; whether this commission is referring to the Indian Bureau under your suggestion the complaints of persecuted people who bring their troubles to this committee?

Senator WHEELER: Let us finish this.

Mrs. KELLOGG: I will be very glad, for the record's sake, too. I do want it.

Senator THOMAS: I move that the Indian Bureau and the Department of the Interior be invited and requested to make a special study of the New York Indian situation and advise the Congress of their legal rights—

The CHAIRMAN: You mean, advise this committee?

Senator THOMAS: That is what it means, of course. They will make the report to Congress, and it will come to this committee, of course. Now, I will continue with my motion and advise the Congress of their legal rights, together with such suggestions for legislation as the Department of the Interior will suggest and recommend. I think that it is broad enough to cover the whole situation.

Senator WHEELER: Yes, it is broad enough to cover it, and if you would include the Attorney General, I think it would be a good idea for the Attorney General to advise us as to the legal status and advise us whether or not we have a right to legislate concerning it.

Senator THOMAS: Would not the Department of the Interior handle that, anyway?

Mr. MERRITT: We will be glad to submit our report and to submit a draft of any legislation to the Attorney General for an expression of the Attorney General's view, before transmitting it to Congress.

(Informal discussion, off the record, here ensued.)

The CHAIRMAN: Are there any further remarks as to Senator Thomas's motion? If not, I will put the motion.

(The question was taken, and the motion was agreed to.)

Mrs. KELLOGG: Mr. Chairman, I am very much concerned about those poor chickens Mr. Merritt referred to, and, really, I should think that I better have another time in which to answer Mr. Merritt.

Mr. MERRITT: You are not answering Mr. Merritt. You are answering the charges made by the Department of Justice and complaints made by the Assistant Attorney General of the United States.

Mrs. KELLOGG: I want to ask Mr. Merritt if he has included in my black record the evidence secured by subornation of perjury in my arrest at Denver, Colo., by one of his officials, and if he recalls the fact that when I was appearing before the other Senate Committee, of 1916—or 1914 or 1917—the chief of the inspection forces, who was our star witness, committed suicide at the National Hotel so as not to appear?

Mr. MERRITT: That has absolutely nothing to do with the case; absolutely nothing whatever.

◆

[In the original document, H. Doc. No. 1590, 63d Cong., 3d sess. was reprinted in the pages that followed the above transcript.]

Appendix

·

Notes

·

References

·

Index

List of Selected Articles from Local, National, and International Newspapers

What follows is a chronological list of newspaper articles we are unable to reprint in full, but which have been very useful to us in piecing together the many facets of a very complex person, writer, and activist. Many of these articles have been digitized and will be available to the interested reader through searches in US databases. Although some of the newspaper accounts are sensationalist and appeal to the public's expectations of "Indian" representations some—if accurate—capture Laura's voice and tone, her quick wit and unwavering determination. Copies of the articles have also been deposited with the Cultural Heritage Department of the Oneida Nation in Wisconsin.

◆

"One Indian Maiden: Her Literary Plans for the Uplifting of Her Race." *New York Tribune*, February 15, 1903. A5.

Laura M. Cornelius (Neoskalita). "The Whites Do Not Understand the Indians; The Indians Do Not Understand Themselves, Says This Oneida Girl." *San Francisco Chronicle*, August 9, 1903, 7.

"Will Be the First Indian Girl Lawyer." *Los Angeles Times*, December 28, 1904, A1.

"An Indian Girl and Glad of It: Miss Cornelius Here to Study Law at Barnard." *The Sun*, February 11, 1906, 7. [Abstract: "Her Purpose to Help Her People—She Would not Be Anything Else than an Indian and She Wants to Prevent a Great Tragedy—Wrong Ideas of White People."]

Hapgood, Joseph. "American Indian Princess Interests Briton Statesmen; Cuts Quite a Dash in the British Metropolis—Unique Figure in Society—Tells Plans for Rehabilitation of Her Race." *Detroit Free Press*, September 19, 1909, C6. [Also reprinted in *Los Angeles Times*, September 26, 1909, II. 14, with new title: "Indian Maid in Europe: Her Mission, the Betterment of Dying Race; Iroquois Princess Gives her Ideas in London; Garden Cities among Others of her Plans."]

"The North American Indians: A Redskin Princess." *Review of Reviews for Australasia*, August 1909, 519–20. [Rubric: "Interviews on Topics of the Month."]

"Refutes Buffalo Bill; Indian Maiden Tells Him His Views of the Red Man Are Wrong." *New York Times*, May 13, 1910, 9.

"Looking for an Indian Booker T. Washington to Lead Their People." *New York Tribune*, August 27, 1911, image 17.

"Princess of Oneida Indians Is Arrested." *El Paso Herald*, October 12, 1913, section A. [Subheading: "Head of Indian Society and Husband Charged with Obtaining Money by Fraud and Impersonating Officers."]

"Asks Indians [to] Live in Model Villages: Woman, Herself of Aboriginal Blood, Urges Government [to] Give Plan Trial." *Washington Times*, May 10, 1914, 8.

"Laura Kellogg, Daughter of Long Line of Indian Chiefs, Laughs at the Old Idea of the Downtrodden Squaw." *Washington Herald*, February 16, 1915, 8. [Rubric: "First American Mothers Had 'Votes for Women.'"]

"Indian Princess Makes Plea for Self-Government." *La Crosse Tribune*, Monday June 26, 1916, 4.

"Would Plead Cause of the Indians before the League of Nations: Wisconsin Woman of Wealth and Education, Granddaughter of Famous Chief, Has Devoted Her Life to Obtaining More Justice for Her People." *Milwaukee Sentinel*, August 17, 1919.

"Indians Will Fight for New York Lands; Legal Battles to Be Begun Soon to Recover Lands Claimed by Indians." *Bemidji Daily Pioneer*, October 19, 1922, 1.

Herdman, Ramona. "A New Six Nations: Laura Cornelius Sees the Old Iroquois Confederacy Reestablished on a Modern Business Basis as the First Fulfillment of a Girlhood Vow Pledging Herself to the Welfare of Her Race." *Syracuse Herald*, November 6, 1927, 1.

"Federal Court Upholds Jones Chief of Six Nations; Judge Bryant Settles Long Tribe Fight; Ruling Powers of Confederacy Upheld in Federal Court; Thomas Loses Claim; Deathbed Testimony Was Taken from Clan Mother." *Syracuse Herald*, August 9, 1929, 4.

Notes

Chronology

1. *Indian Census Rolls, 1885–1940*, 1925, roll M595_203, p. 40, line 28, "Agency: Oneida" (National Archives Microfilm Publication M595, 692 rolls), Records of the Bureau of Indian Affairs, Record Group 75, National Archives, Washington, DC; "Descendants of Laura Miriam Cornelius," Oneida Nation in Wisconsin Cultural Heritage Department, Oneida, Wisconsin.

2. See Laurence M. Hauptman, *Seven Generations of Iroquois Leadership: the Six Nations since 1800* (Syracuse, NY: Syracuse University Press, 2008), 157–61.

3. Laurence Hauptman, *Seven Generations of Iroquois Leadership: The Six Nations since 1800* (Syracuse, NY: Syracuse University Press, 2008), 162; Frederick E. Hoxie, *Talking Back to Civilization: Indian Voices from the Progressive Era* (Boston and New York: Bedford/St. Martin's, 2001), 53.

Introduction

1. *Kalihwisaks*, January 24, 2013.

2. Loretta V. Metoxen, conversation with Kristina Ackley, January 4, 2013.

3. The Oneidas are part of the Six Nations or Iroquois Confederacy, or the Haudenosaunee ("people building a long house" or "people of the long house"), and the other five nations in the Iroquois/Six Nations Confederacy are the Mohawk, the Onondaga, the Cayuga, the Seneca, and the Tuscarora. On Kellogg's involvement in the Oneida land claims see Ackley, "Renewing Haudenosaunee Ties: Laura Cornelius Kellogg and the Idea of Unity in the Oneida Land Claim," *American Indian Culture and Research Journal* 32 (1): 57–81.

4. In 1821 the Oneidas settled in Wisconsin, on land acquired from the Menominee and Ho-Chunk, who initially agreed to a vast land base (8 million in 1822) for the "New York Indians," which included the Oneida, Stockbridge-Munsee, and Brothertown tribes. The Menominee and Ho-Chunk nations soon protested, saying they had thought the agreement stated that the New York Indians were to live upon their lands, not own them. Loretta V. Metoxen, tribal historian, argues that French fur traders who had married Menominee women and the new towns that were set up pressured the federal government to limit the land that the Oneida could hold. In 1831 and 1832, a series of treaties with the Oneida, the

federal government, the Menominee and Ho-Chunk nations, shrunk the vast land base along Lake Michigan to 500,000 acres. In 1838 the New York Indians, including the Oneida, were pressured to leave Wisconsin for Kansas. The 1838 Treaty of Buffalo Creek guaranteed approximately 65,400 acres for Oneida tribal members, and established the current reservation boundaries. See "Treaties in Wisconsin: an Interview with Loretta V. Metoxen," Oneida Nation in Wisconsin, accessed January 9, 2014, http://www.oneidanation.org/culture/page.aspx?id=2462. To understand the complex history of the Oneida Nation in the eighteenth- and nineteenth-centuries, see Karim M. Tiro, *The People of the Standing Stone: the Oneida Nation from the Revolution through the Era of Removal* (Amherst, MA: University of Massachusetts Press, 2011).

5. The changes in Oneida politics caused by this dislocation included the dwindling importance of clan affiliation and the transformation of the Oneida social structure into a patrilineal one, evolving from a traditional Iroquois matrilineal model.

6. After the Dawes General Allotment Act (1887), the Oneidas faced "uncontrolled timber stripping of their lands, serious soil erosion, low leasing arrangements, and increased consumption of alcohol." After the 65,000-acre Oneida reservation was allotted in 1892, a federal "competency" commission was formed in 1918, which "began issuing fee patents to Oneidas of less than one-half Indian blood in order to quicken the process of assimilation." Hauptman, "Designing Woman: Minnie Kellogg, Iroquois Leader," in *Indian Lives: Essays on Nineteenth- and Twentieth-Century Native American Leaders*, edited by L. G. Moses and Raymond Wilson (Albuquerque: University of New Mexico Press, 1985), 162–63.

7. "Salt Lake's Merry Morn in Riverside," *Los Angeles Times*, March 13, 1904, 7.

8. Hauptman, "Designing Woman," 170.

9. It is very likely that Kellogg's papers did not survive. In a conversation with Laurence Hauptman, we learned that her adopted son, Robert E. Kellogg, may have burned her surviving papers. (Robert Kellogg died in 1997.) Laurence M. Hauptman, personal communication with Cristina Stanciu, July 2012. Robert Kellogg's family has expressed interest in learning more about the life of Laura Cornelius Kellogg. Cindy Mill, personal communication with Kristina Ackley, February 2013 and December 2013.

10. Patricia Stovey (146) argues that, "throughout her life, Kellogg demonstrated a high level of comfort using other people's money for projects that some would consider highly risky [. . .], [yet] Kellogg was never convicted of any financial wrongdoing." Stovey, "Opportunities at Home: Laura Cornelius Kellogg and Village Industrialization," in *Oneida Voices in the Age of Allotment, 1860–1920*, edited by Laurence M. Hauptman and L. Gordon McLester III (Norman: University of Oklahoma Press, 2006), 146.

11. "Salt Lake's Merry Morn in Riverside," *Los Angeles Times*, March 13, 1904, 7.

12. In her important essay on Kellogg, Ramona Herdman (1) claims that, although Laura had been courted by many white men, Orrin Kellogg may have been a better suitor for her because of his presumed Seneca ancestry: "32nd degree of Seneca blood mixed with his white ancestry." See "A New Six Nations: Laura Cornelius Sees the Old Iroquois Confederacy Re-established On a Modern Business Basis as the First Fulfillment of a Girlhood Vow Pledging Herself to the Welfare of Her Race," *Syracuse Herald*, November 6, 1927.

13. "Indian New Woman," *Washington Post*, December 4, 1898, 26.

14. "One Indian Maiden: Her Literary Plans for the Uplifting of Her Race," *New York Tribune*, February 15, 1903, A5.

15. Laurence Hauptman's work is foundational in Iroquois Studies and his ground-breaking essay on Kellogg has inspired a generation of scholars. See Hauptman, "Designing Woman," 159–88. We very much respect Professor Hauptman's work and build on it, yet we propose to move the reading of Kellogg's legacy beyond the "tragedy" aura to understand more fully the legacy of this public intellectual woman's work.

16. *Hearings Before the Subcommittee of the Committee on Agriculture and Forestry, United States Senate, 64th Cong., 2nd Session, Pursuant to S. Res. 305, A Resolution Authorizing and Requesting the Senate Committee on Agriculture and Forestry to Hear and Consider Testimony Relative to the Garden City and Garden Suburb Movement* (February 9, 1917) ("The Garden City Movement").

17. "Salt Lake's Merry Morn in Riverside," *Los Angeles Times*, March 13, 1904, 7.

18. "Personals," *Detroit Free Press*, July 13, 1898; *Indiana Democrat* [Indiana, PA], Dec. 28, 1898.

19. "Indian New Woman," *Washington Post*, December 4, 1898, 26.

20. "One Indian Maiden," A5.

21. *Oneida County, N.Y. v. Oneida Indian Nation of New York State*, 470 U.S. 226 (1985). See also Laurence Hauptman, *The Iroquois Struggle for Survival: World War II to Red Power* (Syracuse, NY: Syracuse University Press, 1985), especially 33–34.

22. Society of American Indians, ed., *Report of the Executive Council on the Proceedings of the First Annual Conference of the Society of American Indians* (Washington, DC: Society of American Indians, 1912), 92.

23. Laura Cornelius Kellogg, "Some Facts and Figures on Indian Education," in *Report of the Executive Council*, 34–36.

24. For a look at Seneca "mothers of the nation," see Joy Bilharz, *The Allegany Senecas and the Kinzua Dam: Forced Relocation through Two Generations* (Lincoln:

University of Nebraska Press, 1998), 147–48. Laurence M. Hauptman also highlights this aspect in his work on Seneca activist Alice Lee Jemison in *Seven Generations of Iroquois Leadership: The Six Nations Since 1800* (Syracuse, NY: Syracuse University Press, 2008), especially 194–202.

25. Grant Wallace, "The Exiles of Cupa," *Out West Magazine*, July 1903, 25–41.

26. "An Indian Heroine of Peace: Laura M. Cornelius, the Oneida Girl Who Kept the Copah Tribe from Going on the Warpath," *St. Louis Republic*, December 1904, 1.

27. "Why the Warner Ranch Indians Moved Quietly," *San Francisco Chronicle*, June 14, 1903, 2.

28. "Will Be the First Indian Girl Lawyer," A1. The first-known Indian woman to argue a case in the Supreme Court may have been Lyda Conley (1874–1946), of Wyandott and European ancestry. For more on Lyda Conley, see the biographical entry, "Lyda Conley, Guardian of Huron Cemetery, 1874–1946" by Barbara Magerl, Missouri Valley Special collections. http://www.kchistory.org/cdm4/item_viewer .php?CISOROOT=/Biographies&CISOPTR=21&CISOBOX=1&REC=7. Accessed January 13, 2014

29. "An Indian Girl and Glad of It: Miss Cornelius Here to Study Law at Barnard," *The Sun*, February 11, 1906, 7.

30. Ibid.

31. Joseph Hapgood, "American Indian Princess Interests Briton Statesmen; Cuts Quite a Dash in the British Metropolis—Unique Figure in Society—Tells Plans for Rehabilitation of Her Race," *Detroit Free Press*, September 1909, C6.

32. "Last Indian Princess to Become Mrs. Kellogg," *San Francisco Call*, April 26, 1912, 1.

33. *Galveston Daily News*, October 11, 1910, 1. According to this brief entry in *The Galveston Daily News*, "Princess Neoskalita, chieftainess of the Oneida Iroquois Nation, is at present in London, under the name of Miss Laura Cornelius. She has gone abroad to complete her studies, begun at Leland Stanford University, and later at Columbia University. She is studying the art, social lore, music and literature of the French and English and the system of town planning in Germany. She is an Indian Princess of pure descent and has alms for elevating her people. To illustrate her ideas she has just finished a novel on the manners and customs of the aborigines of America. "Wynnogene," or "A Ray of Light," is the name of the book, and treats of the days before Columbus. She is the first real Indian to write such a work of fiction. From accounts, she is a social toast in the city."

34. "The North American Indians: A Redskin Princess," *The Review of Reviews for Australasia*, August 1909, 519–20, quote on p. 519.

35. Joseph Hapgood, "Indian Maid in Europe: Her Mission, the Betterment of Dying Race; Iroquois Princess Gives Her Ideas in London; Harden Cities among Others of Her Plans," *Los Angeles Times*, September 26, 1909, II 14.

36. Joseph Hapgood, "American Indian Princess Interests Briton Statesmen," C6.

37. "Would Plead Cause of the Indians before the League of Nations: Wisconsin Woman of Wealth and Education, Granddaughter of Famous Chief, Has Devoted Her Life to Obtaining More Justice for her People," *Milwaukee Sentinel*, August 17, 1919, 1.

38. "Laura Kellogg, Daughter of Long Line of Indian Chiefs, Laughs at the Old Idea of the Downtrodden Squaw," *Washington Herald*, February 16, 1915, 8.

39. US Department of the Interior, Office of Indian Affairs, 1-9050, 63879-1908. The Commissioner of Indian Affairs affixed a description of Laura Cornelius in the letter to the secretary of the interior from September 25, 1908. Although she was denied her request of being introduced to court (because the American ambassador wasn't inclined to do so), her request is perhaps more telling than the denial.

40. "Refutes Buffalo Bill; Indian Maiden Tells Him His Views of the Red Man Are Wrong," *New York Times*, May 13, 1910, 9.

41. Joseph Hapgood, "American Indian Princess Interests Briton Statesmen," C6. As A. LaVonne Ruoff's 1997 edition has shown, S. Alice Callahan's *Wynema: A Child of the Forest* (1891) is the first known novel written by a woman of American Indian descent.

42. "The North American Indians: A Redskin Princess," 519.

43. "Laura Cornelius Kellogg to Carlos Montezuma," 15 September 1914, Carlos Montezuma Papers, Roll 3 [page. 8 of letter]. In the same letter, sent almost a year after her dismissal from the SAI, although friendly toward Montezuma, she was not shy to state her feelings for the other SAI members: "You may all think of me what you damn please—you are such a gullible lot of fools" [page 14 of letter].

44. "Trail (The) of the Morning Star: Indian Play in 1 Act by Princess E-gah-tah-yen (i.e., Mrs. O. J. Kellogg). 1916." *Catalog of Copyright Entries*, part 1 (B), group 2. Pamphlets, Etc., New Series 13 (3): 230. (Washington, DC: Government Printing Office).

45. "To Solve Indian Problem: Oneida Princess Is Championing Bill for Autonomous Government of Her Race," *The Edgefield Advertiser*, April 12, 1916, [n.p.].

46. See also Cristina Stanciu, "An Indian Woman of Many Hats: Laura Cornelius Kellogg's Embattled Search for an Indigenous Voice," *Studies in American Indian Literatures* 25, no. 2 and *American Indian Quarterly* 37, no. 3 (2013): 87–115.

47. Jack Campisi, "Ethnic Identity and Boundary Maintenance in Three Oneida Communities," especially 154, 184–85. On the Wisconsin Oneidas receiving the *Katsistowan^*, see "The Fire Comes Home to the Oneida Longhouse," *Kalihwisaks*, September 1, 2005, 7.

48. [Merrill, Frank Wesley, ed.], "The Sacrifice of the White Dog," in *The Church's Mission to the Oneidas* (Oneida Indian Reservation, Wisconsin; Fond du Lac, WI: P. B. Haber, 1902), 57.

49. "One Indian Maiden: Her Literary Plans for the Uplifting of Her Race," *New York Tribune*, February 15, 1903, A5.

50. Overalls, a.k.a. "Mazinita," defies middle class and Victorian conventions as she wears overalls, travels by herself, and rides a wild bronco. The story also sets sharp contrasts between Eastern and Western behaviors and senses of propriety, painting an ideal image of the frontier, especially in the story's happy ending: Overalls falls in love with an Easterner, Tenderfoot. The story *Overalls and Tenderfoot* was originally published in *The Barnard Bear* 2 (2), March 1907, 2. Reproduced in this edition with permission from the Barnard Archives and Special Collections.

51. "A Tribute to the Future of My Race," *Red Man and Helper*, March 20, 1903, 1.

52. *The Church's Mission to the Oneidas* (Oneida Indian Reservation, Wisconsin; Fond du Lac, WI: P. B. Haber, 1902), 55 and 54.

53. The poem is written in 147 trochaic tetrameter lines. The title uses the word "race" in the sense of "people," and reflects early twentieth-century evolutionary thinking and terminology about the various "races of people" (what we would usually call ethnicities today) living in the United States. *A Tribute* was reprinted from *Riverside Daily Press* in the Carlisle Indian Industrial School publication *Red Man and Helper*, March 20, 1903, 1. The poem is also reprinted and annotated in Robert Dale Parker, *Changing Is Not Vanishing: A Collection of American Indian Poetry to 1930* (Philadelphia: University of Pennsylvania Press, 2011), 253–57.

54. "Some Facts and Figures on Indian Education," in *Report of the Executive Council*, 36.

55. *Lorado Taft's Indian Statue "Black Hawk": An Account of the Unveiling Ceremonies at Eagle Nest Bluff, Oregon, Illinois, July the First, Nineteen Hundred and Eleven. Frank O. Lowden Presiding* (Chicago: University of Chicago Press, 1912), 33–34, 44.

56. Source of photo: "Industrial Organization for the Indian," in *Report of the Executive Council on the Proceedings*, 43–55. Photo on page 43.

57. Tom Holm, *The Great Confusion in Indian Affairs: Native Americans and Whites in the Progressive Era* (Austin: University of Texas Press, 2005), 77.

58. "Industrial Organization for the Indian," in *Report of the Executive Council*, 43–55.

59. Ibid., 43, 44, 44–45, 45.

60. Ibid., 50, 54, 55.

61. Hazel Hertzberg attributes this silence to "scheduling pressures," which made impossible the discussion of "most papers on industrial problems." See *The Search for an American Indian Identity: Modern Pan-Indian Movements* (Syracuse, NY: Syracuse University Press, 1971), especially 60–61.

62. "Some Facts and Figures on Indian Education," in *Report of the Executive Council*, 36. Laura Cornelius served as the SAI's vice-president of education in 1912.

63. Laura Cornelius's report on "figures" includes the following: "There are altogether 357 government schools; 70 of these reservation boarding schools, 35 non-reservation boarding schools, and 223 day schools. The enrollment in these schools totals 24,500 children. Besides these, there are 4,300 children in the mission schools and 11,000 in public, of the 11,000, the Five Civilized Tribes of Oklahoma have 6,900. The number of the children of the race in school in the country then is 39,800. The last report shows an increase of nearly 2,000 in attendance over the year before." Society of American Indians, ed., *Report of the Executive Council*, 40.

64. Most SAI members used the term "the Indian" most frequently, but they often referred to "the Indian race" or the "race." Besides these designations, many SAI members and Indian public intellectuals used the phrases "our people" or "the Indian people," with the words "people" and "tribe" being synonymous occasionally. See Hertzberg, *The Search for an American Indian Identity*, 71.

65. "Some Facts and Figures on Indian Education," in *Report of the Executive Council*, 38, 39, 46.

66. Patricia Stovey, "Opportunities at Home: Laura Cornelius Kellogg and Village Industrialization," in *Oneida Voices in the Age of Allotment, 1860–1920*, edited by Laurence M. Hauptman and L. Gordon McLester III, (Norman, OK: University of Oklahoma Press, 2006), 147.

67. "Princess of Oneida Indians Is Arrested," *El Paso Herald*, October 12, 1913, 1.

68. Fellow Iroquois SAI member Arthur C. Parker (Seneca) accused her of dancing "in the nude for the benefit of the Indian people," an allegation never substantiated with any evidence. Arthur C. Parker to J. N. B Hewitt, August 30, 1913. Parker writes in his letter to Hewitt that "clippings are shown from theatrical papers and the Sunday supplement," but no evidence so far has emerged to sustain this accusation. The SAI Papers, quoted in Lucy Maddox, *Citizen Indians: Native American Intellectuals, Race and Reform* (Ithaca: Cornell University Press, 2005), 193n57.

69. "Laura Kellogg, Daughter of Long Line of Indian Chiefs, Laughs at the Old Idea of the Downtrodden Squaw," *Washington Herald*, February 16, 1915, 8.

70. Stovey, "Opportunities at Home," 145.

71. "Laura Cornelius Kellogg, Iroquois, Replies to Secretary Lane's Reform Statement," *Washington Post*, May 2, 1914, 11. *The Washington Times* also picked up the story in "Asks Indians [to] Live in Model Villages: Woman, Herself of

Aboriginal Blood, Urges Government [to] Give Plan Trial," *Washington Times*, May 1914, 8.

72. "Recall of Agents or Superintendents by Indian Tribes Hearings before the United States Senate Committee on Indian Affairs," 64th Congress, *First CIS Hearings* (64) S. 53, 1916, 9–15.

73. According to a newspaper account from 1919, Kellogg's title for this book may have been *The Failure of American Democracy*. She is quoted saying that the book was at that point in the hands of the publisher, which suggests that Burton Publishing altered the title of the book (perhaps for marketing if not also for political reasons). "Would Plead Cause of the Indians before the League of Nations: Wisconsin Woman of Wealth and Education, Granddaughter of Famous Chief, Has Devoted Her Life to Obtaining More Justice for her People," *Milwaukee Sentinel*, August 17, 1919.

74. According to the *Washington Herald*, in May 1913, Kellogg gave a private lecture at the home of Mrs. Josiah Quincy Kern, a member of the District school board in Washington D.C., and wife of Professor Robert Kern (Chair of Sociology, George Washington U). The newspaper records: "Mrs. Kellogg spoke in a forceful way of the deplorable conditions of Indian affairs, and showed striking familiarity with [those] conditions." An elaborate dinner, with music and other entertainments were given in honor of Laura and Orrin J. Kellogg. "Reform in Handling Indian Affairs Needed: Mrs. Laura C. Kellogg, a Member of [the] Oneida Tribe, Lectures Here," *Washington Herald*, May 13, 1913, 2.

75. Warren K. Moorehead, "Review of *Our Democracy and the American Indian*," *Mississippi Valley Historical Review* 8, no. 3 (1921): 281.

76. *Our Democracy and the American Indian*, 17, 22.

77. Ibid., 23–25.

78. Ibid., 29, 30, 28–29, 31.

79. "Lolomi" reflects Kellogg's understanding of a Hopi term to mean "perfect goodness be upon you," 34–35.

80. *Our Democracy and the American Indian*, 41, 63–64, 65–81.

81. Ibid., 82–83, 89, 90, 103.

82. Ibid., 58. Kellogg wrote that she took the name "Lolomi" from what was Hopi for "perfect goodness be upon you."

83. Ibid., 58.

84. Ibid., 38, 83, 85–86, 91, 89.

85. "Indian Maid in Europe: Her Mission, the Betterment of Dying Race; Iroquois Princess Gives her Ideas in London; Harden Cities among Others of her Plans," *Los Angeles Times*, September 26, 1909, 14.

86. *Our Democracy and the American Indian*, 92.

87. "One Indian Maiden: Her Literary Plans for the Uplifting of Her Race," *New York Tribune*, February 15, 1903, A5.

88. Patricia Stovey offers a detailed look at Kellogg's proposal to buy the school in "Opportunities at Home: Laura Cornelius Kellogg and Village Industrialization," 143–75.

89. For more on the federal policy of allotment and the experiences of the Oneida Nation in Wisconsin, an account was prepared by Oneida Nation in Wisconsin Cultural Heritage Department that discusses the rapid land loss that resulted from this policy and includes firsthand accounts of Ida Blackhawk and Jessie Peters. See "Dawes Allotment Act, 1887–1897," accessed December 29, 2013, http://www.oneida nation.org/culture/page.aspx?id=2486.

90. United States, Dept. of the Interior, "Statistics of Indian Tribes, Indian Agencies, and Indian Schools of Every Character," (Washington: Government Printing Office, 1899), 36.

91. *The Church's Mission to the Oneidas*, 52.

92. Ibid., 52.

93. Herbert S. Lewis and L. Gordon McLester, eds., *Oneida Lives: Long-Lost Voices of the Oneida* (Lincoln: University of Nebraska Press, 2005), 401. For a positive recollection of Kellogg in *Oneida Lives*, see Marian Cornelius, "Mothers, Children, and Medicine," 46–48. For a negative one, see John A. Skenandore, "Oneida Boarding School," 304–6.

94. "Students at the Oneida Boarding School," Timeline, 1907–1919, Ernie Stevens, Sr. Collection, Oneida Nation in Wisconsin Division of Land Management (henceforth *ONDLM*), Oneida, WI.

95. The early twentieth century saw great changes in Oneida tribal governance of the reservation, moving away from the hereditary system of government in place during much of the nineteenth century. Correspondence from this time period refers to tribal council meetings as well as to influential Oneida leaders. Kellogg also became involved in the Oneida National Committee, which had a membership that extended beyond the Wisconsin reservation to include other Oneida people in New York State and elsewhere. In 1936 the Oneida Executive Committee (which later became the current Oneida Business Committee) was established as the legislative body of the Oneida Tribe, while the Oneida General Tribal Council is the governing body.

96. In 1919, Superintendent Edgar A. Allen reported on a dispute among the Oneidas as to what should be done with the Oneida Boarding School. Letter to Commissioner of Indian Affairs, October 5, 1919, Oneida Nation Land Management. Complaints were made against Kellogg by Eli Skenandie. Letter to J. C. Hart, January 17, 1919, *ONDLM*.

97. Letter to J. B. Broekman, November 17, 1920, *ONDLM*.

98. The letter was signed by Peter Danforth, Joseph Skenadore, Thomas Skenandore, J. M, Cornelius, Thomas Metoxen, L. King, and L. C. Kellogg. Letter to Hon. John Barton Payne, June 24, 1920, *ONDLM*.

99. The Committee was made up of President Samuel Plantz of Lawrence College, Attorney F. S. Bradford, Attorney T. H. Ryan, and W. E. Fairfield, M.D. Letter to Secretary of the Interior, May 21, 1920, *ONDLM.*

100. Letter to Edward E. Browne, House of Representatives from Commissioner Cato Sells, May 8, 1920, *ONDLM.*

101. Letter to Cato Sells, Commissioner of Indian Affairs, January 31, 1921, *ONDLM.*

102. Kellogg represented a group of Oneidas who were known variously as the Oneida Improvement Association, Oneida Advancement Association, and the Oneida National Council. Letter to Senator Irvine L. Lenroot, February 1, 1922; Letter to Hon. Commissioner Charles C. Burke, September 2, 1924, *ONDLM.*

103. Letter to Edgar A. Allen, December 12, 1922, Oneida Nation Land Management. Letter to Commissioner of Indian Affairs, April 11, 1922, Oneida Nation Land Management. Letter to Commissioner Charles Burke, January 1, 1923, *ONDLM.*

104. Patricia Stovey depicts Kellogg as the individual in charge, almost as if she were working alone, thus putting less of an emphasis on the Oneida National Committee or its members. See Stovey, "Opportunities at Home," 171.

105. In April 15, 1924, Murphy Land and Investment Company submitted a successful bid of $21,744.25, and then transferred title to the Catholic Diocese. In October 13, 1924, the acting assistant commissioner wrote, "As you probably know, from the correspondence in this matter, that the Murphy Land and Investment Company, of which I am secretary is not the real purchaser of the property. As a matter of fact, we are purchasing the property for Anthony J. Koeferl, secretary of the Catholic Diocese of Green Bay." Letter to C. F. Hauke, Acting Assistant Commissioner, October 13, 1924, *ONDLM.*

106. In August 1924 a letter from the Oneida National Committee protested the sale. Members of committee included Thomas King, Hira Doxtator, M. N. Powless, and John Powless. Letter to Commissioner Charles H. Burke, August 28, 1924, *ONDLM.*

107. Letter to Reverend Rhodes, November 18, 1924, *ONDLM.*

108. Letter to Mr. Sam Bell, April 24, 1926, *ONDLM.*

109. Oneidas continued to work at Guardian Angels and some Oneida children resided there along with non-Native children. Many Oneida tribal members worked to have the property returned to the Oneidas. Loretta V. Metoxen, Oneida tribal historian, recounts many afternoons she spent with the bishop of Green Bay informally negotiating to buy the property (she said she "drank quite a bit of tea!"). Kristina Ackley's grandfather, Manuel Torres, Sr., worked at Guardian Angels for the diocese in custodial and landscaping for many years, transitioning to work for the tribe when the land was sold back to the Oneidas. As a child, Kristina remembers using

the property often, mostly for swimming in the small pond behind the old Oneida Boarding School, not realizing at the time that it was owned by the Catholic Diocese.

110. "Council Fires Blaze Again; Oneidas Astir," *Milwaukee Journal*, April 22, 1923, 2.

111. *U.S. v. Boylan*, 265 F. 165 (2d Cir. 1920).

112. See Blue Clark, *Lone Wolf v. Hitchcock: Treaty Rights and Indian Law at the End of the Nineteenth Century*, (Lincoln: University of Nebraska Press, 1999).

113. See especially the arguments in *Deere et al. v. State of New York et al.*, 22 F. 851 (N.D. New York 1927).

114. Laurence M. Hauptman, *The Iroquois and the New Deal* (Syracuse, NY: Syracuse University Press, 1981), 13; Philip O. Geier, "A Peculiar Status: A History of Oneida Indian Treaties and Claims" (PhD diss., Syracuse University, 1980); and Hauptman, *The Iroquois Struggle for Survival: World War II to Red Power* (Syracuse, NY: Syracuse University Press, 1985), 187.

115. Ramona Herdman, "A New Six Nations: Laura Cornelius Sees the Old Iroquois Confederacy Re-established On a Modern Business Basis as the First Fulfillment of a Girlhood Vow Pledging Herself to the Welfare of Her Race," *Syracuse Herald*, November 6, 1927, 1; Hauptman, *The Iroquois Struggle for Survival*, 184, and Campisi, "Ethnic Identity and Boundary Maintenance," 442–43.

116. *Our Democracy and the American Indian*, 26.

117. "Indian Claims to Empire State Outlined," *Fond du Lac Reporter*, October 10, 1922.

118. Laura Cornelius Kellogg to Cato Sells, June 21, 1919, #806-19-69348 (Oneida), BIA, Record Group 75, National Archives.

119. "Indian Leader Calls Occasion a Renaissance," *Fond du Lac Reporter*, October 10, 1922. Jack Campisi has also noted that the movement was important because it signaled a rise in the leadership and influence of Haudenosaunee women in the Wisconsin Oneida community. See Campisi, "Ethnic Identity and Boundary Maintenance," 152–53.

120. For a discussion of the ceremony and Kellogg's role, see Ackley, "Renewing Haudenosaunee Ties," in *American Indian Culture and Research Journal* 32 (1), 57–81.

121. 70th Cong., S. Res. 79 (1928).

122. Senate Subcommittee of the Committee on Indian Affairs, *Survey of Conditions of the Indians of the United States: Hearings on S. Res. 79, New York Indians*, 71st Cong., 2nd sess., 1931, 4862.

123. Ibid., 4894.

124. Ibid., 4887–88.

125. Ibid., 4857.

126. Letter to Cato Sells, January 31, 1921, *ONDLM*.

127. *Survey of Conditions of the Indians of the United States*, 4895.

128. Ibid., 4861.

129. Ibid., 4860.

130. Ibid., 4862.

131. Hauptman, *The Iroquois and the New Deal*, 13–14.

132. *Shenandoah*, August 1984, Oneida Records Management, Oneida, Wisconsin.

133. "Dreamers and Doers," *Kalihwisaks*, March 18, 2010, 1.

134. "Looking for an Indian Booker T. Washington to Lead Their People," *New York Tribune*, August 27, 1911, 1.

Our Democracy and the American Indian

1. The League of Nations—an international organization established at the end of World War I as part of the Treaty of Versailles, promoting international cooperation toward peace. The League of Nations was officially formed in January 1920, a few months before Kellogg's book was published, and it ended in 1946, a few years before her death. In 1919, according to Wisconsin newspapers, Kellogg was expected to "Plead Cause of the Indians before the League of Nations" (*Milwaukee Sentinel*, August 17, 1919).

2. The Turtle Clan—one of the three Oneida clans (Turtle, Wolf, and Bear). According to the Oneida Nation in Wisconsin website, "The Turtle represents the Earth, as well as all the gifts that the earth provides the people. The Turtle teaches patience [. . .]; the Turtle is old and wise and well respected. Turtle Clan people need a strong base where they can live and grow roots. They move slowly to teach patience; lessons learned are not forgotten. Although Turtles may appear slow, their determination allows them to obtain their goals." Oneida Nation Museum, accessed December 29, 2013, http://www.oneidanation.org/museum/clans.aspx.

3. Kipling—reference to British novelist and Rudyard Kipling (1865–1936). The line Laura C. Kellogg cites in full ("He trod the ling like a buck in spring, and he looked like a lance at rest") is from Kipling's poem, "The Ballad of the East and West" (1899).

4. Epictetan—adjective derived from Epictetus (55–135 CE), Stoic Greek philosopher. Kellogg may use it as synonymous for "Stoic" when she refers to the "Epictetan School of the American Indian."

5. Sagoyewhata—also spelled as *Layé•wate*, one of the principal Chiefs of Mohawks, Turtle clan, also known as "Early Riser" (yaw ate). Layé•wate is one of the fifty titles conferred by the Peacemaker. Kellogg refers to his role anticipating the Peacemaker and the creation of the Iroquois Confederacy, and may have wanted to give weight to her words by likening the founding of the Confederacy to her

vision. Kellogg's spelling of Oneida words differs from contemporary spellings, and may have been influenced by written Mohawk translations from the early to mid-eighteenth century. Kellogg started work on publishing a dictionary of the Oneida language but did not finish it. In 1938, a project was funded through the Works Progress Administration (WPA) to employ Oneida writers to work full-time recording stories and interviews in the Oneida language at the reservation in Wisconsin. After WPA funding ran out, the project was re-named the Oneida Ethnological Study and operated from 1940–42. From this work a number of key sources on the Oneida Language emerged, including Floyd G. Lounsbury, *Oneida Verb Morphology* (New Haven: Yale University Press, 1953) and Amos Christjohn et al., *An Oneida Dictionary: Ukwehu•wehneha Tekaw^nate?nyése* (Green Bay: University of Wisconsin-Green Bay Press, 1996). The *Dictionary* is also available online: "Oneida Language Tools," accessed January 12, 2014, http://www.uwgb.edu/oneida /Dictionary.html. For more information on *Layé•wate*, see Bob Brown's translation of the Great Law, *Kayantlako*, unpublished manuscript, Oneida Cultural Heritage Department.

6. The Iroquois Confederacy—The Six Nations (the Senecas, the Cayugas, the Onondogas, the Oneidas, the Mohawk, and the Tuscaroras), or the Haudenosaunee, "People Building a Long House." Initially, it was a confederation of five nations, The League of Five Nations, before the Tuscaroras joined in 1722.

7. ongwe-onwe, odwaganha—[emphasis in the 1920 edition]. Also spelled as *ukwehu-we* ("real people," Haudenosaunee) and *atwa?kanha* (Native Americans other than Iroquois, or Haudenosaunee people). Kellogg's use of "savage" is a bit problematic, as she refers to tribal nations that did not have the Great Law and thus were not members of the Iroquois Confederacy, and she did not likely mean the term to be one of disrespect to other Native Americans.

8. The French General—She may be referring here to German-born French General Dieskau (Ludwig August von Dieskau, 1701–67), the French commander during the French and Indian War (1754–63).

9. The Tuscaroras—members of the Iroquois Confederacy since 1722. After they joined the other five Haudenosaunee nations (the Oneidas, the Mohawks, the Onondagas, the Senecas, and the Cayugas), the Five Nations became the Six Nations.

10. Wampum (or the wampum belt)—used by the Haudenosaunee to communicate important messages, to show status, for ceremonial purposes and in council meetings, also used as mnemonic devices. The Hiawatha wampum belt, the two-row wampum belt, and the George Washington Belt are perhaps the most famous wampum belts for the Haudenosaunee. The Hiawatha belt, in particular, carries special significance in its five geometric patterns: a tree in the middle, representing the Onondaga Nation, or the Keepers of the Central Fire, and four other patterns symbolizing

the other four nations of the confederacy (the Senecas to the West, the Mohawk to the East, and The Cayuga and the Oneida flanking the tree).

11. Galiwhago—*Kayanla?kó* or "Great Law." Kellogg refers to the formation of the Iroquois Confederacy. See Bob Brown, "Translation of the Great Law, *Kayant-lako*" (unpublished manuscript), Collections of Oneida Nation in Wisconsin Cultural Heritage Department, Oneida, WI.

12. The first Awakener—another reference to Sagoyewhata (see note 5 above).

13. Golden Calf—an idol, an object of worship in many cultures (sometimes a bull). According to the Torah, after Moses left his people for forty days as went up Mount Sinai to receive the Ten Commandments, the Israelites were afraid he might not return and asked Aaron to make an image of God. Instead, Aaron made the golden calf, an object of idolatry, which triggered Moses's ire.

14. The words "place," "history," "appreciation," "primitive stock," and "advanced" were emphasized in the 1920 edition.

15. Kellogg was a tireless critic of the Bureau of Indian Affairs, and opposed the paternalistic control that she felt stifled the reservation by limiting its economic potential. Proud of her education and a supporter of Indian education, she was elected vice president of education for the Society of American Indians in 1911. Yet, she was suspicious of federally run Native boarding schools for their lack of innovation and tendency to minimize the worth of the reservation. In this chapter Kellogg is calling out to Native people to reject a mindless acceptance of federal control and instead turn toward self-reliance. Kellogg's acerbic criticism extended to those Native people who worked for the Bureau and promoted the ideas that she found fault with ("syco-phants," or self-seeking, deferential, "yes-men"). See in particular her testimony in the Senate in 1929, in this volume, and Tom Holm, *The Great Confusion in Indian Affairs: Native Americans and Whites in the Progressive Era* (Austin: University of Texas Press, 2005), 79–80.

16. Tecumseh—a nineteenth century Shawnee leader who formed a powerful alliance of tribal nations in the Great Lakes region; the alliance included the Dela-ware, the Shawnee, the Kickapoo, the Miami, the Potawatomi, the Sauk, and the Wyandot. This alliance, or Confederacy, was a serious threat to the United States from 1808 to 1813, during the War of 1812, and what was known as Tecumseh's War in 1811. Tecumseh was well-known to resist Native land dispossession and a propo-nent of Native self-governance. Kellogg refers to both the potential that Tecumseh represented in Native unity and power, and the ultimate dissolution of Tecumseh's Confederacy after his death in 1813. Kellogg sees Tecumseh as a cautionary tale, and warns against tribal in-fighting and allegiance to a colonial power, which uses "divide and conquer" tactics. For more information on Tecumseh, see Gregory Evans Dowd, *A Spirited Resistance: The North American Struggle for Unity, 1745–1815* (Baltimore: John Hopkins University Press, 1992).

17. Kellogg draws on derisive terms in this chapter to call out Native people who take part in the oppression of Native people and Native nations ("warehouse Indians" and "blanket Indians"), putting self-interest against the needs of the reservation community.

18. In using the term "political bosses," Kellogg refers to a common Progressive Era complaint against the political machines, Democrat and Republican, which worked to get politicians elected for the advantage of certain populations. She links the well-known critique of political machines such as the Democratic Tammany Hall, which ran New York City in the late nineteenth and early twentieth century, to the Bureau of Indian Affairs, and the control the federal authorities exerted over the lives of Native people.

19. Lolomi—It is unclear to us why Kellogg decided to use a Hopi term. She clearly wanted her plans for an industrial village to have widespread appeal, so using a term that evokes both aesthetics and intertribal relationships makes sense. Piatote writes that *lolomi* resembles *looloma*, a plural form of *lolma*, meaning "beautiful, good fit, aesthetically pleasing." See Beth H. Piatote, "Home/ward Bound," PhD diss. (Stanford University, 2007), 189; and The Hopi Dictionary Project, *Hopi Dictionary: Hopìikwa Lavàytutuveni* (Tucson: University of Arizona Press, 1998).

20. She attended Grafton Hall, a private school in Fond du Lac, Wisconsin, from which she graduated with honors in 1898.

21. "pinch-back white man"—Kellogg uses here one of G. Stanley Hall's phrases in his 1911 study. According to Hall, the Indian Bureau "is still trying to make a pinch-back white man instead of a noble Indian." This sentence appealed to Kellogg for obvious reasons. See G. Stanley Hall, "The Point of View toward the Primitive Races," in *The Journal of Race Development*, eds. George H. Blakeslee and G. Stanley Hall, (Clark University, 1910–11), 7.

22. The words "BUSINESS," "ECONOMIC," and "LOLOMI" were capitalized in the 1920 edition.

23. The original edition emphasizes the term "self-government." Kellogg believed that the federal government should honor and protect the unique political status of Native nations, most famously known as "domestic dependent nations" in the Supreme Court decision *Cherokee Nation v. Georgia*, 30 U.S. (5 Peters) 1 (1831). Kellogg may have accepted the concept of a domestic dependent nation, but she clearly believed that Native people should not be in a subservient position to the federal or state government. The inherent rights of governance of Indigenous nations and tribal sovereignty continue to be defined and debated today.

24. The Indian Rights Association of Philadelphia, the Boston Citizenship League and the Board of Indian Commissioners—These influential organizations were directed and supported by prominent non-Native philanthropists, and their membership was overwhelmingly non-Native.

25. Wilson—Woodrow Wilson, US president from 1913 to 1921.

26. Clark—James Beauchamp Clark (Missouri), speaker of the House of Representatives from 1911 to 1919.

27. Harry Lane—US senator (Oregon), 1913–17, and reformer of the Progressive Era.

28. The New York Bureau of Municipal Research was created in 1907 to professionalize and expand public service. Other cities formed similar Bureaus during this time. In the Appendix to the 1920 edition, there is a lengthy excerpt, "Municipal Research Document No. 65" (New York Bureau of Municipal Research, 1915).

29. Public Health and Marine Hospital Service, *Contagious and Infectious Diseases Among the Indians*, Document No. 1038, 62nd Cong., 3rd Sess., 1913. (Selections from this document also appear in the Appendix to the 1920 edition.)

30. *The New York Herald*—New York City's first popular, inexpensive, mass circulation newspaper, in operation from 1835 to 1924.

31. Henry Moore Teller—US senator (Colorado), 1876–82 and 1885–1909; US secretary of the interior, 1882–85.

32. Clapp—Moses Edwin Clapp, US senator (Minnesota), 1901–17.

33. Crow Hearings—US Senate, *Opening of the Crow Montana Indian Reservation on S. 2378, a Bill for the Opening and Settlement of a Part of the Crow Indian Reservation in the State of Montana: Hearings Before the Committee on Indian Affairs*, 64th Cong., 1st and 2nd sess., Pt. 1–4, December 6, 1915–December 13, 1916.

34. "Tribal funds"—Kellogg also solicited funds to support litigation and lobbying for different tribal issues, including the Oneida land claim in New York State. Federal officials and other Oneida people viewed her activities with suspicion, particularly since the land claim litigation was not successful during her lifetime. See the introduction to this edition, and Ackley, "Renewing Haudenosaunee Ties."

35. Carlisle Indian Industrial School—An off-reservation boarding school for Native American children founded by Richard H. Pratt in 1879 in Carlisle, Pennsylvania, in operation until 1918. It was a model of education premised on the assimilation of Native Americans and the dissolution of the reservation. See Brenda Child, *Boarding School Seasons: American Indian Families, 1900–1940* (Lincoln: University of Nebraska Press, 1998); Jacqueline Fear-Segal, *White Man's Club: Schools, Race, and the Struggle of Indian Acculturation* (Lincoln: University of Nebraska Press, 2007); David W. Adams, *Education for Extinction: American Indians and the Boarding School Experience, 1875–1928* (Lawrence, KS: University Press of Kansas, 1995).

36. Vladimir Ilyich Lenin (1870–1924) and Leon Trotsky (1879–1940)— Bolshevik leaders in the Russian Revolution of 1917. Kellogg appears to be linking the dismantling of tribal governments to the "revolutionaries" in the United States, who are acting in the interests of the federal government and business interests.

37. Kellogg and her husband, Orrin Joseph Kellogg, lectured and investigated irregularities in oil leases and at an Indian school on the Osage Reservation in Oklahoma in 1913. As a result of their activities, the Kelloggs were arrested for fraud, though they were exonerated of the charges. See Tom Holm, *The Great Confusion in Indian Affairs*, 75, and Laurence Hauptman, *Seven Generations of Iroquois Leadership*, 152.

38. Alexander Fyodorovich Kerensky briefly served as Prime Minister of the Provisional Government of Russia until he was overthrown in the October Revolution by the Bolsheviks. Vladimir Ilyich Lenin assumed power in 1917. Kellogg may have been referring to the mass appeal of the Bolsheviks, as opposed to Kerensky.

39. Edwin S. Johnson—US senator (South Dakota), 1915–21.

40. Charles Elroy Townsend—(Michigan), US senator, 1903–11.

41. Dr. Carlos Montezuma—(c.1866–1923) was a Yavapai-Apache surgeon and prominent intellectual. Montezuma served as an Indian Service physician, worked for Carlisle Indian School, was a founding member of the Society of American Indians, and edited a newsletter, *Wassaja* (1916–22). Well-known for his relentless criticism of the Bureau of Indian Affairs and belief in Native individualism as a means of self-empowerment, Montezuma's views were sometimes at odds with Kellogg's. See Peter Iverson, *Carlos Montezuma and the Changing World of American Indians* (Albuquerque: University of New Mexico Press, 1992).

42. Kellogg is affirming her belief that, while Native people needed to be free of federal paternalism and control, the political status of tribal governments needed to be protected and upheld. She believed the federal government had to uphold its trust responsibilities.

43. Wardship—a political and legal doctrine based on early Supreme Court decisions written by Chief Justice John Marshall, especially in *Worcester v. Georgia*, 31 U.S. 515 (1832). Native nations were ruled to be "domestic dependent nations" whose land was held in "trust" for them by the federal government. Federal policies and court decisions have largely upheld these principles, in some cases using this doctrine to exert overwhelming control of Native Americans. Native Americans were not considered citizens as a group (they were excluded from the Fourteenth Amendment) until 1924, when the Indian Citizenship Act, also known as the Snyder Act, was passed. See Tsianina Lomawaima and David E. Wilkins, *Uneven Ground: American Indian Sovereignty and Federal Law* (Norman: University of Oklahoma Press, 2001).

44. The word "DISSIPATION" was capitalized in the 1920 edition.

45. The Blackfeet Irrigation project of Montana—a Bureau of Reclamation Project intended to irrigate lands located in the central and eastern portions of the reservation and to support Blackfeet farmers. The project was designed with little input from the Blackfeet tribe, however, and was seen to be closely associated with allotment and the break-up of the reservation.

46. "lack of credit"—emphasized in the 1920 edition.

47. Here Kellogg quotes, almost verbatim, from Charles Mahlon Hollingsworth's *From Freedom to Despotism: A Rational Prediction and Forewarning* (Washington, DC: [self-published], 1910), 33. See especially chapter 3, "Constitutionalism and Despotism, as Adapted to Change and Fixity," 24–49.

48. Kellogg most likely means "between the Indian and the American," although this phrase also may also suggest the idea of the Indian *as* an American.

49. Siberia—large region in North Asia, part of the Russian Empire, later the Soviet Union and the Russian Federation, making up three quarters of the Russian territory. Among other things, Kellogg may be referring here to the economic destitution of Siberia during the Soviet era. As Kellogg was preparing this book for publication, President Woodrow Wilson had authorized a US Army force (The Expeditionary Force Siberia) to be stationed in Siberia in 1918. See Gibson Bell Smith, "Guarding the Railroad, Taming the Cossacks: The U.S. Army in Russia, 1918–1920," *Prologue Magazine* 34, no. 4 (Winter 2002), accessed December 29, 2013, http://www.archives.gov/publications/prologue/2002/winter/us-army-in-russia-1.html.

50. Oil trust, of the Beef trust, of the Lumber trust, of the Water trust, of the Coal trust—here Kellogg refers to several forms of industrial monopoly (a common target of Progressive Era reformers), equating them with the control the Bureau of Indian Affairs holds over Native lands. For a discussion of "the trust problem" resonating throughout *Our Democracy*, see contemporaneous Stanford Economics Professor Eliot Jones's *The Trust Problem in the United States* (New York: Macmillan, 1929).

51. The Bureau of Indian Affairs (BIA)—formed in 1824 as a division of the War Department as the Office of Indian Affairs, renamed in 1947 as the BIA, is a federal agency now under the US Department of the Interior. One of its main responsibilities is to administer over 55 million acres of Indian land held in trust by the United States. It is also an institution criticized acerbically by many Native American writers and activists. When Kellogg's book was published, Cato Sells was Commissioner of Indian Affairs (1913–21).

52. Contagious and Infectious Diseases among Indians, Marine Hospital Report, 1914—In 1912 and 1913, the Public Health and Marine Hospital Service conducted an investigation in twenty-five states about American Indians' health conditions. The resulting document, which Kellogg cites here, was recorded as Document No. 1038, 62nd Congress, 3d Session. See Warren K. Moorehead, *The American Indian in the United States; Period 1850–1914* (Massachusetts: Andover Press, 1915), especially 265–77.

53. The Service—or The Office of Indian Services: refers to one of the four offices of the Office of Indian Affairs, tasked with general assistance. (The other three include: the Office of Justice Services, The Office of Trust Services, and the Office of Field Operations.)

54. Talequah—city in the state of Oklahoma (previously The Indian Territory), which became a state in 1907; now the capital of the Cherokee Nation.

55. "[T]he investigation of Osage which I helped to make in 1913"—Here Kellogg refers to the infamous episode which ultimately led to her arrest in Pawhuska, Oklahoma, on October 11, 1913. According to the *El Paso Herald*, reporting the event, Laura and her husband were charged "with having obtained money under false pretenses and impersonating United States officials." The newspaper also insinuates that the arrest may have been "another move in the game now being played in the Osage county between the Department of the Interior and various big factors in the oil world." The charges against the Kelloggs were dropped.

56. " . . . the large interests to defraud the Indian"—Kellogg refers to the fraud that occurred during the allotment of the Osage reservation, begun in 1896, though not formalized until 1906. Fraudulent attempts of non-Natives to gain claim to the Osage oil-rich reservation lands proliferated in the early twentieth-century, from the enrollment of non-Osage to tribal membership rolls to intimidation and outright violence against Osage allottees. The period from 1920 through 1925 is known as "the Reign of Terror" because of more than two dozen murders of Osage allottees who had ties to profitable mineral leases. Though Kellogg is writing just before the spree of murders gained national attention, she clearly had done research in the area and was aware of the issues. See Donald L. Fixico, *The Invasion of Indian Country in the Twentieth Century*, 27–54.

57. " . . . the Indian women of the land"—Kellogg wrote favorably of women's rights elsewhere, including calling for women's suffrage and increased participation by women in national politics. She formed her understanding of the roles and responsibilities of women based on the Iroquois, or Haudenosaunee, who practiced a gender-specific form of governance that was based on an explicit understanding of women's power. Haudenosaunee women could be called to be clan mothers, whose responsibilities included selecting the chiefs who would speak for the people in council. Clan mothers could also remove chiefs, serving as an important check on governance. Haudenosaunee women also controlled cultivated land as owners and protectors, so it makes sense that Kellogg would appeal to women in her discussion of making the reservation a sustainable place for Native people. See Lina Sunseri, *Being Again of One Mind: Oneida Women and the Struggle for Decolonization* (Vancouver: University of British Columbia Press, 2011).

58. "[T]he moral purity which characterized this primitive stock"—here Kellogg is borrowing the lingo of the day, especially as she draws on anthropological ideas of kinship. Many of her SAI colleagues also used similar terms to talk about "race" and "civilization." At Barnard College, Kellogg took two classes in anthropology between 1906 and 1907, and she was also interested in social work, which may explain her use of the racialist terminology and her assumptions.

59. Sycophant—term refers to a servile person, a flatterer, or a slanderer. In this context, it probably alludes to Native people working for the Bureau of Indian Affairs (the BIA), whom Kellogg did not view favorably.

60. [T]he present Commissioner of Indian Affairs—Kellogg is referring to Cato Sells, commissioner of Indian Affairs, 1913–21.

61. Edgar A. Allen—a longtime employee of the Indian Service (1905–22). In 1918, Edgar A. Allen, who had been many years in the Indian Service as a superintendent and supervisor, became superintendent of the Keshena Agency, and thus mediated between the Oneidas and Washington, DC. He generally supported Kellogg's attempts to buy the Oneida Boarding School. See the introduction to the present volume.

62. General Pratt—Richard Henry Pratt (1840–1924), founder and superintendent of Carlisle Indian Industrial School in Carlisle, PA from 1879 until 1904. Kellogg was critical of Pratt's experiment of Americanizing Indian students through the off-reservation boarding school model. Instead, she argued for education at home. Elaine Goodale Eastman's biography of Pratt offers a favorable portrait in *Pratt, the Red Man's Moses* (Norman: University of Oklahoma Press, 1935).

63. "I went into the Service as a classroom teacher"—Here Kellogg refers to her work as an instructor at Sherman Institute, a government Indian school in Riverside, California, where she taught from 1902 until 1904. In 1904 she resigned in order to study law at Stanford University.

64. G. Stanley Hall—Professor of Education at Clark University. Kellogg refers to Hall's following statement, quoted in the hearings before the Committee on Indian Affairs in 1913: "This educational system is making a pinch-back white man instead of good Indian." (*Indian Appropriation Bill; Hearings before the Committee on Indian Affairs*, US Senate, 63rd Congress, 1st session, H.R. 1917 (Washington: Government Printing Office, 1913, 512). See also note 21.

65. Child-labor laws—While child labor laws were a Progressive Era cause, Kellogg was also concerned about federal boarding schools that relied on the labor of Native children. The Oneida Boarding School, or Indian Industrial School, operated from 1893 to 1919 and used children in household labor, farm work, and blacksmithing. See John A. Skenandore's recollection of a laundry-room accident that led to the loss of his arm as a child in *Oneida Lives: Long-Lost Voices of the Oneida*, eds. Herbert S. Lewis and L. Gordon McLester, 304–7.

Short Stories and Poems

1. "Long ago . . ."—By placing the story in the distant past, Kellogg links the story of the bean to the creation of the Haudenosaunee people. In Haudenosaunee cosmology, the bean is planted alongside squash and corn, known collectively as the "Three Sisters." Bean is the third sister, and climbs up through the squash and corn

to bind them all together. See John C. Mohawk, *Iroquois Creation Story: John Arthur Gibson and J. N. B. Hewitt's Myth of the Earth Grasper* (Buffalo, NY: Mohawk Publications, 2005).

2. Kellogg is most likely referring to kidney beans, which are used in corn bread. The Oneidas grew kidney, lima, and green beans, along with white corn and squash (and pumpkins). Today there is a community integrated food system (Tsyunhehkw^) that includes the Oneida Farm, an orchard, a cannery, a buffalo herd, retail stores, and a summer farmer's market. See "Oneida Nation: Tsyunhehkw,^" Oneida Nation in Wisconsin, accessed November 30, 2014, http://www.oneidanation.org/Tsyunhehkwa/.

3. Lalonyhawagon—The name of the Creator, also *Laluhyawá•ku*, "He upholds the Skyworld." Contemporary Haudenosaunee usage of the term is *Tehaluhyawá•ku*, "He is holding up the Skyworld." Randy Cornelius, personal communication, December 22, 2012.

4. " . . . their annual sacrifice of the White Dog"—Kellogg describes one aspect of Midwinter ceremonies. Midwinter is the first in an annual cycle of ceremonies that define the spiritual foundation of the Haudenosaunee people. Samuel Kirkland, a Presbyterian missionary who began his work among the Oneida in 1766, wrote in his journals that the white dog ceremony had not been performed in many years. See James P. Ronda, "Reverend Samuel Kirkland and the Oneida Indians," in *The Oneida Indian Experience*, eds. Jack Campisi and Laurence M. Hauptman (Syracuse, NY: Syracuse University Press, 1988), 26–27.

Essays

1. Richard Henry Pratt—the founder of Carlisle Indian Industrial School. Kellogg was critical of off reservation boarding schools, and believed the education to be inferior because students were not taught to value the potential of the reservation community. See also note 62 to *Our Democracy and the American Indian* (p. 272 in current edition).

2. Tammany Hall—a New York City Democratic political organization (from the late eighteenth to mid-twentieth century) that was characterized by political patronage, graft, and corruption.

3. "The Garden City"—a modern urban planning movement popular in Europe in the late nineteenth and early twentieth century that promoted self-contained communities that were surrounded by greenbelts, thought to provide an aesthetically pleasing and productive refuge from urban decay.

4. Mormon idea of communistic cooperation—Kellogg was impressed by Mormon society and its emphasis on industry and communal values, seeing them as a model and support for the community emphasis she valued for tribal nations.

5. Here Kellogg may refer to the political sentiments that supported Labor rights and social reforms on behalf of oppressed people.

6. "Indian territory"—Kellogg refers to reservations, lands held in common by tribal nations.

7. Patten—Kellogg refers here to Simon Nelson Patten (1852–1922), an economist and author, whose theories on industry, wealth, and economy were influential during the Progressive Era.

8. Kellogg quotes directly from Simon Patten's *The New Basis of Civilization* (Cambridge, MA: Belknap, 1907), 41. See especially the section, "The Basis in Heredity." Patten's book was based on a series of lectures he gave in 1905 for the School of Philanthropy in New York, which Kellogg most likely attended.

9. Kellogg may be referring here to Charles D. Carter (1868–1929), Chickasaw and Cherokee, a US representative from Oklahoma, who served in the US House of representatives for twenty years (1907–27). She may also be referring to Charles Curtis (1860–1936), an enrolled Kaw tribal member who served in the US House of Representatives (1893–1907, US Senate (1907–13 and 1915–29), and 31st vice-president of the United States (1929–33). In later years Kellogg sparred with Curtis in her congressional testimony.

Public Speeches and Congressional Testimonies

1. Here Kellogg quotes several lines from English Victorian poet Lord Alfred Tennyson's poem, "Tears, Idle Tears" (1847), first published as a section of *THE PRINCESS: A Medley*. The last line in Kellogg's version, "In . . . thinking of the days that are no more," is her own conflation of two different lines in the original poem: "In looking on the happy Autumn-fields, / And thinking of the days that are no more," 80–81.

2. " . . . a Dehoadilun, or an Oskanundunah"—two prominent Haudenosaunee leaders, known for their skills in oratory and negotiations on behalf of their people with the newly established United States. Red Jacket (ca. 1750–1830) was a Seneca leader while Oskanundunah (Oskanondonha), also known as Chief Skenandoah, was an Oneida leader. Oskanondonha worked closely with the missionary Samuel Kirkland.

3. Kellogg cites from English critic Walter Besant's "The Art of Fiction," first published in 1884, and reprinted in *Notices of the Proceedings at the Meetings of the Members of the Royal Institution of Great Britain, 1884–1886, with Abstracts of the Discourses Delivered at the Evening Meetings* 11 (London: William Clowes and Sons, 1887), 73.

4. Kellogg may allude here to British diplomat and historian James Bryce (1838–1922), ambassador to the United States, 1907–13, quoted also in the *San Antonio Gazette*, May 10, 1907.

5. Kellogg quotes here lines 2–6 from English Romantic poet John Keats' famous poem, "Ode on a Grecian Urn" (1820).

6. Tawasentha Niagara—Kellogg may refer here to the Tawasentha Valley of Albany County and the Niagara River of the middle and western part of New York State, part of the homeland of the Haudenosaunee people.

7. Stanzas from the last section (22) of Henry Wadsworth Longfellow, *The Song of Hiawatha* (1855), accessed December 12, 2013, http://www.hwlongfellow.org /poems_poem.php?pid=296.

8. Moch-Pe-O-Zon-Za. Kellogg may be using the Oneida word for "leader," which in its contemporary spelling is "*tyohʌ·tú*."

9. These lines seem to be Laura Cornelius Kellogg's conflation of three different lines from two poems by John Keats: "Endymion" ("By every wind that nods the mountain pine") and the unfinished epic poem "Hyperion" ("O aching time! O moments big as years! / All as ye pass swell out the monstrous truth.")

10. Mr. Moorehead—Warren K. Moorehead (1866–1939), prominent archaeologist, also an advocate for Indian rights.

11. Senator from Oklahoma—Robert Latham Owen (Oklahoma), US senator, 1907–25, a Progressive Era reformer of Cherokee descent.

12. CHAIRMAN—William J. Stone, US senator (Missouri), 1903–18.

13. Commissioner ABBOTT—F. H. Abbott, acting commissioner of Indian affairs in 1913.

14. The next section of the hearing begins on page 507 and ends on page 521.

15. Senator TOWNSEND—Charles E. Townsend (Michigan), US Senate, 1911–23.

16. Senator ASHURST—Henry F. Ashurst (Arizona), US Senate, 1912–41.

17. Senator OWEN—Robert L. Owen (Oklahoma), US Senate, 1907–25.

18. Here Kellogg refers to the Dawes Rolls, which listed tribal members in preparation for the allotment of tribal lands in severalty, following the Allotment Act of 1887. Individuals could be listed as tribal members by blood, marriage, or other criteria; as a consequence, there were suspicions that non-Native people were enrolled.

19. Report of the Marine Hospital Service—*Contagious and Infectious Diseases among the Indians*, document no. 1038, 62nd Cong., 3d sess. (1913).

20. Uncle Remus—fictional character in stories ostensibly about African American folklore by Joel Chandler Harris (who was not African American). First published in 1881, the stories were seen as sympathetic to African Americans, but fell out of favor later due to their stereotypical representations.

21. G. Stanley Hall—Granville Stanley Hall (1844–1924), first president of the American Psychological Association and Clark University (Massachusetts). Hall was known for his research in child development and evolutionary theory. See also note 64 above, *Our Democracy and the American Indian* (p. 272 in current edition).

22. Here Kellogg quotes from the work of Walton H. Hamilton, *Readings in Current Economic Problems* (Ann Arbor: University of Michigan, 1914), 444.

23. "Lolomai"—Lolomi, which Kellogg said was Hopi for "perfect blessing be upon you." See also end notes to *Our Democracy and the American Indian*, especially note 19 (p. 267 in current edition).

24. Garden cities of Europe—initially seen as refuges from urban areas for non-Native people. Kellogg saw the model as a possibility for Oneida economic self-sufficiency and tribal sovereignty. See also discussion of garden cities in the Introduction (especially p. 28).

25. "The Mott report"—"The Mott Report Relative to Indian Guardianships in the Probate Courts of Oklahoma" (1912). Written by Marshall Mott and Charles Burke, the report revealed that court-appointed attorneys for Indians in Oklahoma collected extortionate fees of 20 percent, compared to national average of 2–3 percent for the services of professional guardians of whites. Kellogg refers to the report to criticize state and county courts, which oversaw the appointments, as well as federal oversight over Indian trust property, more generally.

26. The Rochdale System—developed by a group of weavers in England in the 1840s. Under the Rochdale system, a cooperative store allowed its shareholders one vote regardless of the number of shares held by any individuals.

27. Senator GRONNA—Asle J. Gronna, US senator (North Dakota), 1911–21.

28. Senator ROBINSON—Joseph Taylor Robinson, US senator (Arkansas), 1913–37.

29. Senator LANE—Harry Lane, US senator (Oregon), 1913–17.

30. Mr. Sloan—Thomas L. Sloan (Omaha), a founding member of the Society of American Indians. Sloan testified earlier during the same hearings.

31. Senator Johnson—Hiram Warren Johnson, US senator (California), 1917–45.

32. Senator Lane—Harry Lane, US senator (Oregon), 1913–17.

33. Senator Page—Carroll Smalley Page, US senator (Vermont), 1908–23.

34. Document No. 65—Municipal Research Document No. 65, September 1915. See also reference on p. 199 as well as note 28, p. 268.

35. Senator CURTIS—Charles Curtis, US senator (Kansas), 1915–29; vice-president United States, 1929–33. Curtis was an enrolled member of the Kaw Nation.

36. Senator Walsh—Thomas James Walsh, US senator (Montana), 1913–33.

37. Untermeyer—Samuel Untermyer, Jewish-American lawyer, civic leader, and wealthy philanthropist.

38. Jacob Schiff—Jacob Henry Schiff, Jewish-American banker, business-owner, and wealthy philanthropist.

39. Senator Clapp—Moses E. Clapp, US senator (Minnesota), 1901–17.

40. Senator Lynn J. Frazier—Lynn Joseph Frazier, US senator (North Dakota), 1923–41.

41. Pine—William B. Pine, US senator (Oklahoma), 1925–31.

42. Wheeler—Burton K. Wheeler, US senator (Montana), 1923–47.

43. Thomas—Elmer Thomas, US senator (Oklahoma), 1927–51.

44. Executive secretary of the Six Nations—Kellogg served as secretary and spokesperson for the Six Nations in the 1920s. This group was comprised of leaders from the Wisconsin Oneida, Onondaga, and Cayuga, including Tadodaho, the political and spiritual head of the confederacy.

45. Treaty of 1784—The Treaty of Fort Stanwix (1784) was signed between members of the Iroquois Confederacy and the United States. Among many provisions, it recognized and affirmed Iroquois territories in what would become New York State.

46. Treaty of 1789—The Treaty of Fort Harmar (1789) was signed by members of the Iroquois Confederacy and the United States. Among many provisions, it recognized and affirmed Iroquois territories in what would become New York State.

47. Sir William Johnson line of property—Sir William Johnson (1715–74) was an official of the British Empire who commanded Iroquois allies and colonial militias in North American military conflicts. Appointed commissioner of Indian Affairs in 1746, Johnson worked closely with the Iroquois Confederacy to settle Indian claims to secure British concerns over colonial expansion. Kellogg refers to the 1768 Treaty of Fort Stanwix, when Johnson adjusted the boundary line between Native lands and British colonial settlements outlined in the Royal Proclamation of 1763. Johnson also worked to ensure that any land cessions or treaties with the Iroquois would be conducted by the British and not by the individual colonies, setting a precedent for federal control over Indian affairs, which Kellogg and the other Haudenosaunee leaders at the congressional hearings affirmed and supported.

48. Gen. Joseph Brant (1743–1807) was a Mohawk military and civil leader who allied with the British during and after the Revolutionary War.

49. General Butler—John Butler (1728–96) commanded a Loyalist militia known as Butler's Rangers during the Revolutionary War. Kellogg refers to the 1777 Battle of Oriskany, where Oneidas who were sympathetic to the patriot cause saw their settlements attacked by Butler-led forces, which included Mohawk fighters. The Battle of Oriskany was a major cause of Iroquois disunity during the Revolutionary War.

50. Stockbridge, Brothertown, and Tuscarora nations—tribal nations allied with the Oneida, the Tuscarora were brought into the Iroquois Confederacy under the protection of the Oneida. The Stockbridge and Brothertown relocated to Wisconsin at approximately the same time of many Oneidas.

51. "The United States Government, however, has never O.K.'d. one of these transactions"—Kellogg refers to the lack of United States presence at the ratification of New York State-negotiated treaties with the Iroquois, calling into question the validity of the treaties. Lack of federal oversight and approval violated the Federal

Trade and Intercourse Act. In the late twentieth century, Native nations would successfully use this argument to challenge the validity of treaties that were not approved by the federal government.

52. MERRITT—Edgar B. Merritt was assistant commissioner of Indian Affairs from 1913 to 1929. Kellogg was very critical of Merritt, and he of her.

53. Mayor Hanna—Charles Hanna was the mayor of Syracuse, New York, 1926–29.

54. Commissioner Burke—Charles Henry Burke was the commissioner of Indian affairs, 1921–29. He also served in the US House of Representatives (South Dakota) from 1808 to 1907, where he was a proponent of allotment.

55. "[O]riginal agreement of 1784"—the 1784 Treaty of Fort Stanwix. See also note 45 above.

56. The Jay Treaty—This treaty, made in 1794, formalized the border between the United States and Britain. Given that the boundary line bisected many Haudenosaunee lands, one of its provisions was to recognize the rights of Iroquois people to pass freely over the border. Kellogg goes on to refer to this right when she discusses her efforts on behalf of the Six Nations. She stresses that the Six Nations Confederacy does not recognize the United States-Canada border or US state borders when they travel on behalf of the confederacy.

57. "[P]inch-back men"—See also notes 21 and 64 (pp. 267 and 277, respectively, in current edition).

58. Laches—Laches is a legal doctrine relating to unreasonable delay in raising a legal claim. It is used as a defense in litigation on the rationale that an unreasonable delay in pursuing a claim can unfairly prejudice the responding party.

59. Boylan case—*United States v. Boylan*, 265 F. 165 (2d Cir. 1920). The court found that the sale of the last remaining Oneida land in New York State to non-Natives was barred without federal approval. The case upholds the trust responsibility of the federal government, based on the treaties, as Kellogg notes.

60. Senator Harreld—John W. Harreld, US senator (Oklahoma), 1921–27.

61. Mohawk chief—Chief Louis P. Oak, whose testimony starts on page 4882 in original text. Kellogg translated for him.

62. Chief Crouse—Chief Livingston Crouse, whose testimony starts on page 4884 in original text.

63. Chief Eels—Chief Elon Eels, whose testimony starts on page 4890 in original text.

64. O. J. Kellogg—a lawyer, was Laura Cornelius Kellogg's husband. They were married in Wisconsin in April 1912. His testimony begins on page 4867 in the original text.

65. Treaty of 1796—the 1796 Jay Treaty. See note 56 above.

66. Senator Frazier—Lynn Joseph Frazier, US senator (North Dakota), 1923–41.

67. Senator WHEELER—Burton K. Wheeler, US senator (Montana), 1923–47.

68. Charles E. Hughes—lawyer and politician from New York State. Served as 11th chief justice of US Supreme Court from 1930 to 1941.

69. Petition is printed in full in the original text.

70. Judge Ray—served as Judge of the United States District Court for the Northern District of New York from 1902 until 1925.

71. Senator THOMAS—Elmer Thomas, US senator (Oklahoma), 1927–51.

72. Contract is printed in full in the original text.

73. "[T]he situation in the Seneca country"—He refers to the controversy surrounding the city of Salamanca, New York, which is on leased land, located on the Allegany Reservation of the Seneca Nation of Indians. O. J. Kellogg wanted the committee to be aware of the nominal fees paid by non-Native leaseholders to the Seneca Nation, which would be contested in the late twentieth century, when the leases ran out.

74. "We are not under the Indian Bureau, but under the control of the United States Government"—Orrin J. Kellogg is asserting one definition of "protected autonomy," a recognition of the trust responsibility of the federal government, yet resisting the paternalism of the Bureau of Indian Affairs.

75. After the unfavorable decision in the 1927 *Deere* ejectment action, individual Haudenosaunee nations began taking up litigation contesting the taking of reservation land. See *Deere et al. v. New York et al.*, 22 F.2d 851 (N.D.N.Y. 1927); *Federal Power Commission v. Tuscarora Indian Nation, Power Authority of (the State of) New York v. Tuscarora Nation*, 362 U.S. 99 (1960); and *Oneida Indian Nation of New York et al. v. County of Oneida, New York*, 414 U.S. 661 (1974).

76. House Document 1590, Sixty-third Congress, third session. The full title of the document is "Senecas and other Indians of the Five Nations of New York: Letter from the Secretary of the Interior, Transmitting Reports of the Interior Department and the Department of Justice on a Bill (H.R. 18735) to Settle the Affairs of the Senecas and Other Indians of the Five Nations in the State of New York."

References

Works by Laura Cornelius Kellogg

Kellogg, Laura Miriam Cornelius. "A Tribute to the Future of My Race." *The Red Man and Helper*, March 20, 1903, 1.

——. "Building the Indian Home." *The Indian's Friend*, May 1901 (13, no. 9), 2 and 11–12.

——. "Industrial Organization for the Indian." In *Report of the Executive Council on the Proceedings of the First Annual Conference of the Society of American Indians*, Society of American Indians, ed., 43–55. Washington, DC: Society of American Indians, 1912.

——. *Our Democracy and the American Indian: A Comprehensive Presentation of the Indian Situation as It Is Today*. Kansas City, MO: Burton, 1920.

——. "Overalls and Tenderfoot." *The Barnard Bear*, March 1907 (2, no. 2), 2. Barnard Archives and Special Collections, Barnard College, New York.

——. "Response to Edgar A. Bancroft's Address, 'The Indian.'" In *Lorado Taft's Indian Statue "Black Hawk": An Account of the Unveiling Ceremonies at Eagle Nest Bluff, Oregon, Illinois, July the First, Nineteen Hundred and Eleven. Frank O. Lowden Presiding*, 71–82. Chicago: University of Chicago Press, 1912.

—— [Laura Minnie Cornelius]. "She Likes Indian Public Opinion." *The Red Man and Helper*, October 10, 1902, 1.

——. "Some Facts and Figures on Indian Education." *Quarterly Journal of the Society of American Indians* 1 (April 1913): 36–46.

——. "The Legend of the Bean." In *The Church's Mission to the Oneidas*, 2nd ed., edited by Frank Wesley Merrill, 55–56. Oneida Indian Reservation, Wisconsin; Fond du Lac, WI: P. B. Haber, 1902.

——. "The Sacrifice of the White Dog." In *The Church's Mission to the Oneidas*, 2nd ed., edited by Frank Wesley Merrill, 57. Oneida Indian Reservation, Wisconsin; Fond du Lac, WI: P. B. Haber, 1902.

———. "Trail (The) of the Morning Star: Indian Play in 1 Act by Princess E-gah-tah-yen (i.e., Mrs. O. J. Kellogg). 1916." *Catalog of Copyright Entries*, part 1 (B), group 2. Pamphlets, Etc., New Series 13 (3): 230. Washington, DC: Government Printing Office.

Archives and Collections

Barnard Archives and Special Collections, Barnard College, New York

Laura Cornelius's Academic Record
Mortarboard
The Barnard Bear (student newspaper)

Stanford University, Stanford, CA

Laura Cornelius's Academic Record

Oneida Nation in Wisconsin, Cultural Heritage Department, Oneida, WI

Census data, including genealogical records and church records
Language Revitalization
WPA Oneida Language and Folklore Project records

Oneida Nation in Wisconsin Division of Land Management (ONDLM), Oneida, WI

Ernie Stevens, Sr. Collection

Oneida Nation in Wisconsin Museum, Oneida, WI

Photo collection

Oneida Nation in Wisconsin Cultural Heritage Department, Oneida, WI

Bob Brown, "Translation of the Great Law, *Kayantlako*" (unpublished manuscript).

National Archives, Washington, DC

RG 75 Correspondence of the Office of Indian Affairs. Letters received: Green Bay Agency. RG 75 Records of the Bureau of Indian Affairs. Central Classified Files, 1907–39, Box 563, Folder 175.

Newberry Library, Chicago

Ayer Collection, The Carlos Montezuma Papers

Ayer Collection, The Society of American Indians (SAI) Papers, microfilm

Government Publications

"Catalog of Copyright Entries." Part 1 [B] group 2. Pamphlets, Etc. New Series 13 (3). Washington, DC: Government Printing Office, 1916.

Hearings to Recall of Agents or Superintendents by Indian Tribes. 64th Cong., 1st sess., pp. 4–15 (1916) (US Senate, Select Committee on Indian Affairs).

Hearing Before the Subcommittee of the Committee on Agriculture and Forestry, United States Senate, Sixty-Fourth Congress, Second Session, Pursuant to S. Res. 305, A Resolution Authorizing and Requesting the Senate Committee on Agriculture and Forestry to Hear and Consider Testimony Relative to the Garden City and Garden Suburb Movement. 64th Cong., 2d sess. (February 9, 1917) (US Senate, Subcommittee of the Committee on Agriculture and Forestry).

Indian Appropriation Bill; Hearings on H.S. 1917. 63d Cong., 1st sess. (1913).

"Senecas and Other Indians of the Five Nations of New York: Letter from the Secretary of the Interior, Transmitting Reports of the Interior Department and the Department of Justice on a Bill (H.R. 18735) to Settle the Affairs of the Senecas and Other Indians of the Five Nations in the State of New York." *House Document 1590.* 63d Cong., 3d sess. (1914) (US House of Representatives).

Survey of Conditions of the Indians of the United States: Hearings on S. Res. 79, New York Indians. 71st Cong., 2d sess. (1929) (US Senate, Select Committee on Indian Affairs).

US Department of the Interior. *Statistics of Indian Tribes, Indian Agencies, and Indian Schools of Every Character.* Washington, DC: Government Printing Office, 1899.

Court Cases

Brief for the Petitioners (filed 1973), *Oneida Indian Nation of New York et al. v. County of Oneida, New York, and the County of Madison, New York,* 414 U.S. 661 (decided 1974).

County of Oneida, New York, et al. v. Oneida Indian Nation of New York State et al., 470 U.S. 226 (1985).

Oneida County, New York v. Oneida Indian Nation of New York State, 470 U.S. 226 (1985).

Oneida Indian Nation v. New York State, 860 F.2d 1145 (2d Cir. 1988).

Oneida Indian Nation v. Oneida and Madison Counties, 414 U.S. 661 (1974).

Oneida Nation v. United States, 26 Ind. Claims Commission 138 (1971).

United States v. Boylan, 265 F. 165 (2d Cir. 1920).

Worcester v. Georgia, 31 U.S. 515 (1832).

Books, Book Chapters, Journal Articles, and Pamphlets

Ackley, Kristina. "Laura Cornelius Kellogg, Lolomi, and Modern Oneida Placemaking." Joint Issue, *Studies in American Indian Literature* 25, no. 2 (2013)/*American Indian Quarterly* 37, no. 3 (2013): 117–38.

———. "Renewing Haudenosaunee Ties: Laura Cornelius Kellogg and the Idea of Unity in the Oneida Land Claim." *American Indian Culture and Research Journal* 32, no. 1 (2008): 57–81.

Adams, David W. *Education for Extinction: American Indians and the Boarding School Experience, 1875–1928.* Lawrence: University Press of Kansas, 1995.

Alfred, Taiaiake. *Wasáse: Indigenous Pathways of Action and Freedom.* Toronto: Broadview, 2005.

Besant, Walter. "The Art of Fiction." In *Notices of the Proceedings at the Meetings of the Members of the Royal Institution of Great Britain, 1884–1886, with Abstracts of the Discourses Delivered at the Evening Meetings* 11, 70–83. London: William Clowes and Sons, 1887.

Bilharz, Joy. *The Allegany Senecas and the Kinzua Dam: Forced Relocation through Two Generations.* Lincoln: University of Nebraska Press, 1998.

Brown, Bob. "Translation of the Great Law, *Kayantlako*" (unpublished manuscript). Oneida Nation in Wisconsin Cultural Heritage Department, Oneida, WI.

Child, Brenda. *Boarding School Seasons: American Indian Families, 1900–1940.* Lincoln: University of Nebraska Press, 1998.

Christjohn, Amos, Maria Hinton, and Clifford Abbott, eds. *An Oneida Dictionary: Ukwehu•wehneha Tekaw^nate?nyése.* Green Bay: University of Wisconsin-Green Bay Press, 1996.

Clark, Blue. *Lone Wolf v. Hitchcock: Treaty Rights and Indian Law at the End of the Nineteenth Century.* Lincoln: University of Nebraska Press, 1999.

Dowd, Gregory Evans. *A Spirited Resistance: The North American Struggle for Unity, 1745–1815.* Baltimore, MD: John Hopkins University Press, 1992.

Eastman, Elaine Goodale. *Pratt, the Red Man's Moses.* Norman: University of Oklahoma Press, 1935.

Fear-Segal, Jacqueline. *White Man's Club: Schools, Race, and the Struggle of Indian Acculturation.* Lincoln: University of Nebraska Press, 2007.

Fixico, Donald L. *The Invasion of Indian Country in the Twentieth Century: American Capitalism and Tribal Natural Resources.* Boulder: University Press of Colorado, 1998.

Hall, G. Stanley. "The Point of View toward the Primitive Races." *Journal of Race Development* 1, nos. 1 and 2 (1910–11): 5–11.

Hamilton, Walton H. *Readings in Current Economic Problems.* Ann Arbor: University of Michigan, 1914.

Harris, Leonard, Scott L. Pratt, and Anne S. Waters, eds. *American Philosophies: An Anthology.* Hoboken, NJ: Wiley-Blackwell, 2001.

Hauptman, Laurence M. "Designing Woman: Minnie Kellogg, Iroquois Leader." In *Indian Lives: Essays on Nineteenth- and Twentieth-Century Native American Leaders,* edited by L. G. Moses and Raymond Wilson. Albuquerque: University of New Mexico Press, 1985.

———. *Seven Generations of Iroquois Leadership: The Six Nations since 1800.* Syracuse, NY: Syracuse University Press, 2008.

———. *The Iroquois Struggle for Survival: World War II to Red Power.* Syracuse, NY: Syracuse University Press, 1985.

Hauptman, Laurence M., and L. Gordon McLester III, eds. *The Oneida Indians in the Age of Allotment, 1860–1920.* Norman: University of Oklahoma Press, 2006.

Hertzberg, Hazel W. *The Search for an American Indian Identity: Modern Pan-Indian Movements.* Syracuse, NY: Syracuse University Press, 1971.

Hilden, Patricia Penn, and Leece M. Lee. "Indigenous Feminism: The Project." In *Indigenous Women and Feminism: Politics, Activism, Culture,* edited by Cheryl Suzack, Shari M. Huhndorf, Jeanne Perreault, and Jean Barman, 56–77. Vancouver: University of British Columbia Press, 2010.

Hollingsworth, Charles Mahon. *From Freedom to Despotism: A Rational Prediction and Forewarning.* Washington, DC: (self published), 1910.

Holm, Tom. *The Great Confusion in Indian Affairs: Native Americans and Whites in the Progressive Era.* Austin: University of Texas Press, 2005.

Hopi Dictionary: Hopìikwa Lavàytutuveni: A Hopi Dictionary of the Third Mesa Dialect with an English-Hopi Finder List and a Sketch of Hopi Grammar. Tucson: University of Arizona Press, 1998.

Hoxie, Frederick E. *Talking Back to Civilization: Voices from the Progressive Era*. Boston and New York: Bedford/St. Martin's, 2001.

Iverson, Peter. *Carlos Montezuma and the Changing World of American Indians*. Albuquerque: University of New Mexico Press, 1992.

Johansen, Bruce Elliott, and Barbara Alice Mann, eds. *Encyclopedia of the Haudenosaunee (Iroquois Confederacy)*. Westport, CT: Greenwood, 2000.

Jones, Eliot. *The Trust Problem in the United States*. New York: Macmillan, 1929.

Kiel, Doug. "Competing Visions of Empowerment: Oneida Progressive-Era Politics and Writing Tribal Histories." *Ethnohistory* 61, no. 3 (Summer 2014): 419–44.

Lewis, Herbert S., and L. Gordon McLester, eds. *Oneida Lives: Long-Lost Voices of the Oneida*. Lincoln: University of Nebraska Press, 2005.

Lounsbury, Floyd G. *Oneida Verb Morphology*. New Haven, CT: Yale University Press, 1953.

Maddox, Lucy. *Citizen Indians: Native American Intellectuals, Race and Reform*. Ithaca, NY: Cornell University Press, 2005.

Martínez, David. *The American Indian Intellectual Tradition: An Anthology of Writings from 1772 to 1972*. Ithaca, NY: Cornell University Press, 2010.

McLester, Thelma. "Oneida Women Leaders" in *Oneida Indian Experience: Two Perspectives*. Edited by Jack Campisi and Laurence M. Hauptman. Syracuse, NY: Syracuse University Press, 1988.

Merrill, Frank Wesley, ed. *The Church's Mission to the Oneidas*. 2nd ed. Oneida Indian Reservation, Wisconsin; Fond du Lac, WI: P. B. Haber, 1902.

Mohawk, John C. *Iroquois Creation Story: John Arthur Gibson and J. N. B. Hewitt's Myth of the Earth Grasper*. Buffalo, NY: Mohawk, 2005.

Moorehead, Warren K. "Review of *Our Democracy and the American Indian*." *Mississippi Valley Historical Review* 8, no. 3 (1921): 281.

———. *The American Indian in the United States; Period 1850–1914*. Andover, MA: Andover Press, 1915.

Parker, Robert Dale, ed. *Changing Is Not Vanishing: A Collection of American Indian Poetry to 1930*. Philadelphia: University of Pennsylvania Press, 2011.

Patten, Simon Nelson. *The New Basis of Civilization*. Cambridge, MA: Belknap Press, 1907.

Peyer, Bernd C. *American Indian Nonfiction: An Anthology of Writings, 1760s–1930s.* Norman: University of Oklahoma Press, 2007.

Society of American Indians, ed. *Report of the Executive Council on the Proceedings of the First Annual Conference of the Society of American Indians.* Washington, DC: Society of American Indians, 1912.

Ruoff, A. LaVonne, ed. Callahan S. Alice, *Wynema: A Child of the Forest.* Lincoln: University of Nebraska Press, 1997 [1891].

Sonneborn, Liz. 2007. "Kellogg, Minnie." *A to Z of American Indian Women,* 108–112. Revised edition. New York: Infobase, 2007.

Stanciu, Cristina. "An Indian Woman of Many Hats: Laura Cornelius Kellogg's Embattled Search for an Indigenous Voice." Joint Issue, *Studies in American Indian Literature* 25, no. 2 (2013)/*American Indian Quarterly* 37, no. 3 (2013): 87–117.

Stovey, Patricia. "Opportunities at Home: Laura Cornelius Kellogg and Village Industrialization." In *Oneida Voices in the Age of Allotment, 1860–1920,* edited by Laurence M. Hauptman and L. Gordon McLester III, 143–75. Norman: University of Oklahoma Press, 2006.

Sunseri, Lina. *Being Again of One Mind: Oneida Women and the Struggle for Decolonization.* Vancouver: University of British Columbia Press, 2011.

Tennyson, Alfred Lord. *THE PRINCESS: A Medley.* Edited by Henry W. Boynton. Boston: Leach, Shewell, and Sanborn, 1896.

"The North American Indians: A Redskin Princess." *The Review of Reviews for Australasia* (August 1909): 519–20.

Tiro, Karim M. *The People of the Standing Stone: The Oneida Nation from the Revolution through the Era of Removal.* Amherst: University of Massachusetts Press, 2011.

Newspaper and Magazine Articles

"An Indian Girl and Glad of It: Miss Cornelius Here to Study Law at Barnard." *The Sun,* February 11, 1906.

"An Indian Heroine of Peace: Laura M. Cornelius, the Oneida Girl Who Kept the Copah Tribe from Going on the Warpath." *St. Louis Republic,* December 1904.

"Asks Indians [to] Live in Model Villages: Woman, Herself of Aboriginal Blood, Urges Government [to] Give Plan Trial." *Washington Times,* May 1914.

"Bright Indian Girl—Miss Laura Miriam Cornelius Has Literary Plans for the Uplifting of Her Race." *Broad Ax*, April 1903.

"Court Instructs Jury to Acquit the Kelloggs." *El Paso Herald*, January 31, 1914.

"Dreamers and Doers," *Kalihwisaks*, March 18, 2010.

Dupuy, William A. "Looking for an Indian Booker T. Washington to Lead Their People." *New York Tribune*, August 27, 1911.

"First American Mothers Had 'Votes for Women.'" *Washington Herald*, February 16, 1915.

Hapgood, Joseph. "American Indian Princess Interests Briton Statesmen; Cuts Quite a Dash in the British Metropolis—Unique Figure in Society—Tells Plans for Rehabilitation of Her Race." *Detroit Free Press*, September 1909.

———. "Indian Maid in Europe: Her Mission, the Betterment of Dying Race; Iroquois Princess Gives her Ideas in London; Harden Cities among Others of her Plans." *Los Angeles Times*, September 26, 1909.

Herdman, Ramona. "A New Six Nations: Laura Cornelius Sees the Old Iroquois Confederacy Re-Established On a Modern Business Basis as the First Fulfillment of a Girlhood Vow Pledging Herself to the Welfare of Her Race." *Syracuse Herald*, November 6, 1927.

"Indian Girl to Study Law at Barnard." *Minneapolis Journal*, February 25, 1906.

"Indian Leader Calls Occasion a Renaissance." *Milwaukee Journal*, October 4, 1925.

"Indian New Woman." *Washington Post*, December 4, 1898.

"Indian Note Book." *Bay View Magazine*, October 1907.

"Indian on Suffrage." *Washington Times*, June 12, 1913.

"Indian Prices Dances to Right People's Wrongs." *Oakland Tribune*, June 1, 1910.

"Indian Princess Is Active Lobbyist in Capital." *Day Book*, February 1916.

"Indian Princess Makes Plea for Self-Government." *La Crosse Tribune*, June 26, 1916.

"Indian Students Immoral." *Washington Herald*, May 15, 1913.

"Last Indian Princess to Become Mrs. Kellogg." *San Francisco Call*, April 26, 1912.

"Last Mother of Oneidas Passes On." *Milwaukee Wisconsin News*, November 14, 1922.

"Laura Cornelius Kellogg, Iroquois, Replies to Secretary Lane's Reform Statement." *Washington Post*, May 2, 1914.

"Laura Kellogg, Daughter of Long Line of Indian Chiefs, Laughs at the Old Idea of the Downtrodden Squaw." *Washington Herald*, February 16, 1915.

"Lolomi Plan." *The Tomahawk*, November 1918.

"Marries Indian Princess." *Eau Claire Leader*, April 27, 1912.

"News and Views of Women." *New-York Tribune*, June 5, 1903.

"One Indian Maiden: Her Literary Plans for the Uplifting of Her Race." *New York Tribune*, February 15, 1903.

"Princess of Oneida Indians Is Arrested." *El Paso Herald*, October 12, 1913.

"Reform in Handling Indian Affairs Needed: Mrs. Laura C. Kellogg, a Member of [the] Oneida Tribe, Lectures Here." *Washington Herald*, May 13, 1913.

"Refutes Buffalo Bill; Indian Maiden Tells Him His Views of the Red Man Are Wrong." *New York Times*, May 13, 1910.

"Salt Lake's Merry Morn in Riverside." *Los Angeles Times*, March 13, 1904.

"Snapshots at Social Leaders." *Washington Post*, April 29, 1912.

"The Whites Do Not Understand the Indians; The Indians Do Not Understand Themselves, Says This Oneida Girl." *San Francisco Chronicle*, August 9, 1903.

"To Solve Indian Problem: Oneida Princess Is Championing Bill for Autonomous Government of Her Race." *Edgefield Advertiser*, April 12, 1916, [n.p.].

Wallace, Grant. "The Exiles of Cupa." *Out West Magazine*, July 1903.

Walschinski, Dawn. "The Fire Comes Home to the Oneida Longhouse." *Kalihwisaks*, September 1, 2005.

"Why the Warner Ranch Indians Moved Quietly." *San Francisco Chronicle*, June 14, 1903.

"Will Be the First Indian Girl Lawyer." *Los Angeles Times*, December 28, 1904.

"Would Plead Cause of the Indians before the League of Nations: Wisconsin Woman of Wealth and Education, Granddaughter of Famous Chief, Has Devoted Her Life to Obtaining More Justice for Her People." *Milwaukee Sentinel*, August 17, 1919.

Dissertations

Campisi, Jack. "Ethnic Identity and Boundary Maintenance in Three Oneida Communities." PhD diss., State University of New York at Albany, 1974.

Geier, Philip O. "A Peculiar Status: A History of Oneida Indian Treaties and Claims." PhD diss., Syracuse University, 1980.

Piatote, Beth H. "Home/ward Bound: The Making of Domestic Relations in Native American Literature and Law, 1886–1936." PhD diss., Stanford University, 2007.

Index

Italic page number denotes illustration.

Abbott, F. H., 174–75
accountability, 47, 51–57
Ackley, Kristina, 262n109
agriculture, 97–98, 179–80, 188–89, 192,
    272n1, 273n2
Allegany Reservation, 279n73
Allen, Edgar A., 104, 261n96, 272n61
allotments: Blackfeet Irrigation project
    (MT) and, 269n45; challenging system
    of, 48, 91, 95, 187–88; defined, 41;
    fraud and, 271n56; laws and legisla-
    tion, 3, 177, 179, 254n6, 275n18;
    pooling together of, 187–88
Aluminum Co., 220–21, 227, 228
American Association of University
    Women (AAUW), 60
Americanization, 30, 272n62
artwork, 24–26, 167–72
Ashurst, Henry F., 175
assimilation, 9–10, 41, 57, 176–77, 184,
    254n6, 268n35
autonomy, "protected," 18–19, 52–57,
    173, 187, 202, 203–4, 279n74

Baird, Ida Skenadore, *53*
Bancroft, Edgar A., 24–25, 167
Barnard College, 6, 13–14, 16, 21–*22*, 28,
    271n58
Battle of Oriskany, 277n49

Blackfeet Irrigation Project (MT), 93–94,
    269n45
Black Hawk statue dedication, 24–26,
    167–72
blindness (trachoma), 83, 87–88, 163,
    177–79
boarding schools: child labor and, 106–7,
    162–63, 272n65; critiques of, 5,
    23, 272n62, 273n1; disease in, 163,
    177–78; federally run, 36, 266n15;
    Lolomi model, 104–8; statistics on,
    159–66, 259n63. *See also* Carlisle
    Industrial School (PA); Oneida Board-
    ing School (WI)
Board of Indian Commissioners, 82, 173,
    190, 240, 267n24
Boas, Franz, 29, 158
Bonnin, Gertrude, 4, 18
borders, 55, 82, 226, 278n56
Boston Citizenship League, 82, 267n24
Boylan, United States v. (1920), 48, 212,
    217, 278n59
Brant, Joseph, 205, 277n48
Bread, Daniel, 2
Britain: garden cities in, 147–48, 186, 187;
    LCK in, 15–16, 17, 256n33, 257n39.
    See also Revolutionary War
Brothertown Nation, 50, 205, 220,
    277n50
Bryant, Frederick H., *58*

Bryce, James, 273n4

Buffalo Bill, 17

"Building the Indian Home" (essay), 133–37

Bureau of Indian Affairs (BIA). *See* U.S. Bureau of Indian Affairs (BIA)

Burke, Charles H., 206, 262n106, 276n25

Butler, John, 205, 277n49

California, 10–12

Callahan, S. Alice, 257n41

Campisi, Jack, 20, 263n119

Canada: Indian bureaus in, 213–14, 243; LCK arrest in, 55–56, 207–10, 243–44; Oneida Nation in, 2–3, 50, 204–5; U.S. border with, 55, 226, 278n56

capitalism, 28–29, 35, 36, 143–46, 152, 189

Carlisle Industrial School (PA): founding of, 85, 268n35, 272n62, 273n1; graduates of, 142, 159, 161; mission of, 23, 85, 89, 96, 268n35; Montezuma and, 89, 138, 269n41; Pratt and, 105, 141–43, 268n35, 272n62, 273n1; publications of, 22, 114, 138

Carter, Charles D., 274n9

Catholic Diocese of Green Bay, 45–47, 262n105, 262n109

Cayuga Nation, 50, 55, 214, 215, 237–40

ceremonies, 20, 51, 52, 113, 265n10, 273n4

Cherokee Nation v. Georgia (1831), 267n23

child labor, 106–7, 162–63, 185, 272n65

Church's Mission to the Oneidas, The (Episcopal Church), 6, 19–20, 42

citizenship, 35, 91, 92–93, 137, 184, 200, 269n43

civilization, stages in development of, 148–49, 152, 178–79, 181–83, 191

clan system, 59, 102–3, 142, 254n5, 271nn57–58

Clapp, Moses Edwin, 84, 201

Clark, James Beauchamp, 82–83

Clinton, George, 206, 216, 231

Columbia University, 158, 256n33

communistic cooperation, 200–201; Mormon idea of, 28–29, 91, 96–97, 149–52, 186–88, 190

community empowerment, 9–10

congressional hearings. *See* Indian Appropriation Bill (H.R. 1917); U.S. Senate Resolution 79 (1929)

Conley, Lyda, 256n28

Cooper, Margaret Summers, *53*

Copahs. *See* Cupeño Tribe

Cornelius, Alice, *53*

Cornelius, Cecilia Bread, 2

corruption and fraud, allegations of: allotments and, 271n56; Crow hearings, 84–85, 158–59; against Kelloggs, 4, 30, 48–52, 55–57, 202, 207–10, 243–45, 254n10, 269n37, 271nn55–56; Mohawk Nation and, 226; Onondaga Nation and, 211, 213; Osage Nation and, 87, 101–2, 269n37, 271nn55–56; police and, 134–35; regarding sale of Oneida Boarding School, 47; Treaty of Fort Stanwix (1784) and, 205–6

court cases: in Canada, 55–56, 207–10, 243–44; *Cherokee Nation v. Georgia* (1831), 267n23; Cupeño Tribe, 10–12; Jones as chief of Six Nations, *58*; *United States v. Boylan* (1920), 48, 212, 217, 278n59; *Worcester v. Georgia* (1832), 269n43; wrongful death, 54. *See also* jurisdiction

credit, 35, 94–97, 151, 188

Crouse, Livingston (Chief), 54, 214, 228–37

Crow Nation, 84–85, 158–59
Cupeño Tribe, 10–12
Curtis, Charles, 197–201, 199, 274n9

Dawes General Allotment Act (1887), 3,
    177, 254n6, 275n18
democracy, origins of, 34, 35–36, 71–74
development, civilization and, 148–49,
    152, 178–79, 181–83, 191
Dieskau, Ludwig August von (general),
    72, 265n8
discrimination, 101, 142, 156, 157, 165,
    180, 182
disease, 38, 83, 87–88, 100, 146–48, 163,
    177–79, 270n52
domestic dependent nations, 267n23
Doxtator, Hira, 262n106
"Dreamers and Doers" tour (Green Bay),
    60

Eastman, Charles A., 24–25, 167
economic sovereignty, 4, 5, 27–28, 30–32,
    180–85. See also communistic coopera-
    tion; governance/self-determination;
    Lolomi Industrial Community
education: funding for, 29, 161–62,
    164–65, 173, 194–96; governance/
    self-determination and, 27–29; identity
    and, 182–83; of LCK, 6–8, 12–17,
    21–22, 256n33, 271n58; LCK presents
    views on to SAI, 29–30; Lolomi
    model of, 104–8; parents and, 135–37;
    role of, 104–8; statistics on, 29–30,
    154–66, 259n63; status of, 182–84;
    testimony regarding, 173, 194–96. See
    also boarding schools
Eels, Elon (Chief), 214, 237–38
elders, value of knowledge and, 9

"Endymion" (Keats), 170–71, 275n5
Episcopal Church, 6, 19–20, 41–42
essays: "Building the Indian Home,"
    133–37; "Industrial Organization for
    the Indian," 27–28, 140–53; "The
    Romans of America," 22; "She Likes
    Indian Public Opinion," 138–39;
    "Some Facts and Figures on Indian
    Education," 29–30, 154–66, 259n63
Europe, LCK in, 15–16, 17
extinction, 176–77, 184

factionalization, 5, 57–59, 76, 84–85
farming, 97–98, 179–80, 188–89, 192,
    272n1, 273n2
Federal Trade and Intercourse Act (1790),
    277n51
Five Civilized Tribes of Oklahoma, 177,
    259n63
Flandreau Indian School (SD), 41
Fourteenth Amendment, 269n43
France, 16, 72, 147–48, 186, 205, 253n4,
    256n33, 265n8
Franklin, Benjamin, 34, 72–73
fraud. See corruption and fraud
Frazier, Lynn J., 203, 204, 216
freedom of movement, 39
French and Indian War, 205, 265n8
funds and fundraising: to buy Oneida
    Boarding School, 45; credit, 35,
    94–97, 151, 188; for education, 29,
    161–62, 164–65, 173, 194–96; in
    Europe, 16; for Indian Commission,
    174; for land claim litigation, 47–52,
    55–57, 85, 219, 220, 268n34; Lolomi
    model, 92, 147, 166, 173, 176, 179,
    188; philanthropic, 80, 82, 86, 176,
    198–99, 267n24; ration system of
    loans, 134; reimbursable, 93–94;

funds and fundraising (*cont.*)
   tribal, 85, 94, 103–4, 179, 268n34;
   U.S. Bureau of Indian Affairs (BIA),
   88, 93–94

garden cities, 28, 37, 147–49, 186–87,
   273n3, 276n24
Garland, Hamlin, 167
geographic isolation, 38–40
George Washington wampum belt,
   265n10
Georgia, Cherokee Nation v. (1831),
   267n23
Georgia, Worcester v. (1832), 269n43
Germany, 16, 37, 147–48, 186, 256n33
"golden calves," 74, 266n13
Goodnough, Edward, 41
governance/self-determination: changes
   in, 261n95; democratic model of, 34,
   35–37; education and, 27–29; essay on,
   133–37
Grafton Hall (WI), 6, 7, 22
Green Bay (WI), 60
Gronna, Asle J., 190
Guardian Angels orphanage (WI), 46–47,
   262n109

Hall, Granville Stanley, 106, 183, 267n21,
   272n64
Hampton Institute (VA), 41
Hanna, Charles, 206
Harreld, John W., 212
Haudenosaunee: acreage, 2–3, 204–6,
   215, 253n4; constitution of, 34,
   72–74, 226, 231, 236; cosmology of,
   19–22; defined, xviii, 253n3, 265n6;
   leadership, 2, 58, 261n95, 271n57,

273n4, 277n44; origins of democracy
   and, 71–74; "Three Sisters," 272n1
Hauptman, Laurence M., xvi, xx, 6,
   253nn2–3, 254n6, 255n15, 259n66,
   263n114
Hawk, Maud Echo, 8
health care. *See* public health
Herdman, Ramona, 255n12
Hertzberg, Hazel W., 29, 258n61
Hiawatha wampum belt, 265n10
Hill, Martha B., 43
Hinton, Maria, 60
Ho-Chunk Nation, 253n4
Holm, Tom, xvi, xx, 26, 258n57, 266n15,
   269n37
H.R. 1917. *See* Indian Appropriation Bill
   (H.R. 1917)
Hughes, Charles E., 216
"Hyperion" (Keats), 170–71, 275n5

identity: destruction of individuality, 105;
   education and, 182–83; placemaking
   and, 37–40, 59–61
income: boarding school employees, 160;
   child labor and, 185; Kelloggs and,
   55–57, 218–21; Lolomi model, 35, 97,
   143–45, 188; Mormons and, 97, 188;
   Navajo Nation and, 179; Onondaga
   Nation and, 213
Indian Appropriation Bill (H.R. 1917),
   31–32, 173–96
Indian Citizenship Act/Snyder Act (1924),
   269n43
Indian Rights Association of Philadelphia,
   82, 267n24
Indian Services. *See* U.S. Bureau of Indian
   Affairs (BIA)
individuality, destruction of, 105

industrial organization, 27–29, 32–37, 140–53. *See also* Lolomi Industrial Community

"Industrial Organization for the Indian" (essay), 27–28, 140–53

Interior Department. *See* U.S. Department of the Interior

Iroquois Confederacy: acreage, 2–3, 204–6, 215, 253n4; constitution of, 34, 72–74, 226, 231, 236; cosmology of, 19–22; defined, xviii, 253n3, 265n6; leadership, 2, *58,* 261n95, 271n57, 273n4, 277n44; origins of democracy and, 71–74; "Three Sisters," 272n1

Iroquois Nation, 16, 53, 71–74

isolation, geographic, 38–40

Jack, Marvin, 164

Jay Treaty, 207, 214, 215, 224, 239–40, 278n56

Johnson, Edwin S., 88

Johnson, E. Pauline, 8

Johnson, Hiram Warren, 197

Johnson, William, 205, 277n47

Joint Commission to Investigate Indian Affairs. *See* U.S. Joint Commission to Investigate Indian Affairs

Jones, Joshua, *58*

Jourdan, Judith L., 60

jurisdiction: borders and, 55; state vs. federal, 225, 233–43, 246; trust responsibility and, 53–54; *United States v. Boylan* and, 48, 212, 217, 278n59; U.S. Court of Claims and, 227

Kansas, 253n4

Katsistowan^, 20, 257n47

Keats, John, 169, 170–71, 274n5, 275n9

Kellogg, Laura Miriam Cornelius, *7, 14, 15, 31, 51, 53, 58*; ambitions and vision of, 3, 8, 15; "a polite Indian," 14–15; arrests of, 6, 30, 55–57, 87, 202, 207–10, 243–44, 248, 269n37, 271n55; birth of, 2; children, 254n9; depictions and portrayals of, 5, 8–9, 13–16, 18–19, 26–27, 37, 60, 61–62; education, 6–8, 12–*17,* 21–*22,* 256n33, 271n58; interviews with, 8, 14–15, 16–17, 21, 30, 40, 47–48, 61; languages spoken, 6–7; legacy of, 3, 4, 6, 57–62; marriage of, 5, 30, 255n12; offices held, 3, 203, 277n44; Oneida ancestry, 2, 3, 18–19; personal papers, 254n9; radicalism of, 5, 27–28, 34, 36–37, 61–62; teaching, 6, 11, 12–13, 22, 106–7, 272n63; travels, 3–4, *12, 13,* 15–16, 17, 30–31, 37, 256n33; writings, 4, 5–6, 18–26

Kellogg, Orrin J.: arrests of, 30, 55–56, 202, 207–10, 243–44, 269n37, 271n55; children, 254n9; legal work of, 5, 55–56, 218–21; marriage of, 5, 30, 255n12; Seneca ancestry, 255n12; testimony of, 54, 57, 202, 214–25, 279n74

Kellogg, Robert E. (son), 254n9

Kerensky, Alexander Fyodorovich, 87, 269n38

Kern, Josiah Quincy, 260n74

Keshena Indian Agency, 45, 104, 272n61

King, Thomas, 262n106

kinship, 36, 59, 102–3, 142, 254n5, 271nn57–58

Kirkland, Samuel, 273n4

Knaebel, Ernest, 240

Koeferl, Anthony J., 262n105

labor, 28, 96–97, 143–52, 184–89; child, 106–7, 156, 185, 272n65

laches, 212, 278n58

land claims/rights: Cupeños Tribe, 10–12; funding for, 47–52, 55–57, 85, 219, 220, 268n34; oil and gas mining, 93–94, 100, 269n37, 270n50, 271nn55–56; origins of, 2–3, 47–48, 59, 204–8; reservation boundaries, 253n4; salt pipeline leases, 231–32. *See also* jurisdiction; treaties

Lane, Harry, 83, 84, 192, 197

Latham, Owen Robert (OK Sen.), 174

laws and legislation: allotments, 3, 177, 179, 254n6, 275n18; child labor, 106–7, 162–63, 272n65; citizenship, 92, 269n43; laches, 212, 278n58. *See also* court cases; Indian Appropriation Bill (H.R. 1917); jurisdiction; treaties; U.S. Senate Resolution 79 (1929)

lawsuits. *See* land claims/rights

League of Five Nations, 4, 71–74

League of Nations, 3, 34, 59, 71–74, 98, 264n1

"Legend of the Bean, The" (story), 19–21, 111–12, 272–73nn1–3

Lenin, Vladimir Illyich, 87, 268n36

Lenroot, Irvine, 55

litigation. *See* court cases; jurisdiction; land claims/rights

Lolomi Industrial Community, 32–40, 79–108; defined, 4, 56–57, 79, 186, 267n19; as democratic and economic model, 35–37; education in, 104–8; funding for, 92, 147, 166, 173, 176, 179, 188; income and, 35, 97, 143–45, 188; placemaking and, 37–40, 59–61; representation in, 35, 149–51, 189, 276n26; social welfare aspects of, 99–108; testimony regarding,

173, 176, 185–96; U.S. Department of the Interior and, 44–45; women in, 102–3

Longfellow, Henry Wadsworth, 22, 25

Longhouse tradition, 20, 51

Lyons, Gretchen, 8

Marine Hospital Service report, 83, 100, 177, 270n52

Menominee Nation, 253n4

Merritt, Edgar B., 53, 54–56, 57, 206, 210, 214, 225, 229, 238–48

Metoxen, Loretta V., 2, 253n4, 262n109

Midwinter ceremonies, 113, 273n4

missionaries, 20, 133–37, 273n4

modernity: indifference and, 35; tradition vs., 8–10, 28, 39

Mohawk, Go-Wan-Go, 8

Mohawk Nation, 207, 208, 213–14, 215, 225–28, 264n5, 277nn48–49

monopolies, 100, 270n50

Montezuma, Carlos, 5, 18, 89, 138, 257n43, 269n41

Moorehead, Warren K., 33, 173

Mormons, communistic cooperation and, 28–29, 91, 96–97, 149–52, 186–88, 190

"Mott report," 187, 276n25

movement, freedom of, 39

Murphy Land and Investment Company, 45, 262n105

Navajo Nation, 98, 149, 176–79

"new Indian," 6, 8, 9, 27

New York: garden cities in, 28, 148–49; Jews in, 200; Oneida Nation in, 2–3, 45–57, 59, 261n95. *See also* land claims/rights; treaties

New York Bureau of Municipal Research, 83, 88, 199, 268n28

Norbert Hill Senior Center (WI), *47,* 48

Oak, Louis P. (Chief), 202, 214, 225–28

"Ode to a Grecian Urn" (Keats), 169, 274n5

oil and gas mining, 93–94, 100, 269n37, 270n50, 271nn55–56

Oklahoma, 30, 48, 50, 159, 162, 177, 182, 259n63, 276n25. *See also* Osage Reservation

Oneida Advancement Association, 262n102

Oneida Boarding School (WI), *40–47,* 261n96, 262nn105–6, 262n109; child labor and, 106–7, 272n65; LCK's request to buy, 43–44, 272n61

Oneida Business Committee, 43–46, 261n95

Oneida Executive Committee, 261n95

Oneida General Tribal Council, 45, 47, 261n95

Oneida Improvement Association, 262n102

Oneida language, 6, 7, 264n5, 265n7

Oneida Nation, *51, 53*; acreage, 2–3, 204–6, 215, 253n4; clans, 264n2; cultural identity, 59–60; differences in, 57–59; integrated food system of, 273n2; relocation and settlement of, 2–3, 20, 47–48, 59, 253n4; during Revolutionary War, 205–6; writings about, 18–26. *See also specific location*

Oneida National Committee, 45–46, 52, 55, 56, 57, 261n95, 262n104, 262n106

Oneida National Council, 43, 262n102

Onondaga Nation: fiscal and social concerns, 56; funding land claims, 48–49; government of, 3; Hiawatha belt and, 265n10; income of, 213; land claims, 54, 206, 211, 213, 214, 215, 224–25, 228–37, 240; salt pipeline leases, 231–32; testimony of Chief Livingston Crouse, 54, 228–37; wrongful death suit, 54

Ontario, Oneida Nation in, 2–3, 45, 50

oppression, 77, 267n17

oral tradition, 20–21

Oriskany, battle of, 277n49

Osage Reservation, 87, 101–2, 269n37, 271nn55–56

Oskanunhunah, 168, 274n2

Our Democracy and the American Indian (book), 4, *32*–40, 63–108; concept of, 37–40; initial title for, 260n73; reviews of, 33; role of education, 104–8; self-government, 79–108; social welfare aspects, 49, 55, 99–108; structure of, 33–37; use of language in, 264nn4–5, 265n7, 267n21, 267nn17–19, 271n58

"Overalls and Tenderfoot" (story), 21–22, 119–32, 258n50

Owen, Robert L., 175

Page, Carroll Smalley, 197

parents, education and, 135–37

Parker, Arthur C., 259n68

paternalism, 38, 142, 173, 180, 266n15, 269n42

Patten, Simon Nelson, 274n7

Patten Jones Cut Stone, 228–29

Pennsylvania, 205, 211, 217, 220, 223. *See also* Carlisle Industrial School (PA)

philanthropy, 80, 82, 86, 176, 198–99, 267n24

Pine, William B., 203

placemaking, identity and, 37–40, 59–61

Poe, Adam, 2

poetry, 169–71, 274n1, 274n5, 275n9; "A Tribute to the Future of My Race," 6, 22–24, 25, 114–18, 258n53

population, Indian, 176–77, 178, 204

Powless, John, 262n106

Powless, M. N., 262n106

Pratt, Richard Henry, 105, 268n35, 272n62, 273n1

"Pratt Ideal," 141–43, 273n1

profits, 149, 231–32, 237

Progressive Era, 267n18

"protected autonomy," 18–19, 52–57, 173, 187, 202, 203–4, 279n74

public health: blindness (trachoma), 83, 87–88, 163, 177–79; creation of public health service, 196; malpractice, 101–2; Marine Hospital Service report, 83, 100, 177, 270n52; sanitation, 36, 38, 100, 103, 146, 186, 189; tuberculosis, 38, 83, 87–88, 100, 146–48, 163, 177–79

public opinion, 138–39

race, terminology and, 271n58

race deterioration, 176–77, 184–85, 190

race-heredity, 156

racism, 101, 142, 156, 157, 165, 180, 182

ration-giving, 133–34

Ray, Judge, 217

"Ray of Light, A" ("Wynnogene") (novel), 18

Red Jacket, 168, 274n2

Reeves, John, 240

"reign of paternalism," 173, 180

"reign of terror," 35, 77, 82, 179, 180, 271n56

reservations: as "industrial villages," 27–28; non-Native paternalism and,

38; as place of opportunity, 9–10, 52–53; sociological environment of, 36

Resolution 79. See U.S. Senate Resolution 79 (1929)

responsibility, 34–35, 42–43, 75–78. See also trust responsibility

Revolutionary War, 72–73, 205–7, 215, 277n47, 277n49

Robinson, Joseph Taylor, 190–96

Rochdale system, 151, 189, 276n26

"Romans of America, The" (essay), 22

Royal Proclamation of 1763, 277n47

Sacred Heart Seminary (WI), 47, 48

"Sacrifice of the White Dog, The" (story), 19–20, 21, 113, 273n4

Sagoyewhata, 71–72, 264n5

SAI. See Society of American Indians (SAI)

Salamanca (NY), 55, 222, 279n73

salaries. See income

salt pipeline leases, 231–32

sanitation, 36, 38, 100, 103, 146, 186, 189

Schiff, Jacob, 200

schools. See boarding schools; specific school

Schurz, Carl, 158–59

Schuyler, Dinah, 53

sculpture, Black Hawk, 24–26, 167–72

self-determination/governance: changes in, 261n95; democratic model of, 34, 35–37; education and, 27–29; essays on, 133–37. See also economic sovereignty; Lolomi Industrial Community

self-reliance, 75–78, 266n15

Senate Resolution 79 (1929). See U.S. Senate Resolution 79 (1929)

Seneca Nation, 222, 237–38, 239, 279n73

"She Likes Indian Public Opinion" (essay), 138–39

Sherman Institute (CA), 6, 12, 22, 114, 159, 272n63

Siberia, 99, 270n49

Six Nations: acreage, 2–3, 204–6, 215, 253n4; constitution of, 34, 72–74, 226, 231, 236; cosmology of, 19–22; defined, xviii, 253n3, 265n6; leadership, 2, *58,* 261n95, 271n57, 273n4, 277n44; origins of democracy and, 71–74; "Three Sisters," 272n1

Six Nations Club, 47–52

Six Nations Confederacy Council, 3, 48–52

Skenandore, Christine, *53*

Sloan, Thomas L., 196

Snyder Act/Indian Citizenship Act (1924), 269n43

socialism, 151–52

social welfare, 49, 55, 56, 99–108

Society of American Indians (SAI), 26–37, 60–61; founding of, 3, 5; inaugural meeting of, 9, 26–29, *27, 28,* 140–53; LCK's dismissal from, 30, 257n43, 259n68; second meeting of, 29–30, 154–66, 259n63; terminology used by, 259n64

"Some Facts and Figures on Indian Education" (essay), 29–30, 154–66, 259n63

Song of Hiawatha, A (Longfellow), 22, 25

sovereignty. *See* economic sovereignty; self-determination/governance; tribal sovereignty

spiritual practices: Golden Calf idol, 74, 266n13; Longhouse tradition, 20, 51; Midwinter ceremonies, 113, 273n4; wampum, 72–73, 265n10; White Dog ceremony, 113, 273n4; in Wisconsin, 20, 51

Stanford University, 6, 12–13, 16

stereotypes: Buffalo Bill and, 17; clans and, 142; of LCK, 5, 8–9, 13–16, 17, 18–19, 26–27, 37; "new Indian," 6, 8–9, 26–27; in sculpture, 24–26, 167–72; "vanishing Indian," 1, 19–27

Stockbridge Nation, 50, 205, 220, 277n50

Stone, William T. (Chairman), 174–75

stories: "The Legend of the Bean," 19–21, 111–12, 272–73nn1–3; "Overalls and Tenderfoot," 21–22, 119–32, 258n50; "The Sacrifice of the White Dog," 19–20, 21, 113, 273n4

Stovey, Patricia, 30, 254n10, 262n104

Syracuse (NY), 54, 206, 210, 212. *See also* Onondaga Nation

Taft, Lorado, 24–25, 167–72

Taft, William Howard, 83

Tammany Hall, 143, 267n18

taxation, 35, 41, 91–92

"Tears, Idle Tears" (Tennyson), 167, 274n1

Tecumseh, 76, 266n16

Teller, Henry Moore, 84

Tennyson, Lord Alfred, 167, 274n1

testimonies. *See* Indian Appropriation Bill (H.R. 1917); U.S. Senate Resolution 79 (1929)

Theambra, Inshta, 8

Thomas, Elmer, 54, 203, 218, 220–22, 229–30, 232–37, 240–48

Thomas, George (Tadohaho), 48, 57–58, *58*

"Three Sisters," 272n1

Tonawanda Nation, 239

Torres, Manuel, Sr., 262n109

Townsend, Charles Elroy, 88, 175, 195

trachoma (blindness), 83, 87–88, 163, 177–79

tradition, modernity vs., 8–10, 28, 39
treaties: Jay Treaty, 207, 214, 215, 224, 239–40, 278n56; Treaty of Buffalo Creek (1838), 253n4; Treaty of Fort Harmar (1789), 204–5, 215, 231, 277n46; Treaty of Fort Stanwix (1784), 204–8, 213, 215, 224, 226, 230–31, 235, 277n45, 277n47; Treaty of New York (1790), 2–3; validation of, 206, 277n51. *See also* jurisdiction; land claims/rights
tribalism, 133–34
tribal sovereignty, 1–2, 22, 37, 39–40, 49, 51, 59, 267n23. *See also* economic sovereignty; governance/ self-determination
"Tribute to the Future of My Race, A" (poem), 6, 22–24, 25, 114–18, 258n53
Trotsky, Leon, 87, 268n36
trust responsibility, 48, 52, 53–54, 269n42, 278n59, 279n74
tuberculosis, 38, 83, 87–88, 100, 146–48, 163, 177–79
Turtle clan, 71–74, 264n2, 264n5
Tuscarora Nation, 72, 205, 265n9, 277n50

Uncle Remus, 182, 275n20
United States v. Boylan (1920), 48, 212, 217, 278n59
University of Wisconsin, 6, 16, *17*
Untermeyer, Samuel, 200
urban planning, 16, 28, 37, 147–49, 186–87, 256n33, 273n3. *See also* garden cities
U.S. Bureau of Indian Affairs (BIA): bureaucracy in, 181; elimination of, 36; formation of, 270n51; funding from, 88, 93–94; indifference of, 35; LCK requests introduction to British court,

17, 257n39; "scientific investigation" of, 83, 193, 197–98; "warehouse Indians" in, 34–35, 76, 266n15, 267n17
U.S. Bureau of Reclamation, 269n45
U.S. Constitution, 34, 72–74, 205–6, 216, 231, 269n43
U.S. Court of Claims, 227, 242
U.S. Department of Justice, 212, 223, 240, 244–48
U.S. Department of the Interior: Competency Commission, 92–93; jurisdiction of, 243; LCK requests introduction to British court, 17, 257n39; LCK requests to buy Oneida Boarding School, 43–44; NYS land claim and, 212, 240, 243, 247–48; Osage Reservation and, 271n55. *See also* U.S. Bureau of Indian Affairs (BIA)
U.S. House of Representatives, 82–83, 104, 239, 240, 279n76
U.S. Joint Commission to Investigate Indian Affairs, 82–85
U.S. Senate, 3–4, 31–32, 52–53, 82–83, 84, 88, 197–201. *See also* Indian Appropriation Bill (H.R. 1917)
U.S. Senate Resolution 79 (1929), 52–57, 60, 202–48; statement of Edgar B. Merritt, 238–48; testimony of Chief Elon Eels, 214, 237–38; testimony of Chief Livingston Crouse, 54, 214, 225–37; testimony of Chief Louis P. Oak, 225–28; testimony of LCK, 203–14, 224–25; testimony of Orrin J. Kellogg, 54, 57, 202, 214–25, 279n74
U.S. Supreme Court, 10–12, 91, 233–34, 267n23, 269n43

"vanishing Indian," 1, 19–27
Vincent, Eugenie, 8

wages. *See* income
Waloron, Jane E., 8
Walsh, James, 198, 200
wampum/wampum belt, 72–73, 265n10
wardship, 65, 91, 142, 163–64, 269n43
Warner Ranch Indians, 10–12
Washington, George, 206, 231
Weller, Reginald H., 43
Wheeler, Burton K., 54, 203, 216–25,
    231
Wheelock, Dennison, 10
White Dog, 19–20, 21, 113, 273n4
Williams, Eleazar, 20
Wilson, Woodrow, 82, 270n49
Wisconsin, Oneida Nation in: Haudeno-
    saunee membership, 220; identity of,
    58–60; payments to Kelloggs, 219,

220; relocation and settlement in, 2–3,
    20, 47–48, 59, 253n4. *See also* Oneida
    Boarding School (WI)
Wise, Whitney, and Parker (law firm), 57,
    219, 222–23
women, 3, 30, 36, 61, 101–3, 263n119,
    271n57
Worcester v. Georgia (1832), 269n43
Works Progress Administration (WPA),
    264n5
Wynema: A Child of the Forest (Callahan),
    257n41
"Wynnogene" ("A Ray of Light") (novel),
    18

Zitkala-Ša, 6, 138